Student Study Guide

to accompany

Abnormal Psychology
Clinical Perspectives on Psychological Disorders

Third Edition

Richard P. Halgin
University of Massachusetts-Amherst

Susan Krauss Whitbourne
University of Massachusetts-Amherst

Prepared by

Elaine Cassel
Lord Fairfax Community College

Boston   Burr Ridge, IL   Dubuque, IA   Madison, WI   New York   San Francisco   St. Louis
Bangkok   Bogotá   Caracas   Lisbon   London   Madrid
Mexico City   Milan   New Delhi   Seoul   Singapore   Sydney   Taipei   Toronto

W9-CFC-316

McGraw-Hill Higher Education 🦋

A Division of The McGraw-Hill Companies

Student Study Guide to accompany

ABNORMAL PSYCHOLOGY: CLINICAL PERSPECTIVES ON
PSYCHOLOGICAL DISORDERS, THIRD EDITION

Copyright © 2000, 1997 by The McGraw-Hill Companies, Inc. All rights reserved.
Printed in the United States of America.

The contents of, or parts thereof, may be reproduced for use with
ABNORMAL PSYCHOLOGY: CLINICAL PERSPECTIVES ON PSYCHOLOGICAL
DISORDERS, THIRD EDITION, by Richard P. Halgin and Susan Krauss Whitbourne,
provided such reproductions bear copyright notice and may not be reproduced in any form
for any other purpose without permission of the publisher.

1 2 3 4 5 6 7 8 9 0 QPD/QPD 9 0 3 2 1 0 9

ISBN 0-07-232387-6

www.mhhe.com

Table of Contents

APPENDIX *Glosssary Cards*

Preface

This **Student Study Guide** continues the tradition set in the previous accompaniments to the first and second editions of **Abnormal Psychology: The Human Experience of Psychological Disorders,** by Richard P. Halgin and Susan Krauss Whitbourne. However, several new features have been introduced that enhance learning by requiring application of your knowledge and critical thinking skills.

This **Study Guide** helps you make efficient use of study time by organizing the material into segments that test your general knowledge of each chapter, as well as assess specific concepts and issues.

Clear and Innovative Study Elements
The first page of each chapter provides an overview of the chapter in a visual context, *Chapter At A Glance*. *Learning Objectives* guide you through the text, *Review At A Glance* fill-in-the-blank recitation tests your specific knowledge of the main points in the chapter, and games, matching, and short answers address main chapter headings. The exercises, as do the text, blend history, theory, and application.

Focus on Critical Thinking and Evaluating Research
New to this edition is an activity that focuses on the case examined in detail in each chapter, *From the Case Files of Dr. Sarah Tobin.* Another new feature is a section called *Focusing on Research* that asks you to evaluate the research methods and conclusions reported in text boxes

Factoring in Diversity
Also new to this edition is an activity titled *How Are We Different?* The questions ask you to think critically about research and theories presented in the text box feature of the same name that focuses on diversity in the human, sociocultural experience of abnormal behavior and psychological disorders. More often than not, as you consider the questions, you will conclude that in the suffering and recovery from mental disorders, generally we are more alike than different—regardless of race, ethnicity, gender, and socioeconomic class. However, you will learn that these factors often impact on whether or not a person will experience a disorder in the first place, and also play a role in certain aspects of treatment and recovery.

Glossary Study Cards
This edition of the **Study Guide** continues the popular feature of *Glossary Study Cards*, but in a better organized format. These cards, which have a glossary term on one side and the term's definition on the other side, are fun and concrete study aids. They are placed at the end of the book. To assist you in your review, the page number on which the term appears in the text is included with the definition. You can sort these cards in any number of ways—chronologically, as they appear in the chapter, according to main headings in the chapters, or according to your level of understanding. You might put the most familiar terms at the end, and spend the greater part of your time working on the terms you know the least.

Answers to Questions

The **Study Guide** provides answers to all objective questions in the Guide, as well as rejoinders to the comprehensive multiple choice review at the end of each chapter. In the rejoinders, you are given the right answer as well as why the other answers are incomplete. General answers are provided for the *From The Case Files of Dr. Sarah Tobin*, *Focusing on Research*, and *How Are We Different?* activities but they are not intended to limit the direction that you may go in your thinking and evaluation.

Suggestions for Study

You have probably developed your own way of studying and using study aids like this **Study Guide**, but here are some suggestions for an effective way to learn the material in this text.

1. Prior to reading the textbook chapter, review the learning objectives in the Study Guide and glance at the *Review At A Glance* feature.
2. Before you read each main section of the text, find the **Study Guide** components that relate to that section and read them over before you read the text. Then complete each activity after you read each section in the text.
3. Before you read the text boxes, look over the *Focusing on Research* and *How Are We Different?* activities in the Study Guide. After reading each of the boxes, complete these activities.
4. After you complete the chapter, complete *Review At A Glance*. Then turn to the *From the Case Files of Dr. Sarah Tobin* and see how the text material helps you better understand the case. Test your comprehensive knowledge by completing the multiple choice questions at the end of each **Study Guide** chapter. Assess your understanding of each chapter's key terms by working with the **Glossary Study Cards** in the way you find most useful.
5. You can check all of your answers as you go along by referring to the answer key at the end of each chapter.
6. Always go back to the text and reexamine material where your answers were inadequate. Do not settle for anything less than a thorough understanding of the text materials.

While the general goal of this **Study Guide** is to help you master the material, it has been designed in a way that encourages you to be an active participant in your learning. Most students consider an Abnormal Psychology course to be one of the most interesting and rewarding of all undergraduate psychology courses. Your excellent text is the foundation for this experience. This **Study Guide** will be a useful, challenging, and engaging companion that will enhance your understanding of psychological disorders.

Elaine Cassel
Lord Fairfax Community College, Middletown, Virginia
Marymount University, Arlington, Virginia

CHAPTER 1
UNDERSTANDING ABNORMALITY:
A LOOK AT HISTORY AND RESEARCH METHODS
CHAPTER AT A GLANCE

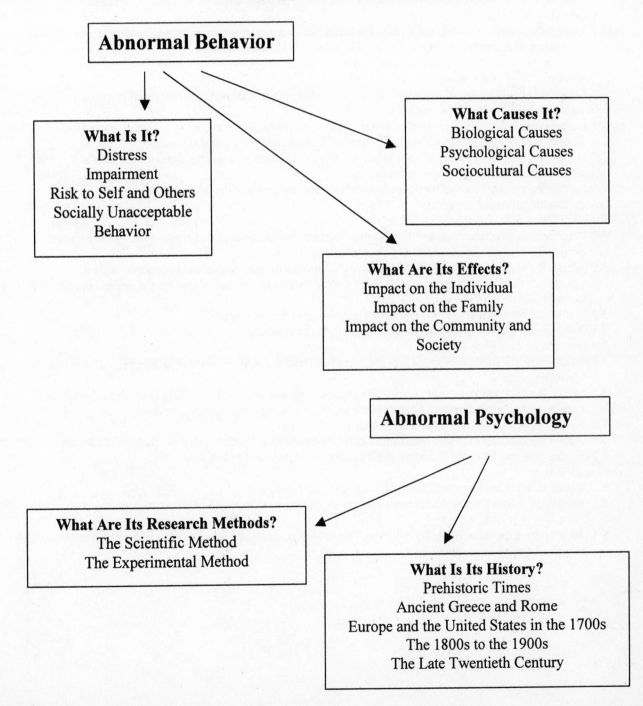

Abnormal Behavior

What Is It?
Distress
Impairment
Risk to Self and Others
Socially Unacceptable
Behavior

What Causes It?
Biological Causes
Psychological Causes
Sociocultural Causes

What Are Its Effects?
Impact on the Individual
Impact on the Family
Impact on the Community and
Society

Abnormal Psychology

What Are Its Research Methods?
The Scientific Method
The Experimental Method

What Is Its History?
Prehistoric Times
Ancient Greece and Rome
Europe and the United States in the 1700s
The 1800s to the 1900s
The Late Twentieth Century

LEARNING OBJECTIVES

1.0 What Is Abnormal Behavior?
   1.1 Recognize that it is difficult to define abnormal behavior because it overlaps with "normal" behavior.
   1.2 Contrast the view of abnormal behavior as deviation from the average with the view of abnormal behavior as deviation from the optimal.
   1.3 Define abnormal behavior as a concept that incorporates biological, psychological, and sociocultural dimensions.
2.0 Abnormal Psychology Throughout History
   2.1 Recognize the influence of beliefs about possession on prehistoric approaches to psychological disorders.
   2.2 Indicate how the beliefs of Hippocrates and Galen contributed to a scientific approach to understanding abnormal behavior.
   2.3 Explain the return in the Middle Ages to the belief that abnormal behavior is caused by demonic or spiritual possession and how this belief was reflected in the treatment of the mentally ill.
   2.4 Describe the reform movement in Europe and the United States in the 1700s and the contributions of Chiarugi, Pinel, Tuke, Rush, and Dix.
   2.5 Explain the contributions of psychiatrists such as Greisinger and Kraepelin to contemporary medical approaches to treating the mentally ill.
   2.6 Describe the influence of Freudian psychoanalysis on the treatment of psychological disorders and the impact of its predecessors such as Braid, Mesmer, Liebault, Bernheim, and Charcot.
   2.7 Indicate how somatic treatments such as psychosurgery and electroconvulsive therapy were used and abused as treatment methods for people in institutions.
   2.8 Explain the pros and cons of the deinstitutionalization movement and the components of successful community treatment programs.
3.0 Research Methods in Abnormal Psychology
   3.1 Describe the essential elements of the scientific method, including observation, hypothesis formation, and sampling.
   3.2 Explain the experimental method and describe the concepts of independent and dependent variables, placebos, treatment and control groups, double-blind technique, the quasi-experimental design, and demand characteristics.
   3.3 Discuss the correlational method and define negative and positive correlations.
   3.4 Outline the survey method and distinguish prevalence from incidence.
   3.5 Describe the case study method.
   3.6 Indicate how the single-subject study is conducted and how the multiple baseline technique is used in this type of research.
   3.7 Explain the logic and procedures involved in studies of genetic influence, including twin studies, adoption studies, cross-fostering studies, biological marker studies, and genetic mapping research.
4.0 The Human Experience of Psychological Disorders
   4.1 Explain the concepts of stigma and distress as they apply to an individual with a psychological disorder.
   4.2 Indicate how psychological disorders affect the family, community, and society.
5.0 Chapter Boxes
   5.1 Discuss cultural variations in defining what is "abnormal" behavior.
   5.2 Indicate the relationship between creativity and mental illness as described in research on writers and artists.

   5.3 Describe the importance of the study in which psychologists disguised themselves as psychiatric patients and sought admission to a hospital.

IDENTIFYING HISTORICAL PERIODS

Put the letter corresponding to the historical period in the blank next to each approach to psychological disorder:

P= Prehistoric
A= Ancient Greece and Rome
M= Middle Ages and Renaissance

S= 1700s
E= 1800s to 1900s (approximately to 1950)
T= Late twentieth century (1950 and later)

Period	Approach to Psychological Disorders
1. ___M___	Reliance on superstition, alchemy, and astrology as explanations of psychological disorders.
2. _____	Emphasis on dysfunction of the brain as the cause of psychological disorder.
3. ___A___	First documented recognition of the role of emotional disturbances in causing psychological disorders.
4. ___E___	Use of mesmerism to redistribute disturbed bodily fluids thought to cause psychological disorder.
5. ___S___	First reform efforts made to remove patients from chains and other physical restraints.
6. ___M___	Punishment and execution of people thought to be witches.
7. _____	Development of managed care as an approach to outpatient treatment.
8. _____	Widespread use of electroconvulsive therapy and psychosurgery for treating psychological disorder.
9. _____	Large-scale release of patients from psychiatric hospitals into treatment sites in the community.
10. ___E___	Transformed poorhouses into asylums where psychologically disturbed individuals were punished.
11. ___T___	Rise of the medical model as an explanation of psychological disorder.
12. ___T___	Development of moral treatment as an approach to care for people with psychological disorder.
13. ___P___	Holes drilled in heads of people with psychological disorders as a method of releasing evil spirits.
14. ___T___	Growth of large publicly funded institutions designed for people with psychological disorders.

"CATTERGORIES"

This puzzle is based on a popular board game in which contestants must think of an item in a specified category that begins with a certain letter. Each of the groups below contains items with the same first letter. Provide the answer in the space provided.

P

___Pussin___ French hospital staff worker in the 1700s who influenced Pinel to free patients from their chains.

_____ Belief based in spirituality that the cause of psychological disorders lies in demonic control.

_____ Model of treatment for psychological disorders based on the notion of unconscious determinants.

3

_____ Control condition in an experiment in which subjects believe they are receiving treatment.

_____ Entire group of people sharing a characteristic of interest to a researcher, from which a sample is derived.

S

Sitigma _____ Negative label that is applied to people with psychological disorders.

Scientific _____ Approach to investigation that involves observations, hypothesis testing, and controls.

Scot, Reginald _____ Englishman living in the 1500s who challenged the belief that demonic possession caused psychological disorder.

Szasz _____ Twentieth century American psychiatrist who claims that mental illness is a "myth."

_____ Explanation of psychological disorders that focuses on violation of norms and potential harm to others.

H

Hippocrates _____ Greek philosopher who proposed that imbalance of bodily fluids produced psychological disorder.

Hypnosis _____ Term coined by English physician Braid to describe the process of putting a person into a trance.

hysteria _____ Disorder treated by Freud and Breuer in which psychological problems are expressed in physical form.

hypothesis _____ Prediction of a certain outcome in an experiment.

Heraclitus _____ Greek philosopher who believed that rationality depended on the nature of fire within the soul.

MATCHING

Put the letter from the right-hand column corresponding to the correct match in the blank next to each item in the left-hand column.

1. ___ Research method in which the association is observed between two variables.
2. _O_ Group in an experiment that does not receive the treatment being tested.
3. _4_ Researcher who conducted a study in which "pseudopatients" were admitted to psychiatric hospitals.
4. _M_ In an experiment, the variable whose value is observed after the manipulation is performed.
5. ___ Research method in which each person is studied in both the experimental and control conditions.
6. _E_ Physician who, in the mid-1500s, criticized the prevailing views of psychological disorder as caused by demonic possession.
7. _I_ American living in the 1800s who was an influential reformer of treatment of psychologically disturbed people.
8. _B_ British psychiatrist who proposed that people who follow society's norms are more disturbed than those who refuse to do so.
9. _D_ In an experiment, the variable whose value is set by the researcher.
10. ___ Treatment method discovered by Freud and Breuer in the case of Anna O. in which the client talks about emotional conflicts.
11. _K_ Roman physician who studied psychological disorder through experimental, scientific methods.
12. _J_ General name for the type of research method in which the investigator attempts to establish cause-effect relations.
13. _G_ Group in an experiment that receives the treatment being tested.
14. ___ Type of study on genetic influences in which children of normal parents are adopted by parents with psychological disorders.
15. _C_ Experimental approach in which neither the researcher nor the subject is aware of which condition the subject is in.

a. experimental method
b. Laing
c. double-blind
d. dependent variable
e. Weyer
f. cathartic
g. experimental group
h. Rosenhan
i. Dix
j. correlational
k. Galen
l. cross-fostering study
m. independent variable
n. single-subject design
o. control group

SHORT ANSWER

1. Place an "X" next to the word or name that does not belong:

   a. R.D. Laing
      X Thomas Szasz
      William Greisinger
      David Rosenhan

   b. Dorothea Dix
      X Vincenzo Chiarugi
      Philippe Pinel
      James Braid

   c. multiple baselines
      representativeness
      demand characteristics
      X mesmerism

   d. X pragmatic
      sanguine
      choleric
      phlegmatic

   e. Jean-Martin Charcot
      Benjamin Rush
      Josef Breuer
      Ambrose-Auguste Liébault

2. Match the period of history with the predominant orientation(s) to understanding and treating psychological disorders by filling in the blank with the letter representing the predominant orientation. Historical periods associated with more than one orientation have two blanks:

Period of history

M	Prehistorical times
S	Ancient Greece and Rome
M H	Middle Ages and Renaissance
H	Europe and the U.S. in the 1700s
S	1800s to 1900s
S H	Late 20th century

Predominant orientation(s)

S= Scientific
H= Humanitarian
M= Mystical

6

3. Using the criteria outlined in the text for defining abnormality as deviation from the "average" (A) vs. deviation from the "optimal" (O), evaluate each of the following behaviors in terms of which of these criteria it meets:

Behavior

Type of deviation

a. A woman receives an unusually high score on a test of depression.

a. _A_

b. A man laughs at the sad part of a movie.

b. _A_

c. A college student makes a mistake when giving a well-prepared oral presentation due to feelings of tension.

c. _O_

d. An athlete is unrealistically self-critical for a team's failure to win a game.

d. _O_

e. A boy is highly active compared with his classmates.

e. _A_

f. A teenager refuses to join her friends for a party because of her extreme shyness.

f. _O_

g. A man with a long record of arrests feels no remorse after robbing a convenience store.

g. _O_

h. A woman is unable to stop herself from pulling out her own hair.

h. _O_

i. A sports fan knows the statistics on all members of nationally known hockey teams.

i. _A_

4. For each of the criteria for deviant behavior, describe the nature of the criterion, its applicability, and its limitations.

Criterion	Definition	Applicability	Limitations
Biological	Disfunction or disorder in a part of the body or aspect of biological functions		
Psychological			
Sociocultural			

7

5. a. Describe four ways in which families are affected by the presence of a psychologically disturbed member:

_____

_____

_____

_____

b. What has been an organized response of groups of families to these difficulties?

_____

_____

c. How are local communities affected by the presence of people with psychological disorder?

_____

_____

6. a. What is the significance of the fact that a disorder has a higher concordance rate among monozygotic than among dizygotic twins?

_____

b. Describe the major difference between an adoption study and a cross-fostering study:

_____

_____

c. What is the purpose of studies on biological markers?

_____

FOCUSING ON RESEARCH

Answer the following questions concerning the Research Focus entitled "How 'Crazy' Are Creative People?"

1. What research method was used by Andreasen?

_____

_____

2. Why was it necessary to include a group of people who were comparable in age, sex, and education to the writers?

_____

_____

3. Why would it have been preferable for Andreasen to have conducted the study without knowing which subjects were creative writers and which were controls?

_____

_____

8

THINKING ABOUT REBECCA'S CASE

Answer the following questions about the case of Rebecca Hasbrouck.

1. Describe the symptoms of distress that Dr. Tobin observed in Rebecca.

_____

_____

2. How was Rebecca's life impaired as a result of her distress symptoms?

_____

_____

3. In what way was Rebecca a threat to herself when she first met Dr. Tobin?

_____

_____

4. In what socially unacceptable behaviors had Rebecca engaged since the onset of her illness?

_____

_____

5. Explain how Rebecca's illness fits the diathesis-stress model of abnormal behavior.

_____

_____

6. What was the course of Rebecca's hospital treatment and what treatment and support did she receive on discharge?

_____

_____

REVIEW AT A GLANCE

Test your knowledge by completing the blank spaces with terms from the chapter. If you need a hint, consult the chapter summary (p. 32).

Abnormality can be defined according to four criteria: ____1____, ____2____, _____3_____, and _____4_____. In trying to understand the reasons people act and feel in ways that are regarded as abnormal, social scientists look at these dimensions: _____5_____, _____6_____, and _____7_____. The term _____8_____ characterizes the interaction among these three sets of influences. The _____9_____ model proposes that people are born with a predisposition that places them at risk for developing a psychological disorder.

Three recurring themes characterize the understanding and treatment of people with psychological disorders. They are the _____10_____, the ____11____, and the _____12_____. The __13__ theme regards abnormality as due to demonic or spiritual possession. The _____14_____ theme regards abnormality as due to psychological or physical disturbances within the person. The ____15____ regards abnormality as due to improper treatment by society.

Researchers use various methods to study the causes and treatment of psychological disorders. The _____16_____ method involves applying an objective set of methods for observing behavior, making a ____17____ about the causes of behavior. In the _____18_____ method, the researcher alters the level of the _____19_____ and observes its effects on the ____20____ variable. The _____21_____ method compares groups who differ on a predetermined characteristic. The ____22____ method studies associations or relationships between variables. The _____23_____ methods enables researchers to estimate the incidence and prevalence of psychological disorders. The ____24____ method studies one individual intensively and conducts a careful and detailed analysis of the individual. In the ____25____ design, one person at a time is studied in experimental and control conditions.

TRUE-FALSE

Indicate whether the following statements are true or false.

1. If you want to prove what causes a psychological illness, conduct a correlational study.
$\quad$ T $\qquad$ F

2. The dependent variable is adjusted or controlled by the experimenter.
$\quad$ T $\qquad$ F

3. The control group consists of the subjects who receive a placebo.
$\quad$ T $\qquad$ F

4. In the double-blind technique, only the person giving the treatment knows whether the subject is in the experimental group or the control group.
$\quad$ T $\qquad$ F

5. Administering an electric shock to treat a mental disorder is known as trephining.
$\quad$ T $\qquad$ F

6. The incidence of a disorder is a figure that tells us the number of people who have ever had a disorder at any given time or over a period of time.
$\quad$ T $\qquad$ F

7. The prevalence of a disorder is the frequency of new cases within a given period of time.
$\quad$ T $\qquad$ F

8. If you and your twin brother both suffer from depression, you may be, in research terms, discordant. $\quad$ T $\qquad$ F

9. The only thing that matters in a survey is the quality of answers you receive.
$\quad$ T $\qquad$ F

10. The purpose of an adoption study is to see how well adopted children adjust to their adoptive families. $\quad$ T $\qquad$ F

MULTIPLE CHOICE

1. Jackson is elated because his exam grade was substantially higher than the mean of the class. Jackson's exam grade would be considered a deviation from
   a. the average.
   b. the optimal.
   c. the mode.
   d. the ideal.

2. Which American psychiatrist has argued that the concept of mental illness is a "myth" created in modern society and put into practice by the mental health profession?
   a. R. D. Laing
   b. David Rosenhan
   c. Thomas Szasz
   d. Marie Balter

3. Trephining is the term used for the procedure in which
   a. holes were drilled in a disturbed person's skull in order to release evil spirits.
   b. a ritual involving fire was used to invoke healthy mental energy as a replacement for unhealthy energy.
   c. blood was released from a person in the belief that an overabundance of blood caused unpredictable mood shifts.
   d. an individual was restrained in a "tranquilizer" chair.

4. Which theorist proposed that bodily fluids—black bile, yellow bile, phlegm, and blood—influence physical and mental health?
   a. Hippocrates
   b. Galen
   c. Eysenck
   d. Pinel

5. Which research method would most likely be used by a researcher interested in determining the relationship between IQ and level of anxiety?
   a. experimental
   b. case study
   c. single-subject design
   d. correlational

6. In 1792, an English Quaker named William Tuke established the York Retreat. Succeeding generations of Tuke's family carried on his work by using methods known as
   a. the "well-cure."
   b. the medical model.
   c. moral treatment.
   d. spiritual treatment.

7. The American Psychiatric Association was greatly influenced by Greisinger's 1845 book on the pathology and treatment of psychological disorders which focused on the role in abnormal behavior of
   a. hormonal imbalances.
   b. demonic influence.
   c. early life experience.
   d. brain dysfunction.

8. Anton Mesmer claimed that psychological cures could be brought about
   a. through the use of hypnosis.
   b. by redistributing the magnetic fluids in a person's body.
   c. through use of the cathartic method.
   d. by using psychoanalytic techniques.

9. The deinstitutionalization movement involved
   a. the restructuring of psychiatric institutions to make them more humane.
   b. the large-scale release of psychiatric clients into the community.
   c. the movement of psychiatric patients from public institutions to private institutions.
   d. the recognition that mental illness is a "myth."

10. A Chinese man who speaks to his dead relatives is an example of which aspect of abnormal behavior?
    a. attempt to fake schizophrenia
    b. genetic mapping
    c. the influence of religious beliefs
    d. mesmerism

11. A researcher tests the effectiveness of a medication so that neither the person administering nor the person receiving the treatment knows whether the subject is in the control or the experimental group. What is this technique?
    a. demand characteristic
    b. correlational
    c. experimental
    d. double-blind

12. Which of the following is considered to be a sociocultural criterion for defining abnormality?
    a. personal distress
    b. maladaptive behavior
    c. statistical deviation
    d. violated social conventions

13. A label that causes certain people to be regarded as different is referred to as a
    a. role.
    b. norm.
    c. stigma.
    d. diagnosis.

14. When did the scientific model of psychological disorders emerge?
    a. prehistoric times
    b. ancient Greece and Rome
    c. the Middle Ages
    d. the 20th century

15. Who is known as the founder of American psychiatry?
    a. Dorothea Dix
    b. Benjamin Rush
    c. William Tuke
    d. Clifford Beers

16. What was the most significant reason for the declining conditions in mental institutions during the later part of the reform period?
    a. overcrowding
    b. lack of funding
    c. undereducated staff
    d. re-emergence of spiritual explanations

17. Who was primarily responsible for reform in American mental institutions?
    a. Benjamin Rush
    b. Clifford Beers
    c. Dorothea Dix
    d. William Godding

18. Which of the following methods is most effective for determining cause and effect relationships?
    a. case study
    b. correlational
    c. survey method
    d. experimental

19. Which perspective on abnormality is based on the interaction of several sets of influences?
    a. humanitarian
    b. medical
    c. biopsychosocial
    d. supernatural

20. Which type of explanation of psychological disorders regards abnormal behavior as the product of possession by evil or demonic spirits?
    a. mystical
    b. scientific
    c. humanitarian
    d. psychological

21. The philosophy of Chiarugi, Pinel, and Tuke that people can, with the proper care, develop self-control over their own disturbing behaviors is referred to as
    a. psychotherapy.
    b. hypnosis.
    c. moral treatment.
    d. deinstitutionalization.

22. The method of using suggestion to induce a trance state is called
    a. somnambulism.
    b. trephining.
    c. hypnotism.
    d. psychotherapy.

23. The theory and system of practice that relies on the concepts of the unconscious mind, inhibited sexual impulses, early development, and the use of free association and dream analysis is called
    a. psychoanalysis
    b. hypnotherapy
    c. lobotomy
    d. person-centered theory

24. The variable whose level is adjusted or controlled by the experimenter is referred to as the _____ variable.
   a. placebo.
   b. dependent.
   c. independent.
   d. correlational.

25. The attempt by biological researchers to identify the characteristics controlled by each gene is referred to as
   a. biological marking.
   b. cognitive mapping.
   c. genetic mapping.
   d. sensory gating.

ANSWERS

IDENTIFYING HISTORICAL PERIODS
1. M
2. E
3. A
4. E
5. S
6. M
7. T
8. T
9. T
10. M
11. E
12. S
13. P
14. E

"CATTERGORIES"

P
Pussin
Possession
Psychoanalysis
Placebo
Population

S
Stigma
Scientific
Scot
Szasz
Sociocultural

H
Hippocrates
Hypnosis
Hysteria
Hypothesis
Heraclitus

MATCHING

1. j
2. o
3. h
4. d
5. n
6. e
7. i
8. b
9. m
10. f
11. k
12. a
13. g
14. l
15. c

SHORT ANSWER

1. a. William   contemporary critics of medical model   2. M
        Greisinger   18th century reformers of treatment   S
    b. James Braid   terms related to research methods   M & H
    c. mesmerism   the dispositions proposed by Hippocrates   H
    d. pragmatic   physicians who developed hypnosis   S
    e. Benjamin Rush   S & H

3. a. average; b. average; c. optimal; d. optimal; e. average; f. optimal; g. optimal; h. optimal; i. average

4.

Criterion	Definition	Applicability	Limitations
Biological	Disorder or dysfunction in a part of the body or aspect of biological functioning	Biological factors play important role in cause, expression, and treatment of abnormal behavior.	Not relevant to all disorders
Psychological	Disorder of emotional state, intellect, memory, language use, adaptation, ability to satisfy personal needs; feelings of personal distress	Feelings of unhappiness and maladjustment are useful indicators of dysfunction.	People may show maladaptive behavior but not necessarily feel distressed.
Sociocultural	Violation of social norms	Situations in which people behave unacceptably or cause harm to others	Not every member of a society agrees regarding what is "acceptable."

5. a. Feeling the pain of the affected member.
        Worrying that the affected member will be harmed.
        Experiencing the stigma of the affected family member.
        Feeling blamed by the mental health profession for the person's problems.
    b. Families have formed support and education groups such as the National Alliance for the Mentally Ill.
        Books have also been written that specifically concern family issues.

15

c. Halfway houses and day treatment centers may need to be established for deinstitutionalized individuals. In the absence of sufficient treatment programs, psychologically disturbed people may become part of the homeless population of a community.

6. a. The disorder probably has a genetic basis because monozygotic twins have identical genetic inheritance.

   b. In an adoption study, a child of biologically disordered parents is adopted by parents who have no psychological disorder; in a cross-fostering study, a child of normal parents is adopted by parents who have psychological disorders.

   c. In studies of biological markers, researchers attempt to understand the specific mechanisms involved in models of genetic transmission.

FOCUSING ON RESEARCH

1. Correlational, because she was investigating the relationship between two naturally occurring phenomena

2. A control group of people with comparable age, sex, and education was needed to rule out the possibility that any observed relationship between creativity and psychological disorder was due to factors other than the backgrounds of the writers. This was an important aspect of the study, because, as it turned out, there was a higher rate of psychological disorder in the "controls" than would be expected on statistical grounds.

3. Because Andreasen knew the identity of her subjects, it might have been difficult for her to evaluate her hypothesis objectively. However, the fact that Andreasen found a relationship between creativity and mood disorder (not schizophrenia, as she had predicted), suggests that her awareness of the subjects' identity did not bias her evaluation of their psychological status.

THINKING ABOUT REBECCA'S CASE

From the case files of Dr. Rebecca Tobin:

Here are some suggestions for possible answers, not a comprehensive discussion of the topics.

1. Rebecca was disheveled, with dirty hair and torn and stained clothing. She was homeless and said she wanted to return to the world she had left three years earlier.

2. Rebecca lost her career and her home after the illness that took her to such depths of despair. She heard voices that were not there and had delusions about where her husband and children were.

3. Rebecca was a threat to herself because she was homeless and, at times, incoherent. She had reported hearing voices.

4. Her joblessness, homelessness, unkempt and dirty physical appearance, hearing voices and having delusions.

5. Since her mother suffered from depression, Rebecca may have inherited a predisposition to depression (diathesis). The loss of her husband and children in an accident in which she survived led to her breakdown. She may have felt guilt for surviving (stress). Her mother and mother-in-law wanted nothing to do with her after the tragedy, so Rebecca was left without loved ones with whom to grieve (stress). The tragedy overwhelmed Rebecca, and she lost the ability to continue in her work.

6. During her hospital stay, Rebecca received a comprehensive physical and mental evaluation. She attended group therapy and had individual therapy. Dr. Tobin consulted with a social worker, who began to help Rebecca reconnect with her family and find her a place to live and employment. After 2 weeks in the hospital, Rebecca went to a halfway house for women who had suffered similar breaks with reality. After being there a month, she found an apartment and a new line of work that was less stressful. She continued in individual therapy with Dr. Tobin for a year.

GUIDED REVIEW

1. distress
2. impairment
3. risk to self or others
4. behavior that deviates from social and cultural norms
5. biological
6. psychological

7. sociocultural
8. biopsychosocial
9. diathesis-stress
10. mystical
11. scientific
12. humanitarian
13. mystical
14. scientific
15. humanitarian
16. scientific
17. hypothesis
18. experimental
19. independent variable
20. dependent
21. quasi-experimental
22. correlational
23. survey
24. case study
25. single-subject

TRUE-FALSE

1. False-Only an experiment can prove causation. Correlational studies may indicate a relationship between variables, but not causation.
2. False-The independent variable is adjusted or controlled by the experimenter in order to study its effect on the dependent variable.
3. True-The experimental group receives the treatment.
4. False-Neither the person giving the treatment nor the experimenter knows which subjects are getting the treatment.
5. False-Trephining was an ancient technique that involved drilling holes in the heads of people manifesting abnormal behavior.
6. False-Incidence is the frequency of new cases within a given period of time. See answer to #7.
7. False-Prevalence of a disorder is a figure that indicates the number of people who have ever had a disorder at any given time or over a period of time. See answer to #6.
8. False-You would be considered "concordant" for expressing the disorder, meaning that you both express it. If you were discordant, one of you would not have the disorder.
9. False-Among other things, the number of people that respond to a survey, as well as the types of questions and how they are framed, are important indicators of a survey's research value.
10. False-Adoption studies attempt to determine what aspects of a person's makeup are genetic (from their biological parents) and what are environmental.

MULTIPLE CHOICE

1. The answer is (a), deviation from the average (a statistic derived by adding all the scores and dividing that number by the number of persons taking the test). (b) Optimal means the "best" under certain conditions; (c) is a statistic meaning the most frequently appearing number in a set of numbers; (d) the "ideal" has nothing to do with an exam grade, but a perfect score would be ideal.
2. The answer is (c), Thomas Szasz. (a) R.D. Laing contended that modern society dehumanized the individual; (b) David Rosenhan conducted the research into mental institutions (that is discussed in your text).
3. The answer is (c).
4. The answer is (a). (b) Galen conducted experiments on animals to understand human anatomy; (c) Eysenck is a contemporary theorist whose personality theory builds on Hippocrates' idea of the bodily fluids; (d) Pinel was an 18th century French reformer.

5. The answer is (d). The correlational method examines relationships between two variables. (a) The experimental method seeks to prove causation by using experimental and control groups; (b) case study is an in-depth study of one person; (c) single-subject design studies one person in both experimental and control conditions.

6. The answer is (c). (a) The "well-cure" is not a method of treatment; (b) the medical model treats mental illness with drugs or other medical means; (d) spiritual treatment relies on prayer and religious practices.

7. The answer is (d). Greisinger's book did not deal with (a), (b), or (c).

8. The answer is (b). (a) Hypnosis was espoused by Charcot; (c) Rush believed in the cathartic method; (d) Freud pioneered psychoanalytic techniques.

9. The answer is (b). The other answers are wrong because of the definition of the word "deinstitutionalization". It means releasing people from institutions, not (a) making institutions more human, (c) privatizing institutions, or (d) making a statement about mental illness.

10. The answer is (c). (a) is wrong because suggesting that people who believe they commune with the dead are mentally ill is a sociocultural bias; (b) "genetic mapping" means identifying the human genes; (d) mesmerism was the technique of attempting to "redistribute" the body's "magnetic fluids" in an effort to treat mental illness.

11. The answer is (d). (a) Demand characteristic involves subjects trying to behave in the way they think will support the research hypothesis; (b) correlational studies examine relationships between variables and does not involved giving a treatment; (c) the experimental method relies on the double-blind technique to ensure maximum validity of research results.

12. The answer is (d). (a) and (b) are individual criteria; (c) is a scientific criterion.

13. The answer is (c). (a) is involves behaving according to expectations; (b) is a behavioral standard; and (d) is the name given a disorder.

14. The answer is (b), as supported by historical texts.

15. The answer is (b). (a) Dorothea Dix sought to reform mental institutions to make them more humane; (c) William Tuke first proposed moral treatment; (d) Clifford Beers followed in Dix's path to continue reform of psychiatric institutions.

16. The answer is (a). (b) and (c) Both lack of funding and undereducated staff contributed to declining conditions but were not as significant as overcrowding; (d) There was not a re-emergence of spiritual explanations for mental illness at the end of the reform period.

17. The answer is (c). (a) Benjamin Rush is considered the founder of American psychiatry; (b) Clifford Beers was involved in reform efforts as a result of Dix's pioneering efforts.

18. The answer is (d). Neither (a), (b), nor (c) can ever result in a determination of cause and effect between variables.

19. The answer is (c). (a) and (d) are not perspectives on abnormality; (b) does not involve interaction with any other influence.

20. The answer is (a). (c) is not an explanation of disorders; (b) explains disorders by empirical data; (d) explains disorders as a function of individual cognitive and emotional processes.

21. The answer is (c). (a) involves methods to make the unconscious impulses surface; (b) involves being put into a trance; and (d).

22. The answer is (c). (a) is sleepwalking; (b) involved drilling holes in the head; and (d) does not include putting clients into a trance.

23. The answer is (a). (b) involves a being put into a trance-like state; (c) is a surgical procedure; and (4) emphasizes client-therapist relationship.

24. The answer is (c). (b) remains constant; (a) is what the control group receives instead of the treatment; and (d) is a research method.

25. The answer is (c). (a) can lead to genetic mapping; (b) and (c) are not research methods or procedures.

CHAPTER 2
CLASSIFICATION AND TREATMENT PLANS

CHAPTER AT A GLANCE

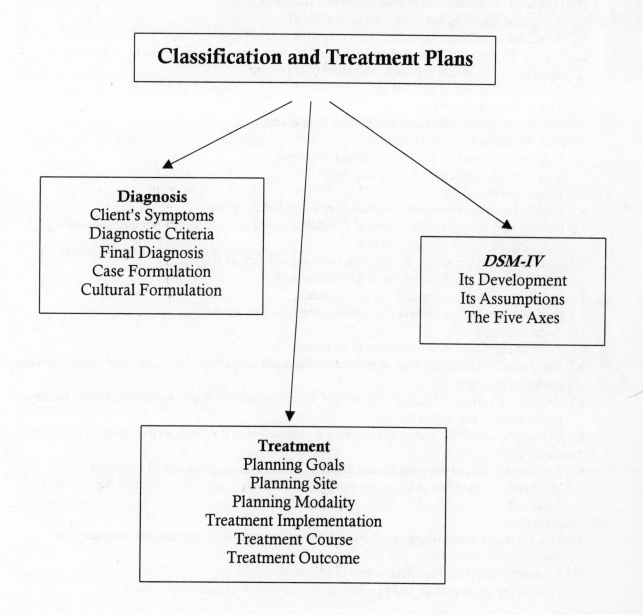

Classification and Treatment Plans

Diagnosis
Client's Symptoms
Diagnostic Criteria
Final Diagnosis
Case Formulation
Cultural Formulation

DSM-IV
Its Development
Its Assumptions
The Five Axes

Treatment
Planning Goals
Planning Site
Planning Modality
Treatment Implementation
Treatment Course
Treatment Outcome

Learning Objectives

1.0 Psychological Disorder: Experiences of Client and Clinician
    1.1 Distinguish the concept of a client from that of a patient as the individual who is the focus of psychological treatment.
    1.2 Describe the prevalence of psychological disorders in the United States.
    1.3 Describe the types of clinicians who provide psychological treatment.

2.0 The Diagnostic and Statistical Manual of Mental Disorders
    2.1 Outline the history of the development of *DSM-IV*.
    2.2 Define the term "mental disorder" as it is used in *DSM-IV*.
    2.3 Explain the assumptions underlying the *DSM-IV*, including the medical model, a theoretical orientation, categorical approach, and multiaxial system.
    2.4 Define the five axes of *DSM-IV*.
        Axis I: Clinical Disorders
        Axis II: Personality Disorders and Mental Retardation
        Axis III: General Medical Conditions
        Axis IV: Psychosocial and Environmental Problems
        Axis V: Global Assessment of Functioning

3.0 The Diagnostic Process
    3.1 Explain how the clinician obtains the client's reported symptoms.
    3.2 Indicate how the diagnostic criteria of *DSM-IV* are used in identifying a possible diagnosis, including the role of the decision tree.
    3.3 Discuss the ways in which the clinician rules out differential diagnoses.
    3.4 Explain how the clinician arrives at a final diagnosis.
    3.5. Indicate how a case formulation is constructed.
    3.6 Describe the need for cultural formulations and how they are written.

4.0 Treatment Planning
    4.1 Contrast short- and long-term goals of treatment.
    4.2 Distinguish the treatment sites of psychiatric hospitals, outpatient clinics, halfway houses, and day treatment programs.
    4.3 Explain the various modalities of treatment, including individual psychotherapy, family therapy, group therapy, and milieu therapy.
    4.4 Discuss the role of the clinician's theoretical perspective as it influences the nature of treatment.

5.0 Treatment Implementation
    5.1 Indicate the roles of the clinician and client as they influence the course of treatment.
    5.2 Discuss the frustrations and possible limitations involved in providing effective psychological treatment.

6.0 Chapter Boxes
    6.1 Discuss the evidence regarding whether minority individuals are particularly vulnerable to psychological disorders.
    6.2 Evaluate research on the effectiveness of psychotherapy.
    6.3 Discuss the arguments for and against use of the *DSM-IV* as a diagnostic tool.

Matching

Put the letter from the right-hand column corresponding to the correct match in the blank next to each item in the left-hand column.

1. ___ Consistency of measures or diagnoses.

2. ___ Term meaning the form in which psychotherapy is offered.

3. ___ Diagnostic dimension that applies to clinical syndromes.

4. ___ Illness seen in Latinos in which a frightening event causes the "soul" to leave the body, resulting in depression and somatic symptoms.

5. ___ Structured, community-based treatment program similar to that found in a psychiatric hospital.

6. ___ DSM scale that rates an individual's overall health.

7. ___ Common term that refers to behavior involving loss of contact with reality.

8. ___ Accuracy of a diagnosis or measure.

9. ___ Approach to treatment in a psychiatric hospital in which the total environment is structured to be therapeutic.

10. ___ A client's likelihood of recovering from a disorder.

11. ___ Process through which a clinician systematically rules out alternative diagnoses.

12. ___ Axis in DSM for designating long-standing, maladaptive features of personality.

13. ___ Explanation of a client's psychological status that accompanies a diagnosis.

14. ___ Primary disorder for which the client is seeking treatment.

15. ___ Disorder found in Malaysia in which a man experiences a violent outburst, usually following an insult.

a. validity

b. modality

c. milieu therapy

d. differential diagnosis

e. Axis II of the DSM

f. susto

g. amok

h. case formulation

i. reliability

j. Axis I of the DSM

k. day treatment

l. principal diagnosis

m. psychosis

n. Global Assessment of Functioning

o. prognosis

Identifying the Axis

Put the Roman numeral corresponding to the axis on the *DSM* represented by each of the symptoms or characteristics below:

I = Clinical syndromes
II = Personality disorders and mental retardation
III = Physical disorders or conditions

IV = Psychosocial and environmental problems
V = Global Assessment of Functioning

Axis	Symptoms or characteristics		Axis	Symptoms or characteristics
1. ____	Brain damage that interferes with memory	7.	____	Recent unemployment
2. ____	Extreme sadness, guilt, and suicidality	8.	____	Gastric ulcer
3. ____	Mental retardation	9.	____	Symptom severity ratings
4. ____	Death of a spouse	10.	____	Severe anxiety in social social situations.
5. ____	Chronic bronchitis			
6. ____	Personality characterized by constant dependency on others	11.	____	Deficient ability to carry out tasks of everyday living

Short Answer

1. Explain the three main assumptions of the *DSM* regarding mental disorders:

Assumption about mental disorder	Explanation
The disorder is clinically significant.	
The disorder is reflected in a syndrome.	
The disorder is associated with present distress, impairment, or risk.	
The disorder is not a culturally sanctioned response.	

2. For each step of the diagnostic process, describe elements that the clinician must consider:

Step in diagnostic process	Elements that clinician considers
Client's reported symptoms	
Diagnostic criteria	
Differential diagnosis	
Final diagnosis	
Case formulation	

3. For each of the following treatment sites, describe the type of services provided and the reasons for referring clients to each site:

Treatment site	Type of service provided	Reasons for referral
Psychiatric hospital		
Outpatient treatment		
Halfway house		
Day treatment		

4. Answer the following questions about the process of implementing treatment for psychological disorders:

a. What would lead a clinician to recommend family therapy rather than individual therapy?

_____

_____

b. How does family therapy differ from group therapy?

_____

_____

c. What is the role of a clinician's theoretical orientation in providing treatment?

_____

_____

d. How might the clinician's reactions to a client influence the course of treatment?

_____

_____

e. What is the client's role in the treatment process?

_____

_____

f. What are some of the obstacles that can interfere with successful outcomes of treatment?

_____

_____

5. Describe the aims of each successive edition of the *DSM*:

DSM Edition	Goal	Limitations
I		
II		
III		
III-R		
IV		

Focusing on Research

Answer the following questions concerning the Research Focus entitled "How Do Experts Determine Which Treatments Really Work?"

1. Compare and contrast the goals and research methods of "efficacy research" and "effectiveness research" in terms of analyzing psychotherapy.

_____

_____

_____

2. Briefly summarize Seligman's argument that "efficacy studies" don't tell the whole story about the value of psychotherapy.

_____
_____
_____

3. As a potential consumer of psychotherapy, which types of study would you pay most attention to and why?

_____
_____
_____

From The Case Files of Dr. Sarah Tobin: Thinking About Peter's Case

Answer the following questions about the case of Peter Dickinson.

1. Briefly list Peter's symptoms reported by Peter and his brother, Don.

_____
_____

2. What symptoms did Dr. Tobin observe in Peter?

_____
_____

3. What was Dr. Tobin's diagnosis of Peter?

_____
_____

4. Describe the course of Peter's treatment, both in the hospital and after discharge.

_____
_____

5. Concerning the outcome of Peter's treatment, would you characterize his treatment as effective? Why or why not?

_____
_____

Review At a Glance

Nearly (1)_____ the population is afflicted with a diagnosable psychological disorder at some time in life. Approximately (2)_____ percent of these people seek professional help from clinicians, (3)_____ percent from other processional sources. The remainder turn to informal sources of support or go without help. Clinicians are found within several professions, such as (4)_____, (5)_____, (6)_____, (7)_____, and (8)_____ counseling.

Clinicians and researchers use the (9)_____, which contains descriptions of all psychological disorders. In recent editions the authors have tried to meet the criterion of (10)_____ so that a given diagnosis will be consistently applied to anyone showing a particular set of symptoms. Researchers have also worked to ensure the (11)_____ of the classification system so that the

various diagnoses represent real and distinct clinical phenomenon. The *DSM-IV* is based on a
(12)_____ model orientation in which disorders are viewed as (13)_____. Diagnoses are
categorized in terms of relevant areas of functioning called (14)_____. Axis I includes
(15)_____; Axis II, (16)_____; Axis III, (17)_____; Axis IV;
(18)_____; and Axis V contains the (19)_____ scale.

The diagnostic process involves using all relevant information to arrive at a label that characterizes a
client's disorder. After attending to a client's reported and observable symptoms, the clinician uses the
DSM-IV criteria and a strategy known as a (20)_____. The clinician rules out
(21)_____ and tries to assign a (22)_____. After the diagnostic process,
clinicians develop a (23)_____, in an effort to understand the processes and factors that
might have influenced the client's current psychological status. Once diagnosis is determined, a
(24)_____ plan is developed, which includes issues pertaining to (25)_____,
(26)_____, and (27)_____. A (28)_____ is recommended. Possibilities
include a (29)_____, (30)_____, (31)_____,
(32)_____ or other appropriate setting. The treatment (33)_____ is specified,
and may involve (34)_____, (35)_____, (36)_____, or
(37)_____therapy. After a plan is developed, clinicians implement treatment with
particular attention to the fact that the (38)_____ is a crucial determinant of whether therapy
will succeed.

Multiple Choice

1. A doctoral-level clinician who has been trained as a medical doctor is called a
    a. clinical psychologist.
    b. clinician.
    c. psychiatrist.
    d. neurophysiologist.

2. The *DSM* was developed to ensure that a given diagnosis would be consistently applied. This criterion is referred to as
    a. reliability.
    b. validity.
    c. predictability.
    d. base rate.

3. What is the commonly used term for behavior involving a person's loss of contact with reality?
    a. neurosis
    b. psychosis
    c. derealization
    d. syndrome

4. Upon admission to a psychiatric hospital for bizarre behavior, Carlos states that he has diabetes. This medical information would be noted on ___ of *DSM-IV:*
    a. Axis I
    b. Axis II
    c. Axis III
    d. Axis IV

5. Matthew has recently been discharged from a psychiatric hospital and is moving to a facility with other discharged residents until ready to live independently. Such a facility is called a
    a. day treatment center.
    b. community mental health center.
    c. milieu therapy center.
    d. halfway house

6. In epidemiological research on racial differences in rates of psychological disorders, reports of higher rates among African-Americans appear due to
   a. methodological problems.
   b. true racial differences.
   c. lack of recent data.
   d. prejudice by the researchers.

7. What is the term that refers to a client's likelihood of recovering from a disorder?
   a. prediction
   b. syndrome
   c. prognosis
   d. base rate

8. A collection of symptoms that together form a definable pattern is a
   a. diagnosis.
   b. syndrome.
   c. prognosis.
   d. disorder.

9. Which model does the *DSM* adhere to?
   a. psychoanalytic
   b. behavioral
   c. mystical
   d. medical

10. Axis II of the *DSM* is used for
    a. clinical syndromes.
    b. personality disorders and mental retardation.
    c. organic brain disorders.
    d. substance abuse disorders.

11. The process of ruling out possible alternative diagnoses is called
    a. differential diagnosis.
    b. compound diagnosis.
    c. assessment of functioning.
    d. multiaxial diagnosis.

12. An analysis of the client's development and the factors that may have influenced the client's current emotional state is called
    a. diagnosis.
    b. prognosis.
    c. classification.
    d. case formulation.

13. What treatment site is usually recommended by a clinician when the client presents a risk of harming self or others?
    a. community mental health center
    b. psychiatric hospital
    c. halfway house
    d. outpatient treatment center

14. A man arrives one hour late for work every day because he is compelled to read every street sign on the road to his workplace. Which of the following components of a mental disorder is exemplified by his behavior?
    a. It reflects a behavioral syndrome.
    b. It is associated with impairment in life.
    c. It is a culturally sanctioned response.
    d. It reflects a serious risk.

15. The first step for a clinician in the diagnostic process involves
    a. ruling out differential diagnoses.
    b. planning a treatment strategy.
    c. reviewing the *DSM* criteria for disorders matching the client's symptoms.
    d. commencing the treatment program.

16. Roger is in the stage of therapy where he and his therapist are working on altering his long-standing patterns of dependent behavior. What phase of therapy is Roger in?
    a. immediate management
    b. assessment of objectives
    c. management of short-term goals
    d. management of long-term goals

17. An outpatient clinic that provides psychological services on a sliding fee scale and serves individuals who live in a certain geographic region is called a(n)
    a. halfway house.
    b. psychiatric hospital.
    c. community mental health center.
    d. asylum.

18. Structured programs in a community treatment facility that provides activities similar to those provided in a psychiatric hospital are called
    a. day treatment programs.
    b. CMHCs.
    c. asylums.
    d. halfway houses.

27

19. A treatment approach used in an inpatient psychiatric facility in which all facets of the environment are components of the treatment is referred to as _____ therapy.
   a. psychoanalytic
   b. person-centered
   c. milieu
   d. group

20. What is the current trend with regard to theoretical perspectives and treatment of psychological disorders?
   a. person centered theory
   b. psychodynamic theory
   c. object relations theory
   d. the combination of elements from various orientation

ANSWERS

MATCHING

1.	i	6.	b	11.	d
2.	k	7.	m	12.	e
3.	l	8.	o	13.	h
4.	j	9.	a	14.	n
5.	f	10.	c	15.	g

IDENTIFYING THE AXIS

1. I
2. I
3. II
4. IV
5. III
6. II
7. IV
8. III
9. V
10. I

SHORT ANSWER

1. a. 3
   b. 7
   c. 5
   d. 1
   e. 6
   f. 2
   g. 4

1.

Assumption about mental disorder	Explanation
The disorder is clinically significant.	Symptoms must be present to a significant degree and for a significant period of time.
The disorder is reflected in a syndrome.	Individual symptoms or problematic behaviors are not sufficient for diagnosis as a mental disorder.
The disorder is associated with present distress, impairment, or risk.	The behaviors or symptoms must involve personal or social cost.
The disorder is not culturally sanctioned.	The disorder is not expectable for one□s society or culture.

2.

Step in diagnostic process	Elements that clinician considers
Client's reported symptoms	Compare the client's statement of problems with diagnostic terms and concepts
Diagnostic criteria	Clarify the nature of the client's symptoms and attempt to match them with diagnostic criteria by following the decision tree
Differential diagnosis	Rule out alternative diagnoses
Final diagnosis	Provide diagnoses and ratings on the five axes of the *DSM*
Case formulation	Place into perspective the client's diagnosis in the context of the client's life history

3.

Treatment site	Type of service provided	Reasons for referral
Psychiatric hospital	24-hour inpatient treatment, which may include medical and psychotherapeutic interventions best offered in a setting with close monitoring and supervision	Client at risk of harming self or others
Outpatient treatment	Psychotherapy and counseling	Treatment site most frequently recommended unless hospitalization is needed
Halfway house	Interaction with other deinstitutionalized clients and supervision by professional staff who can help clients develop skills needed for independent living	Client is recently deinstitutionalized and is not yet ready for independent living.
Day treatment	Milieu treatment similar to that provided in a psychiatric hospital.	Client does not need to be hospitalized but needs structured support during the day.

4. a. The clinician determines that, although one person is the "patient," this person's difficulties reflect problems in the family as a whole.
   b. In group therapy, participants are unrelated clients who work together to share their difficulties and problems in a setting where they can receive feedback, develop trust, and improve their interpersonal skills. In family therapy, the therapist works with related individuals as a system to help alleviate the distress of one member.
   c. Clinicians are often trained with particular theoretical orientations that form the basis for the services they provide. However, most clinicians adapt their own perspective and combine it with elements of other perspectives to tailor their treatment to the needs of the individual client.
   d. Each client stimulates a different reaction in the clinician, who must be alert to these reactions.
   e. The client has the responsibility for presenting and clarifying the nature of his or her symptoms and reactions to therapy as it progresses and to implement changes suggested in treatment. These areas of responsibility can be complicated by the nature of therapy, which is highly personal and demanding, and by the nature of the client's psychological difficulties, which can interfere with the progress of therapy.

f. Client's unwillingness to change, financial constraints, refusal by another party to cooperate with therapy, and a variety of practical difficulties in the client's life

5.

DSM Edition	Goal	Limitations
I	Search for a standard set of diagnostic criteria	Criteria were vague and based on unfounded theoretical assumptions.
II	Attempt to use atheoretical concepts that would fit with the ICD system	Criteria were actually based on psychoanalytic concepts. Criteria were too loose.
III	Precise rating criteria and definitions for each disorder	Criteria were incompletely specified.
III-R	Further refinement of diagnostic criteria	Became outdated with collection of new research evidence on the disorders.
IV	Incorporation of current research evidence on validity and reliability of diagnoses	

FOCUSING ON RESEARCH

1. Efficacy research takes place under experimental conditions, usually in university-based clinics where therapists are carefully selected, trained, and monitored. Patients with multiple problems are usually excluded. Effectiveness studies are conducted in the "field" (in real-world therapy settings), where clients are not assigned to random groups, for fixed durations, and treated according to a predetermined script.
2. Efficacy studies do not take into account real-world situations. Clients' diagnoses often do not fit neatly into one clearly delineated category, which can be treated with a predetermined script. Efficacy studies don't take into account one of the main reasons therapy is successful (when it is), the client-therapist relationship.
3. Probably both. Efficacy studies have a place because they are conducted under experimental conditions. But I would also want to know about real-life experiences from effectiveness studies.

FROM THE CASE FILES OF DR. SARAH TOBIN: THINKING ABOUT PETER'S CASE

1. Peter reported recent bouts of anxiety, feeling "hyper," and restless. However, he reported depression and suicidal ideation 4 months prior. Don, Peter's brother, corroborated that Peter had been acting "hyper." Peter's mother reported that Peter's landlord observed "odd" behaviors, such as staying up all night, playing his guitar, writing what Peter said was a "million-dollar recording hit." He sometimes ran from room to room, waking up other boarders, telling them to come watch his genius at work. He spent hours on the phone, trying to contact recording executives. He had spent large sums of money, filled out an application to buy a $50,000 car, and looked at expensive homes, as if he could afford these purchases. He hung out in bars in the evening, and, after spending 48 hours with a woman, he asked her to marry him. She did not show up at city hall to get the marriage license, infuriating Peter.
2. Dr. Tobin observed Peter to be "hyper," edgy, irritable, and annoyed when she questioned him. She noticed an air of bravado. He was loud and demanding but had some endearing qualities. She believed that, beneath the brave front, he was terrified by his experiences since his wife had left him.
3. Dr. Tobin diagnosed Peter with mania, a mood disorder.

4. Dr. Tobin hospitalized Peter voluntarily and ordered lithium to stabilize his mood, individual therapy, family therapy (with his mother and brother), and group therapy with others who were suffering with the same disorder. He stayed in the hospital for 14 days, during which his mania resolved and he ate and slept with more normalcy. He had six sessions of individual therapy, which went well, as did his family therapy. Peter refused to participate in group therapy, saying he had nothing in common with the "psychos" in the group. After discharge, Peter continued individual therapy once every other week for six months, continued to take lithium, and had no return of manic symptoms. He applied for a job in a bank that offered educational benefits. After six months Peter stopped talking the lithium, saying he didn't need it any longer. He cut back his sessions with Dr. Tobin to once a month. After five months of no medication, he exhibited manic symptoms again and Dr. Tobin convinced him to resume his medication. He continued to see Dr. Tobin once monthly for another year, and then therapy was terminated. Since termination of therapy, Peter contacts Dr. Tobin yearly and he reports that "all is well."

5. It appears that Peter's treatment was effective. Though he is not "cured," the symptoms are controlled by lithium. He got and maintained a job and reports periodically to Dr. Tobin that things are going well.

REVIEW AT A GLANCE

1. half
2. 25
3. 15
4. psychiatry
5. psychology
6. social work
7. nursing
8. family
9. Diagnostic and Statistical Manual of Mental Disorders, 4th Ed (DSM-IV)
10. reliability
11. validity
12. medical
13. diseases
14. axes
15. clinical disorders
16. personality disorders and mental retardation
17. general medical conditions
18. psychosocial and environmental problems
19. Global Assessment of Functioning (GAF)
20. decision tree
21. differential diagnoses
22. principal diagnosis
23. case formulation
24. treatment
25. immediate management
26. short-term goals
27. long-term goals
28. treatment site
29. psychiatric hospital
30. outpatient service
31. halfway house
32. day treatment program
33. modality
34. individual psychotherapy
35. couple or family therapy
36. group therapy
37. milieu therapy
38. quality of the client-clinician relationship

MULTIPLE CHOICE

1. The answer is (c). None of the other choices is a licensed medical doctor.
2. The answer is (a). (b) and (c) apply to test instruments and (d) is a measurement used in some types of assessment.
3. The answer is (b). (a) and (c) don't involve loss of contact with reality, and (d) is a collection of symptoms associated with a certain disorder.
4. The answer is (c). (a) and (b) concern mental health disorders, and (c) is the axis on which functioning is assessed.
5. The answer is (d). The others are not residential facilities.
6. The answer is (a). There is no reason to think that any of the other factors play a part.
7. The answer is (c). (b) is a collection of symptoms that may be present in a disorder, (a) involves the likelihood of someone having a disorder, and (d) is involved in certain types of assessment.

8. The answer is (b). (a) is what a clinician does when he or she names the disorder (d), and (c) is the likelihood of recovery from a disorder.

9. The answer is (d). The *DSM* is atheoretical, so (a), (b), and (c) are incorrect.

10 The answer is (b). (a) is not a *DSM*-related term; (b) and (d) are coded on Axis I.

11. The answer is (a). (c) refers to an assessment issue; (b) is not a term used by diagnosticians; and (d) is related to diagnoses under the *DSM*.

12. The answer is (d). (a) involves relating the symptoms to a known disorder; (b) is the prospect of recovery; and (c) is how the *DSM* categorizes disorder.

13. The answer is (b). None of the others is a residential treatment facility.

14. The answer is (d). There is not enough evidence for (b); (a) is not a *DSM*-related diagnostic requirement; and the behavior would not be culturally sanctioned (c).

15. The answer is (c). All the other answers are involved after diagnosis.

16. The only correct answer is (d) because they are working on long-standing patterns, not immediate (a) and (c) short-term issues. They would have resolved (b) at the beginning of treatment..

17. The answer is (c). There are no more asylums (d); (a) and (b) are not outpatient venues.

18. The answer is (a). (d) is where people may live after release from a hospital; (b) is an abbreviation for Community Health Centers; (c) no longer exist.

19. The answer is (c). (a) and (b) involve other models of psychology; and (d) is a type of psychotherapy involving several clients.

20. The answer is (d). (a), (b), and (c) may be included in (d), which is an integrative approach.

CHAPTER 3
ASSESSMENT

CHAPTER AT A GLANCE

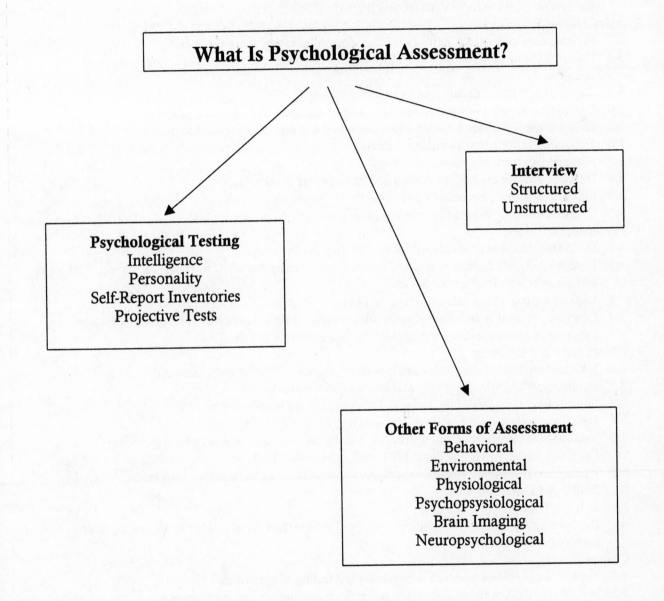

What Is Psychological Assessment?

Interview
Structured
Unstructured

Psychological Testing
Intelligence
Personality
Self-Report Inventories
Projective Tests

Other Forms of Assessment
Behavioral
Environmental
Physiological
Psychopsysiological
Brain Imaging
Neuropsychological

1.0 What Is a Psychological Assessment?
    1.1 Describe the goals and basic types of assessment procedures.

2.0 Interview
    2.1 Describe the rationale and procedures involved in an unstructured interview.
    2.2 Explain how a structured interview is used in diagnosis and be familiar with examples such as the SADS, SCID, ADIS-IV, CIDI, and IPDE.

3.0 Mental Status Examination
    3.1 Indicate how appearance and behavior are assessed and why these are important.
    3.2 Describe the methods used to evaluate a client's orientation or awareness of time, place, and identity.
    3.3 Explain the types of disturbance in content of thought.
    3.4 Distinguish among the various forms of thought disorders and provide examples.
    3.5 Describe the difference between affect and mood and how they are used in diagnosis.
    3.6 Define the various forms of hallucinations.
    3.7 Explain disturbances in sense of self or identity.
    3.8 Describe how motivation is assessed and its relevance to therapy.
    3.9 Indicate how cognitive deficits and strengths are assessed.
    3.10 Describe the assessment of insight and judgment.

4.0 Psychological Testing
    4.1 Define the concepts of standardization, reliability, and validity.
    4.2 Describe how intelligence is assessed through tests such as the Stanford-Binet Intelligence Test and the Wechsler Intelligence Scales.
    4.3 Explain the role of cultural considerations in the assessment of intelligence.
    4.4 Describe personality and diagnostic tests such as the MMPI-2 and other self-report inventories.
    4.5 Describe projective testing methods such as the Rorschach and the TAT.

5.0 Other Forms of Assessment
    5.1 Indicate how behavioral assessment is used, including self-report and observation.
    5.2 Explain how and why environmental assessments are conducted.
    5.3 Indicate how measures of physiological functioning are used in assessment.
    5.4 Describe psychophysiological measures such as ECG, EMG, and GSR.
    5.5 Indicate how measures of brain structure and function are used in assessment, including the EEG, CAT scan, MRI, functional MRI, PET scan, and SPECT.
    5.5 Explain the role of neuropsychological assessment and describe measures such as the Halstead-Reitan and Luria-Nebraska.

6.0 Putting It All Together
    6.1 Describe how clinicians use multiple sources of information about a client in putting together a comprehensive assessment.

7.0 Chapter Boxes
    7.1 Explain the problems involved in psychological testing of minorities.
    7.2 Indicate the controversies involved in research on intelligence and achievement.
    7.3 Outline the ethical issues involved in personnel selection.

Matching

Put the letter from the right-hand column corresponding to the correct match in the blank next to each item in the left-hand column.

1. ___ Altered experience of one's body.
2. ___ Assessment of a client's current functioning in such areas as orientation, thinking style, affect, insight, and motivation.
3. ___ Flow of thoughts that is vague, unfocused, and illogical.
4. ___ Expression of emotion that does not match the nature of the situation.
5. ___ False perception of a sound.
6. ___ Lack of clear sense of who one is.
7. ___ False perception of seeing a person or an object.
8. ___ Fabricating facts or events to fill voids in one's memory.
9. ___ Type of test in which test-taker interprets ambiguous stimuli.
10. ___ Behavioral assessment conducted in a specific setting.
11. ___ Experience of losing one's thought in the middle of speaking, leading to a period of silence ranging from seconds to minutes.
12. ___ False perception of a smell.
13. ___ Strength of emotional expression.
14. ___ Type of psychological test comprised of standardized questions with fixed response categories, completed by the test-taker.
15. ___ Thoughts that are odd but not bizarre or deeply entrenched.

a. confabulation
b. blocking
c. auditory hallucination
d. intensity of affect
e. analog observation
f. olfactory hallucination
g. depersonalization
h. overvalued idea
i. self-report clinical inventory
j. mental status examination
k. loosening of associations
l. inappropriate affect
m. identity confusion
n. projective test
o. visual hallucination

Identifying Symptoms

Write the name of the symptom in the blank next to the behavioral description on the right.

1. _____ Abnormally energized physical activity characterized by rapid movements and speech.
2. _____ Grossly exaggerated conception of one's own importance.
3. _____ Illogical and peculiar connection between objects or events that others see as unrelated.
4. _____ Unpleasant feelings such as sadness or irritability.
5. _____ False belief that one has no money or other material possessions.
6. _____ Abnormally rapid bodily movements involving an obvious level of personal discomfort in which the individual appears to be stirred up.
7. _____ Mood that is neither happy nor sad but shows ordinary day-to-day variations.
8. _____ Erroneous belief that other people are attempting to inflict harm on one.

35

9. _____ Mood that is more cheerful and elated than average, perhaps even ecstatic.
10. _____ False belief that one's thoughts are being transmitted to others who hear these thoughts.
11. _____ Abnormally slow bodily movements and lethargy.
12. _____ False belief that other people are putting thoughts into one's mind.

Identifying Tests

1. Write in the blank next to each test the aspect(s) of functioning it is designed to assess:

| **I** = intelligence | **D** = diagnosis | **H** = physical |
| **P** = personality | **S** = psychophysiological | **N** = neuropsychological |

a. ____ Stanford-Binet	g. ____ TAT	m ____ GSR
b. ____ Luria-Nebraska	h. ____ EEG	n. ____ WISC-III
c. ____ Rorschach	i. ____ NEO-PI-R	o. ____ PET scan
d. ____ IPDE	j. ____ Halstead-Reitan	p. ____ MRI (or NMR)
e. ____ WAIS-R	k. ____ CAT scan	q. ____ MCMI-IIII
f. ____ MMPI-2	l. ____ Bender- Gestalt	

Letter Find Puzzle

The following letters are all used in the definitions below. As you fill in each definition, cross out the letters that you have used until there are none left:

```
O I Y S E R T S O A
N T D O M C O Y P N
N I I S I S S C U I
E T O T D L O E P F
O T B N A L M H C N
A A S T S A H F L S
C O S A N C S U E H
I S C E M E N T U A
R S O S L I R N T O
I P C A N I O I S E
```

1. Unwanted repetitive thoughts or images that persist in an individual's consciousness.   _ _ _ _ _ _ _ _ _

2. Deeply entrenched false beliefs that are not consistent with an individual's level of intelligence or cultural background.   _ _ _ _ _ _ _ _

3. Repetitive behaviors that seem to have no purpose and that are performed in response to a person's uncontrollable urges or according to a ritualistic set of rules.   _ _ _ _ _ _ _ _ _ _

4. Disturbance of motor behavior in a psychotic disorder that does not have a physiological cause.   _ _ _ _ _ _ _ _

5. Term referring to the "measurement of the mind" and used in describing standards for good psychological tests.   _ _ _ _ _ _ _ _ _ _ _

6. False perception that does not correspond to any objective stimuli in a person's surroundings.   _ _ _ _ _ _ _ _ _ _ _

7. Adjective used to describe sadness, used in abnormal psychology to apply to a person's sad mood.   _ _ _ _ _ _ _ _

8. An individual's awareness of time, place, and personal identity.   _ _ _ _ _ _ _ _ _ _

9. Outward expression of an emotion.   _ _ _ _ _ _

10. Process of evaluating an individual's psychological or physical status.   _ _ _ _ _ _ _ _ _ _

Short Answer

For each of the methods of assessment listed in the chart, describe the procedures involved in the assessment, the advantages of this method, and its disadvantages.

1.

Assessment method	Assessment procedure	Advantages	Disadvantages
Unstructured interview			
Structured interview			
Individual intelligence testing			
Self-report clinical inventory			
Projective test			
Behavioral self-report			
Behavioral observation			

2. Answer each of the following questions about the MMPI/MMPI-2:

a. How does the MMPI-2 determine whether a test-taker has falsified responses, been excessively defensive, or been careless in responding?

_____

_____

b.   Identify the MMPI-2 scale that is intended to reflect each of the following personality or diagnostic attributes:

_____1.   Feelings of unhappiness and low self-esteem
_____2.   Asocial and delinquent behaviors
_____3.   Elevated mood
_____4.   Obsessions, compulsions, and unrealistic fears
_____5.   Bodily reactions to stress, denial of psychological problems
_____6.   Preoccupation with physical problems and illness
_____7.   Bizarre thinking and behavior

c. What was the original intent of the MMPI?

_____

_____

d. How were the MMPI scales developed?

_____

_____

e. Specify three criticisms of the MMPI that the authors of MMPI-2 attempted to address.

_____

_____

f. What five improvements were made in the MMPI-2 in response to criticisms of the MMPI?

_____

_____

3. Identify the types of reliability or validity described in each of the following items:

a. The extent to which two raters agree on how to score a particular
    response.
b. How closely test scores correspond to related measures at the
    same point in time.
c. The degree to which items on a test are correlated with each
    other.
d. How well test scores on one occasion predict performance on
    other measures at a later occasion.
e. General term applying to how closely test scores correspond to
    other measures with which they are expected to relate.
f. The extent to which scores taken on the same test at two
    different occasions relate to each other.
g. How closely a test measures a body of knowledge that it is
    designed to assess.
h. The degree to which a test measures a concept based on a
    theoretically derived attribute.

a. _____

b. _____

c. _____

d. _____

e. _____

f. _____

g. _____

h. _____

4. The following questions relate to the concept and measurement of intelligence:

a. How was the "IQ," or intelligence quotient, originally calculated in the Stanford-Binet measurement of intelligence?

_____

_____

b. How does the "deviation IQ" used in the Wechsler scales differ from the original Stanford-Binet IQ?

_____

_____

c. What three forms of IQ are derived from the Wechsler measures of intelligence?

_____

_____

d. What types of measures are used to assess the three forms of IQ?

_____

_____

e. How do clinicians interpret scores on the Wechsler IQ scales?

_____

_____

Focusing on Research

Answer the following questions about the Research Focus entitled "Is Intelligence Destiny?"

1. What is the main thesis of _The Bell Curve_ by Herrnstein and Murray?

_____

_____

2. What racial differences in intelligence are proposed by Herrnstein and Murray?

_____

_____

3. List three criticisms that have been made of the Herrnstein and Murray position.

_____

_____

From The Case Files of Dr. Sarah Tobin: Thinking About Ben's Case

Answer the following questions about the case of Ben Robsham.

1. What was Ben's reason for wanting to see Dr. Tobin?

    _____

    _____

2. What behaviors did Dr. Tobin observe in Ben?

    _____

    _____

3. Summarize what Dr. Tobin believed to be Ben's history relevant to his current mental state.

    _____

    _____

4. What evaluation procedures did Dr. Tobin use to assess Ben?

    _____

    _____

5. According to Dr. Tobin, what psychological disturbances was Ben manifesting?

    _____

    _____

6. What treatment recommendations and referrals did Dr. Tobin make for Ben?

    _____

    _____

How Are We Different?

Answer these questions about "How People Differ: Psychological Testing of Minorities."

1. Summarize the general questions raised about the validity of using common psychological tests with people from diverse cultural and ethnic backgrounds.

    _____

    _____

2. Describe SOMPA and explain how it might be better suited than a standard IQ test (such as the WISC-III) for cognitive assessments of minority children.

_____

_____

3. Briefly state the debate about the validity of using standard personality tests for assessment of ethnic minorities.

_____

_____

4. How is the TEMAS test different from the TAT and other traditional personality instruments and how might its use contribute to a more valid assessment of adaptive and maladaptive aspects of the personalities of minority children living in urban areas?

_____

_____

Review At a Glance

(1)_____ is a procedure in which a clinician evaluates a person in terms of (2)_____, (3)_____, and (4)_____ factors that influence an individual's functioning. Clinicians who undertake assessments have many different goals, depending on the needs of the client. These include (5)_____, (6)_____, and (7)_____. Some assessment tools focus on (8)_____, others assess (9)_____, and others are oriented toward (10)_____.

The (11)_____ is the most commonly used assessment tool for developing an understanding of a client's current problems, past history, and future aspiration. An (12) _____ interview is a series of open-ended questions. The (13)_____ interview consists of a standardized series of questions.

Clinicians use the (14)_____ to assess a client's behavior and functioning in several areas. They include (15)_____, (16)_____, (17)_____, (18)_____, (19)_____, (20)_____, (21)_____, (22)_____, (23)_____, and (24)_____.

Scorable information about psychological functioning is collected through the use of (25)_____, developed and administered according to psychometric principles such as (26)_____, (27)_____, and (28)_____. Information about an individual's cognitive function is obtained through (29)_____. Useful data about a person's thoughts, behaviors, and emotions are obtained through (30)_____, such as the (31)_____, a self-report clinical inventory, and the (32)_____, a projective technique.

Other forms of assessment include behavioral assessment that measures a person's (33)_____, environmental assessments that provide information about (34)_____, physiological techniques, which measure (35)_____, and brain imaging techniques, such as (36)_____. A commonly used neuropsychological assessment is the (37)_____.

42

Based upon information from a wide variety of sources, clinicians formulate an understanding of the (38)_____, (39)_____, and (40)_____ factors that may be important in assessing and treating the client.

Multiple Choice

1. Dr. Tobin uses an assessment approach with open-ended questions on reasons for coming to therapy, health symptoms, family background, and life history. This is called a(n)
   a. unstructured interview.
   b. structured interview.
   c. mental status examination.
   d. self-report.

2. A researcher studying depression has each research assistant ask the same questions in the same order to each subject. This is called a(n)
   a. unstructured interview.
   b. structured interview.
   c. mental status examination.
   d. personal history interview.

3. What term would a clinician use to describe a client's understanding and awareness of self and world?
   a. judgment
   b. reactivity
   c. self-monitoring
   d. insight

4. Edward believes that his thoughts, feelings, and behaviors are controlled by the window fan in his room. This symptom is called a
   a. delusion of control.
   b. visual hallucinations.
   c. somatic delusion.
   d. delusion of nihilism.

5. Marnie cannot rid her mind of thoughts of contamination. This symptom is called a(n)
   a. compulsion.
   b. obsession.
   c. thought disorder.
   d. delusion.

6. An assessment method in which the individual rates family or social context is known as a(n)
   a. behavioral observation.
   b. *in vivo* observation.
   c. behavioral interview.
   d. environmental assessment.

7. A psychologist constructs a measure of "optimism" intended to correlate with other characteristics reflective of optimism. This is known as _____ validity.
   a. construct
   b. criterion
   c. concurrent
   d. content

8. A school psychologist measuring the IQ of a fourth-grade boy could administer the
   a. WAIS-R.
   b. WISC-III.
   c. WPPSI-R.
   d. WBIS.

9. The "mental age" approach used with the Stanford-Binet was abandoned because
   a. scores were hard to determine for adults.
   b. the term "mental" has a negative meaning.
   c. it did not yield performance and verbal IQ.
   d. it was based on a deviation measure of IQ.

10. A clinician concerned about whether or not a client has faked responses on the MMPI-2 would pay careful attention to
    a. the number of items answered.
    b. the elevation of the clinical scales.
    c. the elevation of the validity scales.
    d. the elevation of the reliability scales.

11. Which test used ambiguous evoked unusual and idiosyncratic responses in the textbook case of Ben Robsham?
    a. Rorschach
    b. MCMI-III
    c. MMPI-2
    d. SCL-90-R

12. A technique for studying the brain involving a computerized combination of X rays is called
    a. computerized axial tomography.
    b. magnetic resonance imaging.
    c. nuclear magnetic resonance.
    d. positron emission tomography.

13. A disturbance in thought or the use of language is referred to as a(n)
    a. thought disorder.
    b. illusion.
    c. delusion.
    d. obsession.

14. Dispute over the issue of using personality tests in personnel selection has focused on whether
    a. test scores should relate to brain scans.
    b. minority applicants may be unfairly judged.
    c. there are no ethical guidelines for their use.
    d. personality tests have no validity.

15. Inconsistency between the person's expression of emotion and the content of speech is called
    a. mobility of mood.
    b. perseveration.
    c. inappropriateness of affect.
    d. flat affect.

16. A good psychological test is one that follows standardized procedures for scoring and
    a. diagnosis.
    b. classification.
    c. organization.
    d. administration.

17. What kind of psychological test yields information about cognitive deficits and strengths?
    a. projective test
    b. intelligence test
    c. behavioral assessment
    d. self-report questionnaire

18. Which of the following is the most commonly administered self-report inventory?
    a. Wechsler Adult Intelligence Scale-R
    b. *Diagnostic and Statistical Manual of Mental Disorders*
    c. Minnesota Multiphasic Personality Inventory
    d. Rorschach Inkblot Test

19. Dr. Schwartz asks his client to keep a tally of the number of times per hour he says negative things to his wife. This assessment technique is
    a. behavioral interviewing.
    b. self-actualization keying.
    c. self-monitoring.
    d. behavioral observation.

20. Which of the following is an assessment measure specifically designed for use with individuals from diverse cultural and ethnic backgrounds?
    a. NEO-PI-R
    b. SCORS
    c. WISC-III
    d. SOMPA

21. Which of the following is NOT one of the areas of functioning assessed by the mental status examination?
    a. behavior
    b. content of thought
    c. socioeconomic status
    d. motivation

44

22. Donnie's dad has asked him to turn the radio off, and Donnie responds by repeating, "Radio, radio, radio, radio." This repetition is an example of
   a. habituation.
   b. clanging.
   c. echolalia.
   d. confabulation.

22. All of the Wechsler IQ tests have two sets of scales—one yields a verbal IQ and the other yields
   a. mathematical IQ.
   b. Cognitive IQ.
   c. Performance IQ.
   d. Psychomotor IQ.

24. Pat's therapist is showing him various inkblots and asking him to tell her what he sees in each. Pat's therapist is administering the
   a. Rorschach
   b. TAT
   c. MMPI-2
   d. BCT.

25. Which of the following is the psychological test specifically designed to assess neurological functioning?
   a. the Wechsler Intelligence Scale for Children
   b. the Electroenchephalogram
   c. the Luria-Nebraska Neuropsychological Battery
   d. the Minnesota Multiphasic Personality Inventory

Answers

MATCHING

1. g	4. l	7. o	10. e	13. d
2. j	5. c	8. a	11. b	14. i
3. k	6. m	9. n	12. f	15. h

IDENTIFYING SYMPTOMS

1. hyperactivity
2. delusion of grandeur
3. magical thinking
4. dysphoric mood
5. delusion of poverty
6. psychomotor agitation
7. normal or euthymic mood
8. delusion of persecution
9. euphoric mood
10. thought broadcasting
11. psychomotor retardation
12. thought insertion

IDENTIFYING TESTS

1. a. I
   b. N
   c. P
   d. D
   e. I
   f. D+P
   g. P
   h. S
   i. P
   j. N
   k. H
   l. N
   m. S
   n. I
   o. H
   p. H
   q. D+P

LETTER FIND PUZZLE

1. OBSESSIONS
2. DELUSIONS
3. COMPULSION
4. CATATONIA
5. PSYCHOMETRICS
6. HALLUCINATION
7. DYSPHORIC
8. ORIENTATION
9. AFFECT
10. ASSESSMENT

SHORT ANSWER

1.

Assessment method	Assessment procedure	Advantages	Disadvantages
Unstructured interview	Open-ended questions about personal and family history, symptoms, and reasons for seeking treatment	Flexibility allows interviewer to adapt questions and questioning style to client's responses.	Variation from interviewer to interviewer in nature of questions; skill and experience are necessary
Structured interview	Highly structured set of questions with predetermined wording and order	No extensive knowledge of interviewing techniques required. Standardized ratings based on research criteria can be obtained.	None are stated in text.
Individual intelligence testing	Standardized questions that tap different verbal and nonverbal abilities	Rich qualitative information about the client's thought processes and judgment	Cultural bias; lack of clear support for validity of test scores in terms of relation to behaviors in everyday life
Self-report clinical inventory	Standardized questions with fixed response categories that test-taker completes on his or her own	Are "objective" in that scoring does not require judgment by clinician; can be given to large numbers of people	Questions are "subjective" in that they often have a theoretical basis, and interpretation of scores can be affected by clinician's biases.
Projective test	Test-taker is presented with ambiguous item or task and asked to "project" his or her own meaning onto it.	Assumed to tap unconscious determinants of personality	Difficulties in establishing reliability and validity
Behavioral self-report	Behavioral interviews, self-monitoring, and checklist	Detailed information about symptoms, goals for intervention, and basis for evaluation	It is difficult for client to report certain behaviors. Detailed background information is hard to obtain.
Behavioral observation	*In vivo* or analog observations of the target behavior(s)	Avoids the problem of clients attempting to present themselves in a favorable light on self-report measures.	Observations affect the people whose behavior is being observed.

2. a. There are three validity scales that ascertain how defensive the test-taker was and whether the individual may have been careless, confused, or intentionally lying.

   b. (1) Depression (2); (2) Psychopathic deviate (4); (3) Hypomania (9); (4) Psychasthenia (7); (5) Hysteria (3); (6)Hypochondriasis (1); (7) Schizophrenia (8).

   c. To provide an assessment device that was efficient to administer and score, and that could be used for the purposes of objectively arriving at diagnoses of psychological disorders (a "cookbook")

   d. The procedure of "empirical criterion keying" was used. Items developed by the test authors were administered to psychiatric patients, nonpsychiatric hospital patients, and others. Items on which these groups differed and which were sensitive to psychiatric diagnosis were included in the final scales of the MMPI.

   e. The comparison group of "normals" did not reflect the population diversity of the United States.
   Many items were outdated or offensive by current standards.
   The psychometric data in support of the MMPI were only moderate.

   f. A more representative sample was used to collect data on normal individuals as well as on psychiatric patients.
   The items were brought up-to-date.
   Subcultural biases were eliminated.
   More subtle validity scales were included.
   Additional personality assessment scales were included.

3. a. interjudge reliability
   b. concurrent validity
   c. internal consistency
   d. predictive validity
   e. criterion validity
   f. test-retest reliability
   g. content validity
   h. construct validity

4. a. IQ was originally calculated as the ratio of "mental age" to "chronological age."

   b. The deviation IQ is based on conversion of a person's actual test score to a score that reflects how high or low the score compares with the scores of others in that person's age and gender group.

   c. Verbal IQ
   Performance IQ
   Full Scale IQ

   d. Verbal IQ: vocabulary, factual knowledge, short-term memory, and verbal reasoning
   Performance IQ: psychomotor abilities, nonverbal reasoning, and ability to learn new relationships
   Full Scale IQ: the total of scores on both the Verbal and Performance IQ measures

   e. Scores on the Wechsler scales are interpreted by clinicians by referring to published guidelines and by formulating a picture of the client's cognitive strengths and weaknesses on the basis of how the test-taker responded to particular items and the test situation in general. The interpretation must also take into account a person's background, especially when that person's background does not match the backgrounds of those on whom the test was standardized.

FOCUSING ON RESEARCH

1. Intelligence is a heritable trait that predicts and possibly causes a variety of social outcomes, including social attainment or failure of the individual as well as problems for society as a whole.

2. Higher overall IQs for Asians compared with those for Whites and Blacks; higher IQs for Whites compared with those for Blacks.

3. There is considerable evidence for environmental contributions to intelligence.
Intelligence may be a multifaceted trait, and tests of intelligence do not take all abilities into account.
The definition of distinct races is difficult to make.

FROM THE CASE FILES OF DR. SARAH TOBIN: THINKING ABOUT BEN'S CASE

1. Ben said he wanted to find out about psychological testing.
2. Dr. Tobin observed Ben to be sitting in a corner of the room, staring at the floor, muttering or humming to himself. Although it was a warm day, he had on a wool hat that covered his hair and ears and he had on black leather sports gloves. His voice sounded fearful. Dr. Tobin believed that Ben was experiencing emotional instability and was feeling needy and frightened. Ben reported that police officers had been following him, since he collided with a police car while riding his bike. He was fearful of being prosecuted by the police. He said he wore the hat and gloves to cover up his identifying characteristics in case "someone is trying to find you." But then he laughed at himself and said he was just kidding.
3. He spent his time in solitary hobbies and had no close friends. His family system was dysfunctional. He said that his mother was a "nut case," who had been in psychiatric hospitals at least twice. Dr. Tobin believed that her behavior and history suggested that she was a schizophrenic. Ben said that his teachers commented about his failure to maintain eye contact with people. He said he found teachers' questions sometimes hard to understand, but teachers thought he was being a "wise guy." After the collision between his bike and a police car, Ben started feeling frightened of police and believed that they were looking for him to arrest him. He worried that his phone was tapped, his mail read, and his food treated with truth serum. He also believed that "Nazi police," sent by the local police, were trailing him.
4. Diagnostic interview, WAIS-III, MMPI-2, Rorschach, Tat, and evaluation by neurologist that included an MRI
5. Delusional thinking, hallucinations, and extreme anxiety
6. Referral for psychiatric consultation, recommended evaluation for antipsychotic medication, and long-term psychotherapy to help him develop more adaptive behaviors

HOW ARE WE DIFFERENT?

1. Some experts contend that test content is biased in favor of white, middle-class American culture and values, and that minorities get lower scores than Whites not because they are less intelligent or have more psychological disorders but because the assessment instruments are flawed.
2. SOMPA is a cognitive assessment along three dimensions, medical, social, and pluralistic, that take into account cultural and linguistic differences of minority children. Assessment items take into account the child's culture and how it differs from dominant Anglo-American culture. SOMPA seems to be suited for predicting academic placement and achievement, but some question its validity for assessing cognitive abilities.
3. It is suggested that some objective personality measures, such as the MMPI, have items that are inapplicable to different ethnic groups. The TAT, a commonly used projective assessment, contains no depictions of minority members. These criticisms question the validity of these tests for minority populations when the content is tied to the dominant culture.
4. TEMAS was designed specifically for Hispanic and African American children and adolescents as an alternative to traditional personality instruments such as the TAT. It consists of 23 pictures depicting minority children in ambiguous interpersonal situations, which children are asked to interpret. For instance, one picture could be interpreted as an act of stealing or helping behavior. Responses to the ambiguous depictions provide data about adaptive and maladaptive aspects of personality.

REVIEW AT A GLANCE

1. Assessment
2. psychological
3. physical
4. social
5. determining a person's intellectual capacity
6. predicting a person's appropriateness for a job
7. evaluating competence to stand trial
8. brain structure and functioning
9. personality
10. intellectual functioning
11. clinical interview
12. unstructured
13. structured
14. mental status examination

48

15. appearance and behavior
16. orientation
17. thought content
18. thinking style and language
19. affect and mood
20. perceptual experiences
21. sense of self
22. motivation
23. cognitive functioning
24. insight and judgment
25. psychological testing
26. validity
27. reliability
28. standardization
29. intelligence tests
30. personality tests
31. MMPI-2
32. Rorschach
33. behavior
34. family environment or other dimension that influences behavior
35. bodily function and structure
36. EEG, CAT scan, and MRI
37. Halstead-Reitan Neuropsychological Test Battery
38. biological
39. psychological
40. sociocultural

MULTIPLE CHOICE

1. The answer is (a). (b) does not involve open-ended questions; (c) does not involve assessment of reasons for therapy, and background, and (d) involves a written questions which the client answers.
2. The answer is (b). (a) is incorrect (see answer to number (1); (c) is incorrect (see answer to number (1) and there is no assessment procedure known as (d).
3. The answer is (d). (a) is a decision-making process; (b) is a response to something, and (c) is a client's awareness of his or her own behavior.
4. The answer is (a). (b) involves seeing things for which there is no physical basis; (c) and (d) are not recognized symptoms.
5. The answer is (b). (a) involves an act; (d) is a form of disordered thinking (c).
6. The answer is (d). (a) and (b) involve observing a behavior in the client; (c) involves asking the client questions about behavior.
7. The answer is (a).
8. The answer is (b), the IQ assessment for children. The other answers are not IQ assessment scales for children.
9. The answer is (a).
10. The answer is (c). The other answers have nothing to do with determining a client's faking.
11. The answer is (a). The other answers do not involve projective tests that are analyzed for idiosyncratic responses.
12. The answer is (a). The other answers do not involve X ray-type procedures.
13. The answer is (a). (b) involves an unrealistic belief about something that itself is based in reality; (c) is a thought that is not based in reality; and (c) is a repetitive, intrusive thought.
14. The answer is (b). There is no way yet to measure (a); (c) and (d) are false statements.
15. The answer is (c). (a) involves shifts in mood; (b) involves incessantly talking about one topic; and (d) indicates a lack of emotional expression.
16. The answer is (d). The other answers are not involved in the administration and scoring of assessment instruments.
17. The answer is (b). The other processes do not assess cognitive deficits and strengths.
18. The answer is (c). (a) and (d) are not self-administered; (b) is not an assessment instrument, but a diagnostic manual.
19. The answer is (c). (a) and (d) involve therapist questioning and observation; (b) is not a recognized assessment procedure.
20. The answer is (d). (a), (b), and (c) are not, as such, designed for use with diverse populations.
21. The answer is (c). (a), (b), and (d) are assessed by using the mental status examination.
22. The answer is (c). (a) is not related to language; (d) involves fabricating information and (b) involves making up or using words that have similar sounds.

23. The answer is (c). (a), (b), and (d) are not IQ measures.
24. The answer is (a). (b), (c), and (d) do not utilize inkblots.
25. The answer is (c). (a), (b), and (d) do not assess neurological functioning.

50

CHAPTER **4**
THEORETICAL PERSPECTIVES

CHAPTER AT A GLANCE

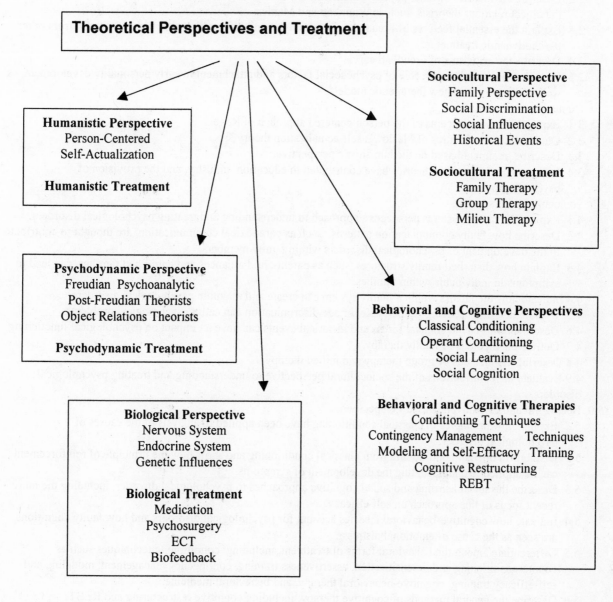

Theoretical Perspectives and Treatment

Sociocultural Perspective
Family Perspective
Social Discrimination
Social Influences
Historical Events

Sociocultural Treatment
Family Therapy
Group Therapy
Milieu Therapy

Humanistic Perspective
Person-Centered
Self-Actualization

Humanistic Treatment

Psychodynamic Perspective
Freudian Psychoanalytic
Post-Freudian Theorists
Object Relations Theorists

Psychodynamic Treatment

Behavioral and Cognitive Perspectives
Classical Conditioning
Operant Conditioning
Social Learning
Social Cognition

Behavioral and Cognitive Therapies
Conditioning Techniques
Contingency Management   Techniques
Modeling and Self-Efficacy   Training
Cognitive Restructuring
REBT

Biological Perspective
Nervous System
Endocrine System
Genetic Influences

Biological Treatment
Medication
Psychosurgery
ECT
Biofeedback

LEARNING OBJECTIVES

1.0 The Purpose of Theoretical Perspectives in Abnormal Psychology
    1.1 Describe the purpose of theories as the basis for understanding and treating abnormal behavior.

2.0 Psychodynamic Perspective
    2.1 Describe the main concepts of Freud's theory, including the structure of personality, psychodynamics, defense mechanisms, stages of psychosexual development, and Freud's place in history.
    2.2 Describe the theories of other psychodynamic theorists including Jung, Adler, Horney, and Erikson, and the object relations theorists, such as Winnicott and Mahler.
    2.3 Explain the essential features of Freudian psychoanalysis and differentiate this form of therapy from other psychodynamic treatments.
    2.4 Describe the criticisms of Freud's theory.
    2.5 Discuss the research on the role of psychosocial factors and attachment in early personality development, as well as the growth of new therapeutic models.

3.0 Humanistic Perspective
    3.1 Explain the main concepts of the person-centered approach of Rogers.
    3.2 Outline the main features of Maslow's self-actualization theory.
    3.3 Describe treatment based on the humanistic perspective.
    3.4 Indicate how humanistic theories have contributed to education, industry, and the provision of psychotherapy.

4.0 Sociocultural Perspective
    4.1 Explain the family systems perspective approach to understanding and treating psychological disorders.
    4.2 Describe how faulty communication patterns, such as paradoxical communication, are thought to contribute to the development of psychological disorders within family members.
    4.3 Explain how disturbed family structures, such as parent-child alliances and enmeshed families, can lead to symptoms in individuals within families.
    4.4 Indicate how the factors within a family system can create and maintain psychological disorders.
    4.5 Explain how experiencing gender, race, or age discrimination can cause psychological problems.
    4.6 Describe how general societal forces and historical events can have an impact on psychological functioning.
    4.7 Outline the methods of family therapy.
    4.8 Describe the methods of group therapy and milieu therapy.
    4.9 Evaluate the contributions of the sociocultural perspective to understanding and treating psychological disorders.

5.0 Behavioral and Cognitively Based Perspectives
    5.1 Explain how principles of classical conditioning have been applied to analysis of the causes of psychological disorder.
    5.2 Distinguish operant conditioning from classical conditioning and show how the principle of reinforcement can be applied to understanding the development of symptoms.
    5.3 Describe the social learning and social cognitive approaches to psychological disorder, including the more recent focus of this approach on self-efficacy.
    5.4 Indicate how cognitive-behavioral theories account for psychological disorders and how faulty cognitions are seen as the cause of emotional distress.
    5.5 Differentiate among the behavioral forms of treatment, including conditioning techniques such as counterconditioning and desensitization, assertiveness training, contingency management, modeling and self-efficacy training, cognitive-behavioral therapy, and behavioral medicine.
    5.6 Describe the general methods of cognitive therapy, including cognitive restructuring and REBT.
    5.7 Describe the evidence in support of the effectiveness of cognitive and behavioral approaches to understanding and treating psychological disorders.

6.0 Biological Perspective

    6 .1 Outline the structure and functions within the central nervous system, the neuron and synapse, neurotransmitters, the structures within the brain, and the autonomic nervous system.

    6.2 Describe the role of the endocrine system in behavior, including the effect of hormones.

    6.3 Explain basic concepts in genetics, such as genes, chromosomes, genotype, and phenotype.

    6.4 Indicate the major models of genetic transmission of inherited traits and diseases.

    6.5 Outline the forms of biologically based therapies, including medication, psychosurgery, ECT, and biofeedback.

    6.6 Evaluate the contributions of the biological perspective, including the search for genetic causes, to understanding and treating mental disorders.

7.0 Developing a Perspective: An Integrative Approach

    7.1 Explain how integrative models of psychotherapy put together the concepts and methods of the major perspectives in abnormal psychology.

8.0 Chapter Boxes

    8.1 Outline the controversy regarding the issue of repressed memories.

    8.2 Describe feminist approaches to psychotherapy and how they contrast with traditional psychoanalysis.

MATCHING

Put the letter from the right-hand column corresponding to the correct match in the blank next to each item in the left-hand column.

1. ___ The ego's logical and rational style of thinking.
2. ___ Freud's proposed view of the basis of feminine psychology.
3. ___ Method used by psychoanalysts to encourage clients to talk openly about their unconscious thought processes.
4. ___ Stage of development in Freud's theory in which the infant experiences hostile urges toward caregivers.
5. ___ What Adler and Horney regard as the attempt by a maladjusted individual to avoid facing the weaknesses of the real self.
6. ___ Object relations theorist who emphasized the infant's fantasy life.
7. ___ What Rogers called the optimally adjusted individual.
8. ___ Psychological process characterized by a lack of gratification, according to Maslow.
9. ___ English psychologist who criticized psychoanalysis as ineffective.
10. ___ Process in Freud's theory in which the young child feels romantic love toward the opposite-sex parent.
11. ___ The id's distorted cognitive representation of the world.
12. ___ Researcher who developed the □Strange Situation□ to study attachment processes in infants.
13. ___ According to Rogers, parental communications that cause children to feel they are loved only if certain demands are fulfilled.
14. ___ Interpretation rejected by Freud that the patients with hysteria he treated were victims of incest.
15. ___ According to Mahler, the most important phase of development.
16. ___ The learning of an association between a neutral stimulus and a behavior that usually occurs reflexively.
17. ___ System in the body involved in controlling automatic, involuntary processes necessary for survival.
18. ___ Brain region involved in controlling balance and motor coordination.
19. ___ Part of the neuron that transmits information to other neurons.
20. ___ Form of behavioral treatment in which a client receives rewards for performing desired behaviors and not for performing undesired behaviors.

a. free association
b. Oedipal complex
c. Hans Eysenck
d. primary process thinking
e. fully-functioning person
f. Mary Ainsworth
g. conditions of worth
h. rapprochement
i. secondary process thinking
j. seduction hypothesis
k. oral-aggressive phase
l. penis envy
m. Melanie Klein
n. neurotic excuses
o. deficit need
p. cognitive restructuring
q. operant conditioning
r. central nervous system
s. dysfunctional attitudes

21. ___ System in the body containing the brain and spinal cord.
22. ___ Treatment method in family therapy in which a family is instructed to interact in problematic ways.
23. ___ Type of learning in which the individual acquires new behaviors by being reinforced for performing them.
24. ___ Part of the cortex involved in abstract planning and judgment.
25. ___ Area of the neuron that receives neural transmissions.
26. ___ Assumptions or personal rules that interfere with an individual's adjustment.
27. ___ Method of therapy in which a person's negative assumptions and ideas are reframed in more positive ways.
28. ___ Point of communication between two or more neurons.
29. ___ Unit of inheritance on which genes are located.
30. ___ Chemical substance produced by endocrine glands.

t. synapse
u. classical conditioning
v. paradoxical intervention
w. prefrontal cortex
x. synaptic terminal
y. contingency management
z. hormone
aa. dendrite
bb. basal ganglia
cc. autonomic nervous system
dd. chromosome

IDENTIFYING THEORY

Put the letter corresponding to the theoretical perspective in the blank next to the concept.
F= Freudian psychoanalysis
P= Post-Freudian psychodynamic (Jung, Adler, Horney, and Erikson)
O= Object relations (Klein, Winnicott, Kohut, Mahler)
P= Post-Freudian psychodynamic (Jung, Adler, Horney, and Erikson)
O= Object Relations (Klein, Winnicott, Kohut, and Mahler)
H= Humanistic (Rogers and Maslow)
BI= Biological
FS= Family systems
CB= Cognitive-behavioral
BE= Behavioral
SL= Social Learning

PERSPECTIVE CONCEPT

1. _____ Double bind
2. _____ Automatic thought
3. _____ A-B-C model
4. _____ Extinction
5. _____ Concordance rate
6. _____ Vicarious reinforcement
7. _____ Penetrance
8. _____ Shaping
9. _____ Identified patient
10. _____ Reticular formation
11. _____ Generalization
12. _____ Cross-fostering
13. _____ Self-efficacy
14. _____ Heritability
15. _____ Neurosis results from the individual's misguided efforts to live up to the image of the idealized self.
16. _____ Psychological disorder results from defects in the self created by faulty parenting.
17. _____ Personality continues to develop throughout life in a series of psychosocial □crises.□
18. _____ Psychologically healthy people boost their feelings of well-being by their ability to have peak experiences.

19. _____ Fantasized images in infancy of parents as "good" and "bad" form the basis of the later development of the self.
20. _____ Severe psychological disturbance is the result of faulty communication patterns learned in early life.
21. _____ Psychological disorder is the result of id-ego-superego imbalances.
22. _____ The deepest layer of the unconscious mind is made up of archetypal images representing universal human themes.
23. _____ Psychological disturbance results from incongruence between one's self-concept and one's experiences.
24. _____ Unconscious sexual and aggressive impulses provide the fundamental motivation for human behavior.

MIND BOGGLE PUZZLE

Each box contains a term that is defined in the clue below it.   The letters of the term are connected to each other in the box, but they may follow any direction.   Indicate your answer by drawing a line connecting the letters in the box.

S U G S C	B C O X F	C R F H J	Y E X V Q	T R B W E
I J P N K	G P N G R	L A Q W S	S B I S T	X V A N X
Q E G E R	H J T Y U	U C T X M	C W M N E	I U E F S
Y C V E I	A Q O R E	P O E N B	O Q T H J	N E R O C
P X G O W	T V E C N	Z Y P C Y	V I A L P	C E K H G
The structure of personality that, according to Freud, contains the conscience and the ego-ideal	Term used by Rogers to describe a psychological state in which an individual's self-concept is consistent with experiences	Psychosexual development stage in late childhood in which sexual urges become relatively unimportant forces in personality	Theory in psychology that emphasizes living each moment to the fullest	Process in psychotherapy in which the client carries over feelings toward parents onto the therapist

56

SHORT ANSWER

1. Match the theorist or researcher with the concept:

   Theorist

   ___ a. Freud
   ___ b. Jung
   ___ c. Adler
   ___ d. Horney
   ___ e. Erikson
   ___ f. Winnicott
   ___ g. Kohut
   ___ h. Mahler
   ___ i. Rogers
   ___ j. Maslow
   ___ k. Watson
   ___ l. Bandura
   ___ m. Minuchin
   ___ n. Ellis
   ___ o. Wolpe
   ___ p. Skinner
   ___ q. Pavlov
   ___ r. Bowen
   ___ s. Haley

   Concept

   1. psychosocial crisis
   2. narcissism
   3. hierarchy of needs
   4. idealized self
   5. person-centered
   6. separation-individuation
   7. social interest
   8. transitional object
   9. libido
   10. archetypes
   11. power relationships within families
   12. irrational beliefs
   13. intergenerational approach to family perspective
   14. counterconditioning
   15. classical conditioning
   16. conditioned fear
   17. self-efficacy
   18. operant conditioning
   19. enmeshed families

2. For each of the following theorists, summarize his position on the role of early parenting in the healthy development of the self and the development of psychological disorder:

Theorist	Healthy development	Psychological disorder
Kohut		
Mahler		
Rogers		

3. Describe the contributions, criticisms, and type of research associated with each of the following theoretical perspectives:

Perspective	Contributions	Criticisms	Current evaluation
Psychoanalytic			
Psychodynamic (post-Freudian)			

Perspective	Contributions	Criticisms	Current evaluation
Humanistic			

4. For each of the following theorists, summarize the goals of treatment and approach or approaches used in therapy:

Theorist	Goals of treatment	Approaches in therapy
Freud		
Adler		
Horney		
Erikson		
Object relations theorists		
Rogers		

5. Describe the main points, criticisms, and current evaluation of each of the following theoretical perspectives:

Perspective	Underlying assumptions about the causes of psychological disorder	Current evaluation
Family Systems		
Behavioral (conditioning models)		

Social learning		
Cognitive-behavioral		
Biological		

6. For each of the following theoretical perspectives summarize the goals of treatment approaches used in therapy:

Theory	Goals of treatment	Approach in therapy
Family systems		
Behavioral (conditioning models)		
Social learning		
Cognitive-behavioral		
Biological		

7. The following behaviors are examples of each of the ego defense mechanisms identified in Freudian theory. In the blank to the left of each example, name the defense mechanism it represents:

a. _____ Asserting that alcohol is not a problem in one's life, even though one drinks heavily.
b. _____ A person is angry with a roommate and intentionally breaks a glass.
c. _____ After being turned down by a prospective dating partner, a person goes to her room and sulks.
d. _____ A student fails a test and falsely attributes the failure to feeling ill.
e. _____ A daughter insists that she "hates" her mother completely after her mother refuses to lend her money.
f. _____ One mentally relives a tragic situation and makes it come out all right.
g. _____ A soccer player talks about her painful knee operation in a detached and impersonal way.
h. _____ A student forgets about the time he made a fool out of himself at a friend's party.
i. _____ A woman is excessively nice to an acquaintance of whom she is acutely jealous.
j _____ Someone wrongly accuses a person to whom she is attracted of flirting with her.

8. Write in the blanks the psychosexual stage with which each characteristic is most closely associated:

O=Oral   **A**=Anal   **P**=Phallic   **G**=Genital

___ a. Smoking
___ b. Being unusually tidy
___ c. Failing to establish a stable career
___ d. Being sarcastic

___ e. Having overly sloppy living habits
___ f. Holding extremely harsh standards of moralistic behavior
___ g. Being unable to share in romantic relationships
___ h. Failing to establish a sense of morality

9. Indicate in the blank next to each item which aspect of Maslow's theory it pertains to, using the following codes:

P= peak experiences   **H**= hierarchy of needs   **S**= self-actualization

a. ___ The fulfillment of security needs before the fulfillment of self-esteem needs.

b. ___ Feeling a tremendous surge of inner happiness and harmony with the outside world.

c. ___ The need for physical comfort and safety take priority over reading a good book.

d. ___ Feeling that one can accept one's own weaknesses.

e. ___ Liking people without having to approve of what they do.

f. ___ Achieving a strong sense of spiritual fulfillment.

g. ___ Having a sense of purpose or mission in life.

h. ___ Feeling loved enough by others to go on and seek ways to improve one's self-understanding.

10. As a child, Sandy became terrified when she almost fell out of a fast-moving roller coaster. Now, as an adult, Sandy feels panicky when she takes her children to a park or fair where there is a roller coaster. Apply the terms from the classical conditioning model of Pavlov to Sandy's experience:

Unconditioned stimulus_____   Unconditioned response _____
Conditioned stimulus _____   Conditioned response_____

BONUS PUZZLE

This is an acrostic puzzle in which the letters in the clues, when rearranged, form a quotation. The clues are common words, and when you put the letter in each clue in the numbered space in the puzzle, the quote will contain Sigmund Freud's perspective on the use of dreams in understanding personality:

___ ___ ___ ___   Sound made by a lion.
1 18 8 6

___ ___ ___ ___ ___   What you do when you say ☐One, two, three.☐
17 2 24 19 12

___ ___ ___   Sodium hydroxide (rhymes with ☐pie☐).
5 3 14

___ ___ ___ ___   Sound made by an owl.
13 7 23 10

___ ___ ___   The opposite of happy.
25 4 9

___ ___ ___ ___ ___ ___   Son of your aunt and uncle.
21 11 15 20 22 16

| 1 | 2 | 3 | 4 | 5 | | 6 | 7 | 8 | 9 | | 10 | 11 | | 12 | 13 | 14 | | 15 | 16 | 17 | 18 | 19 | 20 | 21 | 22 | 23 | 24 | 25 |

60

FROM THE CASE FILES OF DR. SARAH TOBIN: THINKING ABOUT KRISTIN'S CASE

Answer the following questions about the case of Kristin Pierpont.

1. Summarize Kristin's thoughts and feelings that had led to her see Dr. Tobin as a therapist.

_____

_____

2. What was Dr. Tobin's diagnosis of Kristin?

_____

_____

3. Identify the theoretical perspectives Dr. Tobin considered in developing her case formulation (for instance, what models did she use to explain Kristin's psychological state?).

_____

_____

4. Describe how Dr. Tobin's treatment plan integrated several theoretical models. Be sure to identify the models and their contributions to Kristin's treatment.

_____

_____

_____

5. Referring to the text box on the feminist-relational approach to therapy, explain how this perspective could contribute to understanding and treating Kristin's psychological distress.

_____

_____

HOW ARE WE DIFFERENT?

Answer these questions about "How People Differ: Feminist-Relational Approaches to Therapy."

1. Explain how the feminist-relational perspective differs from the psychodynamic perspective in explaining the causes of psychological problems.

_____

_____

2. Describe how a feminist-relational therapist differs from a psychodynamic therapist in terms of goals of treatment.

_____

_____

3. Do you think the feminist-relational approach has some value for men? If so, for what types of psychological problems?

_____

_____

REVIEW AT A GLANCE

The five major theoretical perspectives that influence the ways in which clinicians and researchers interpret and organize their observations about behavior are _____1_____, _____2_____, _____3_____, _____4_____, and _____5_____. The _____6_____ approach brings together aspects and techniques of more than one theoretical perspective.

The _____7_____ perspective emphasizes unconscious determinants of behavior, and is derived from the _____8_____ approach of Sigmund Freud. The term _____9_____ is used to describe the processes of interaction among the ____10_____, _____11_____, and the ____12_____. According to this theory, people use _____13_____ to keep unacceptable thoughts, instincts, and feelings out of conscious awareness. Freud proposed that people develop though a series of _____14_____stages, with each stage focusing on a different sexually excitable zone of the body: _____15_____, _____16_____, _____17_____and ____18_____. Post-Freudian theorists, such as _____19_____, ____20_____, _____21_____and _____22_____ departed from Freud's emphasis of sexual and aggressive instincts. _____23_____ theorists, such as _____24_____, _____25_____, _____26_____, and _____27_____, proposed that _____28_____ lie at the core of personality.

Traditional psychodynamic treatment incorporates techniques such as _____29_____, _____30_____, _____31_____, and _____32_____. Newer approaches, based on object relations theory, have adapted the concept of _____33_____ to understanding the ways that individuals relate as adults to significant people in their lives.

The _____34_____ perspective believes that people are motivated to strive for _____35_____ and _____36____ in life. The person-centered theory of _____37_____, focuses on the uniqueness of each individual and the need to confront honestly the reality of his or her experiences in the world. _____38_____ self-actualization theory focuses on the maximum realization of the individual's potential for _____39_____growth. In _____40_____ therapy, Rogers recommended that therapists treat their clients with _____41_____ and _____42_____, while providing a model of _____43_____ and a _____44_____.

Theorists within the _____45_____perspective emphasize the ways individuals are influenced by _____46_____, _____47_____, and _____48_____. The four major approaches to the _____49_____ perspective are: _____50_____, _____51_____, _____52_____, and _____53_____. Psychological disturbances can arise as a result of _____54_____, _____55_____, or _____56_____discrimination. Treatments within the sociocultural perspective depend upon the nature of social forces contributing to their distress, and include _____57_____, _____58_____, and _____59_____.

According to the _____60_____perspective, abnormality is caused by faulty _____61_____. According to the _____62_____perspective, abnormality is caused by _____63_____processes. Emotional reactions may be acquired through _____64_____ and behaviors through _____65_____. Behavioral therapists believe that clients can acquire new emotional and behavioral responses by ____66_____ the behavior of others. The _____67_____ theories of Beck and Ellis emphasize changing _____68_____.

The _____69_____perspective sees abnormal emotions, behaviors and cognitive processes as being caused by _____70_____, such as the _____71_____ and ____72_____and _____73_____. A person's _____74_____ makeup can play an important role in determining certain disorders. In trying to assess the relative role of _____75_____and _____76_____, researchers have come to accept an interactionist perspective. Biological treatments usually consist of _____77_____. _____78_____ is an intervention in which clients learn to control various bodily reactions associated with stress.

In contemporary practice, most clinicians take an _____79_____approach, combining different models by means of _____80_____, _____81_____, and _____82_____.

MULTIPLE CHOICE

1. Freud's statement that "the child is father to the man" means that
   a. early life experiences play a formative role in the development of personality.
   b. children are often more psychologically healthy than adults.
   c. adults can learn a great deal by observing the behavior of children.
   d. resolution of the Oedipal conflict is needed for healthy adult functioning.

2. Id is to ego as
   a. instinct is to conscience.
   b. secondary is to primary process thinking.
   c. pleasure principle is to reality principle.
   d. ego is to superego.

3. As discussed in the Critical Issue on repressed memories of early childhood abuse
   a. memory of early life events is highly accurate and reliable.
   b. adults accused of abuse confess to their behavior when confronted.
   c. children's memories are not necessarily accurate and are subject to distortion.
   d. clinicians agree that such memories should not be discussed in therapy.

4. According to Freudian theory, which behavior would suggest fixation at the anal stage?
   a. compulsive pursuit of gratification
   b. a drive to "work and love"
   c. hostility and a critical attitude
   d. rigid overcontrol and hoarding

5. Every time that Alyssa enters her therapist's office, she feels anxious and apprehensive, feelings similar to her fearful reactions to her father. Psychodynamic theorists would call this response
   a. transference.
   b. countertransference.
   c. resistance.
   d. a defense mechanism.

6. The Q-sort was used by Carl Rogers to measure
   a. incongruence between actual and ideal self.
   b. incongruence between actual and real self.
   c. degree of an individual's self-actualization.
   d. an individual's capacity for empathy.

7. Which theorist conceptualized a pyramid-like structure called the hierarchy of needs, specifying the order in which human needs must be fulfilled?
   a. Mahler
   b. Laing
   c. Maslow
   d. Rogers

8. Existential theorists believe that
   a. it is important to appreciate fully each moment as it occurs.
   b. fundamental flaws in human nature cause psychological disorders.
   c. unconscious factors are the basis of human behavior and existence.
   d. human existence represents a continual struggle between good and evil.

9. What is the term for the phase of psychodynamic treatment in which the client is helped to achieve a healthier resolution of earlier childhood issues?
   a. transference
   b. working through
   c. dream analysis
   d. free association

10. Feminist-relational approaches to therapy emphasize which themes?
    a. the need of the client to establish herself independently of her relationships
    b. the client's need to understand her relationships in terms of penis envy
    c. the relationship between the client's physical and psychological symptoms
    d. the client's feelings about significant relationships and connections in her life

11. Which of the following statements best characterizes current thinking regarding the theoretical perspective that should be assumed by a clinician?
    a. Clinicians typically adopt one perspective from which to treat all individuals.
    b. Most clinicians tend to identify with one perspective but borrow from other perspectives when appropriate.
    c. Most clinicians view the psychodynamic perspective as outdated and therefore utilize the humanistic perspective.
    d. Currently, most clinicians are disillusioned by the psychological perspectives and have adopted the medical perspective.

12. When defense mechanisms are used in a rigid or extreme fashion, they become the source of:
    a. adjustment.
    b. psychological disorders.
    c. ego strength.
    d. unconscious impulses.

13. Each of Freud's psychosexual stages centers around
    a. the mother-infant bond.
    b. one of the body's erogenous zones.
    c. psychosocial crises in childhood.
    d. development of adequate defense mechanisms.

14. Which post-Freudian theorist postulated that each individual progresses through a life-long set of eight crises?
    a. Adler
    b. Erikson
    c. Sullivan
    d. Horney

15. George's psychoanalyst is urging him to sit back, relax, and say whatever is on his mind. This technique is known as:
    a. dream analysis.
    b. free association.
    c. client centering.
    d. word association.

16. To counteract the conditions of worth a person experienced in childhood, Rogers believed that clients should be treated with
    a. sympathy
    b. unconditional positive regard
    c. courtesy
    d. dream analysis

17. The family perspective was developed in the late 1960s within the emerging framework of:
    a. humanistic theory.
    b. systems theory.
    c. behavioral theory.
    d. integrative theory.

18. Eduardo's therapist recommends biofeedback for his high blood pressure because this technique:
    a. helps a person to learn how to regulate autonomic functions.
    b. teaches a person to learn how to regulate peripheral nervous functions.
    c. incorporates structured techniques for managing diet and exercise.
    d. is an effective adjunct to systematic desensitization.

19. The pattern of interrelationships among members of a family is referred to as
    a. family dynamics.
    b. family structure.
    c. interindividual paradigm.
    d. psychodynamics.

20. _____ conditioning is a learning process in which an individual acquires a set of behaviors through reinforcement.
    a. Respondent
    b. Operant
    c. Classical
    d. Pavlovian

21. Which learning technique have parents and animal trainers known for many years as a way of establishing complex behaviors through gradual steps?
    a. discrimination training
    b. classical conditioning
    c. punishment
    d. shaping

22. Ideas so deeply entrenched that an individual is not even aware that they lead to disturbing feelings of unhappiness and discouragement are referred to by Beck as
    a. dysfunctional attitudes.
    b. automatic thoughts.
    c. false cognitions.
    d. irrational beliefs.

23. "I must be liked or loved by virtually every other person I come in contact with, otherwise I am worthless." This statement, in Ellis' terms is an example of a(n)
a. faulty cognition.
b. dysfunctional attitude.
c. irrational belief.
d. activating experience.

24. Although Karen is an extremely competent and effective administrator who gets along well with her subordinates and is well liked, she still feels as though she is not doing a good job. In Rogers' terms Karen is in a state of
a. congruence.
b. alienation.
c. conflict.
d. incongruence.

25. "I get so mad at my wife for bothering me while I try to get my office work done at home." Which of the following statements represents, in Rogers' terms, a reflection of the previous comment?
a. "You really don't mean that; after all you married her so you can't be angry with her."
b. "It really must anger you when she interrupts."
c. "You must have some unconscious hostility toward your mother."
d. "Your work frustrates you."

26. Jeremy continually gets drunk in a smoke-filled bar, where the jukebox always plays loud country music. Eventually, even before he starts drinking in this bar, his speech gets slurred. The slurring of his speech in response to the smoke-filled room and the country music is a(n)
a. unconditioned response.
b. conditioned stimulus.
c. conditioned response.
d. unconditioned stimulus.

27. Which perspective argues that indirect reinforcement can also affect behavior?
a. family systems
b. humanism
c. psychoanalysis
d. social learning

28. A form of counterconditioning in which the individual is trained to replace intimidated behaviors with more forceful behaviors is called
a. systematic sensitization.
b. contingency management.
c. rational-emotive therapy.
d. assertiveness training.

29. Excesses of which neurotransmitter are related to schizophrenia, while diminished amounts are associated with Parkinson's disease?
a. serotonin
b. dopamine
c. GABA
d. norepinephrine

30. Judy has asthma and is being taught by her therapist how to identify the onset of an attack and what steps to take in order to control her attacks. This form of treatment is known as
a. relaxation therapy.
b. self-monitoring therapy.
c. biofeedback.
d. ECT.

ANSWERS

MATCHING

1.	i	11.	d	21.	r
2.	l	12.	f	22.	v
3.	a	13.	g	23.	q
4.	k	14.	j	24.	w
5.	n	15.	h	25.	aa
6.	m	16.	u	26.	s
7.	e	17.	cc	27.	p
8.	o	18.	bb	28.	t
9.	c	19.	x	29.	dd
10.	b	20.	y	30.	z

IDENTIFYING THEORIES

1.	FS	8.	BE	
2.	CB	9.	FS	
3.	CB	10.	BI	
4.	BE	11.	BE	
5.	BI	12.	BI	
6.	SL	13.	CB	
7.	BI	14.	BI	

MIND BOGGLE PUZZLE

15.	P (Adler and Horney)	23.	H (Rogers)
16.	O	24.	F
17.	P (Erikson)		SUPEREGO
18.	H (Maslow)		CONGRUENCE
19.	O (Klein)		LATENCY
20.	P		EXISTENTIAL
21.	F		TRANSFERENCE
22.	P (Jung)		

SHORT ANSWER

1.		l.	17	
a.	9	m.	19	
b.	1074	n.	12	
e.	18	o.	14	
g.	2	p.	18	
h.	6	q.	15	
i.	5	r.	13	
j.	3	s.	11	
k.	6			

2.

Theorist	Healthy development	Psychological disorder
Kohut	Parents communicate to the child their pride in the child's accomplishments, which helps the child develop a favorable sense of self-esteem.	Child develops a disturbed sense of self as a result of parents who fail to show their pride in and approval of in the child's activities.
Mahler	Infant develops through phases in which an autonomous self develops; healthy development results when the caregiver establishes an appropriate balance between supporting dependence and independence.	Disturbance in the sense of self results from being raised by a caregiver who fails to provide adequate nurturance or who does not support the child's establishment of autonomy.
Rogers	Parents who help the child feel accepted for who the child is promote healthy self-development and congruence between self and experiences.	When parents establish conditions of worth, the child feels loved only when certain demands are fulfilled. This situation ultimately leads to the development of incongruence.

3.

Perspective	Contributions	Criticisms	Current evaluation
Psychoanalytic	First modern psychological theory; First systematic approach to psychological disorder; First approach to emphasize psychological causes of disturbed behavior; Emphasized importance of the unconscious	Difficult to test empirically; difficult to disprove on logical grounds; negative view of women in idea of penis envy; Freud's rejection of seduction hypothesis may have been motivated by political reasons; traditional psychoanalysis ineffective	Some supportive evidence in experimental studies of unconscious processes; brief therapy makes it possible to evaluate therapeutic interventions in controlled studies; Freud's theory now viewed increasingly in terms of the context in which it was developed
Psychodynamic (post-Freudian)	Incorporated into psychological theory the importance of cognitive processes, interpersonal relations, and social factors; many important ideas introduced by individual theorists; expanded psychotherapy beyond psychoanalysis	Many concepts are difficult to test experimentally; evidence to support theories biased by the nature of the methods used to collect the evidence	Large number of research studies have supported the ideas of these theorists, including research on Erikson's theory, Adler, and attachment styles.

67

Perspective	Contributions	Criticisms	Current evaluation
Humanistic	More positive view of human behavior than that offered by psychodynamic perspective; widespread influence of humanistic ideas has occurred throughout psychology	Methods of therapy rely heavily on self-report, making them inappropriate for certain disorders; downplays role of the unconscious and may therefore be overly simplistic; given the nature of disorders the perspective can explain, there is a narrow range of clients for whom therapy is appropriate	Maslow's theory not well supported by research. Applications of Maslow to business and industry not widely supported; emphasis by Rogers on research using the Q-sort and factors affecting therapy outcome give the theory an empirical base and support the importance of empathy

4.

Theory	Goals of treatment	Approaches in therapy
Freud	Bring into conscious awareness the individual's unconscious conflicts	Free association; dream analysis; analysis of transference issues; interpretation of resistance
Adler	Help the individual lead a more productive life	Collaboration between the client and therapist to examine the client's feelings of inferiority and boost sense of inner confidence
Horney	Help the individual regain lost connections to the inner self	Help the client explore unrealistic demands imposed by the idealized self's expectations and instead accept the flawed but "true□ self
Erikson	Achieve more favorable resolutions of psychosocial crises	Help the client discover factors impeding the his or her successful resolution of the psychosocial crisis
Object relations theorists	Reverse destructive processes that occurred early in the client's life	Through good □parenting,□ the therapist tries to restore the client's sense of self and control over the self's boundaries; empathy in therapeutic relationship helps the client feel appreciated and accepted as an individual (Kohut).
Rogers	Help the client discover inherent goodness; achieve greater self-understanding	Provide unconditional positive regard; use empathy to see the client's situation as it appears to the client; provide reflection and clarification of client's feelings and thoughts; provide a model of genuineness and willingness to self-disclose

5.

Perspective	Underlying assumption about the causes of psychological disorder	Current evaluation
Family systems	An individual's disorder is a function of disturbance in the family as a whole.	Importance of family is increasingly recognized as an influential determinant of some disorders, but rarely are family problems considered the sole basis of serious psychological disturbance.
Behavioral (conditioning models)	Psychological disorder is seen as a set of behavioral responses controlled by the environment.	These theories are empirically based and straightforward but lack in-depth approach to understanding the causes of disorders. Cognitive-behavioral models address some of the criticisms of behaviorism but are limited in their application to specific aspects of personality and psychological disorder.
Social learning	Psychological disorder can be acquired through observing the behavior of others.	
Cognitive-behavioral	Dysfunctional emotions are the result of faulty cognitions about the self and others.	
Biological	Psychological disorder has biological origins.	Increasing evidence is accumulating in favor of biological causes of certain disorders, but there is recognition of the importance of interactions with environmental causes.

6.

Theory	Goals of treatment	Approach in therapy
Family systems	Help the client by changing the family system of which the client is a part	Working with the family as a whole, the therapist attempts to change the dynamics of the family. In some cases, paradoxical interventions may be used.
Behavioral (conditioning models)	Provide corrective learning experiences that reduce the frequency of maladaptive behaviors	Counterconditioning; systematic desensitization; assertiveness training; contingency management
Social learning	Help the client develop more positive self-expectations	Modeling; Self-efficacy training
Cognitive-behavioral	Change the dysfunctional thoughts that produce maladaptive emotions	Cognitive restructuring; Rational-emotive therapy; Stress inoculation training
Biological	Alter faulty biological processes	Electroconvulsive therapy; Biofeedback

7.
   a. denial
   b. displacement
   c. regression
   d. rationalizlation
   e. splitting
   f. undoing
   g. isolation of affect
   h. repression
   i. reaction formation
   j. projection

8.
   a. O
   b. A
   c. G
   d. O
   e. A
   f. P
   g. G
   h. P

9.
   a. H
   b. P
   c. H
   d. S
   e. S
   f. P
   g. S
   h. H

BONUS PUZZLE FINAL ANSWER: □ROYAL ROAD TO THE UNCONSCIOUS□

ROAR
COUNT
LYE
HOOT
SAD
COUSIN

10. The experience of almost falling from
    a fast-moving roller-coaster.   Fear
    The sight of a roller coaster.   Fear

70

FROM THE CASE FILES OF DR. SARAH TOBIN: THINKING ABOUT KRISTIN'S CASE

1. Kristin said she was seeking therapy to deal with feelings of isolation, loneliness, and sadness as a result of her father's suicide a year earlier. She said that the year since his death had been the worst year of her life. She saw herself as a failure because of her low income, lack of any friends, and lack of a boyfriend. She had little contact with her mother and refused to go out when people asked her to join them. She said she was sad and furious about what her father had done.
2. Mood disorder and identity problem
3. Dr. Tobin used psychodynamic (object relations), cognitive-behavioral, and sociocultural models. Kristin's lack of closeness with her mother early in life made her insecure about other important relationships. She turned to her father for emotional support and affection. She needed to feel good about herself again (humanistic), and she needed to improve her relationship with her mother (family).
4. The foundation of the treatment plan was rooted in object relations (psychodynamic). Dr. Tobin would conduct the therapy with strong positive regard for and acceptance of Kristin (humanistic). One goal of therapy would be for Kristin to alter the way she views herself, her family, and other significant people in the world (cognitive). Family therapy would be designed to explore family issues with her mother and sister (sociocultural).
5. This approach stresses the value of relationships to women. Kristin's disturbance arose with the loss of the parent closest to her. Dr. Tobin realized this, and the goals of therapy included improving relationships with her sister, mother, and friends.

HOW ARE WE DIFFERENT?

1. The psychodynamic perspective traditionally focuses on deficits and problems in early development and stresses the need to achieve autonomy and independence. The feminist-relational approach stresses the importance of relationships.
2. The goals of psychodynamic therapy are self-knowledge, autonomy, and independence, which enable the individual to separate from parents or parent-figures. The goals of feminist-relational therapy are to help women develop a sense of self based on their ability to care for themselves in the context of caring for others, stressing connectedness with others rather than independence from others.
3. There is every reason to believe that men value relationships and closeness, too, but the importance of them and the skills to make and maintain relationships do not necessarily come naturally to them (due to gender roles and expectations). Boys are taught when very young that they must be self-sufficient and independent. This puts pressure on them not to "need" anyone but themselves. Many men complain that they don't have close friends and that they have problems relating to women in healthy ways. The feminist-relational approach would help men who wanted to improve their relationships develop a sense of self in the context of caring for others.

REVIEW AT A GLANCE

1. psychodynamic
2. humanistic
3. sociocultural
4. behavioral-cognitive
5. biological
6. integrative
7. psychodynamic
8. psychoanalytic
9. psychodynamic
10. id
11. ego
12. superego
13. defense mechanisms
14. psychosexual

15. oral
16. anal
17. phallic
18. genital
19. Jung
20. Adler
21. Horney
22. Erikson
23. Object relations
24. Klein
25. Winnicott
26. Kohut
27. Mahler
28. interpersonal relationships
29. free association
30. dream analysis
31. analysis of transference
32. analysis of resistance
33. infant attachment style
34. humanistic
35. self-fulfillment
36. meaning
37. Carl Rogers
38. Maslow's
39. psychological
40. client-centered
41. unconditional positive regard
42. empathy
43. genuineness
44. a willingness to disclose
45. sociocultural
46. people
47. social institutions
48. social forces
49. family
50. intergenerational
51. structural
52. strategic
53. experiential
54. gender
55. race
56. age
57. family therapy
58. group therapy
59. milieu therapy
60. behavioral
61. learning experiences
62. cognitive
63. maladaptive thought
64. classical conditioning
65. operant conditioning
66. modeling
67. cognitive
68. maladaptive thought patterns

69. biological
70. abnormal bodily functioning
71. brain
72. nervous system
73. endocrine system
74. genetic
75. mature
76. nurture
77. medication
78. biofeedback
79. integrative
80. technical eclecticism
81. theoretical integration
82. attention to common factors

MULTIPLE CHOICE

1. (a) is correct. (b) and (c) may be true, and (d) is a Freudian theory, but neither of these address Freud's quoted statement.
2. (c) is correct. (a) involves the id and the superego; (b) is incorrect since secondary process thinking belongs to the ego, not the id; and (d) is incorrect.
3. (c) is correct. There is no empirical support for (a), (b), and (d).
4. (d) is correct. (a), (b), and (c) are not associated with the anal stage.
5. (a) is correct. (b) involves the feelings a client invokes in the therapist; (c) is a client's reluctance to do the therapeutic work; and (d) is a mechanism to protect the ego.
6. (a) is correct. (b) is incorrect and (c) and (d) have no bearing on the Q-sort assessment.
7. (c)is correct. Mahler (a) was concerned with infant development; (b) Laing was a critic of the diagnostic process; and Rogers (d) was concerned with the humanistic perspective.
8. (a) is correct. (b), (c), and (d) are unrelated to existential theory.
9. (b) is correct. (a), (b), and (c) are also utilized in psychodynamic therapy, but do not relate to resolution of issues.
10. (d) is correct. (a), (b), and (c) are not associated with feminist-relational approaches.
11. (b) is correct. (a), (c), and (d) may be true for some clinicians, but not for the majority.
12. (b) is correct. Defense mechanisms may arise as a result of (d); they are not associated with (a) and (c).
13. (b) is correct. (a) and (d) are issues in Freud's perspective; (c) is associated with Erik Erikson, not Freud.
14. (c) is correct. (a), (b), and (d) did not propose stage theories of development.
15. (b) is correct. Psychoanalysts may sometimes use (a); (d) was used in the early days of clinical work, but is not generally in use today; and (c) is not clinical technique.
16. (b) is correct. Rogers did not utilize (d) and (a); he would likely express (c) but not as a technique.
17. (b) is correct. (a), (c) and (d) were not related to the development of the family perspective.
18. (a) is correct. (d) may be correct sometimes; (b) cannot be regulated by biofeedback; and (c) has nothing to do with biofeedback.
19. (a) is correct. (b), (c), and (d) are not terms dealing with family interaction.
20. (b) is correct. (a) and (d) are not terms for learning processes; (c) involves reflexive biological responses.
21. (d) is correct. (b) involves biological, reflexive responses; (a) involves a form of operant conditioning; and (c) may be used with operant conditioning, but it does not help one learn new behaviors.
22. (b) is correct. (a), (c), and (d), though they may correctly state the idea, are not associated with Beck.
23. (c) is correct. (a), (b), and (d) are not associated with Ellis.
24. (d) is correct. (a) is the opposite of (d); and there is no evidence for (b) or (c).

25. (b) is correct. (a) is a verbal challenge; (c) and (d) are conclusions.
26. (c) is correct. (b) and (d) are incorrect, because Jeremy's drunkenness is not a stimulus, but a response; (a) is incorrect, because the response was learned.
27. (d) is correct. (a), (b), and (c) do not concern reinforcement as an aspect of learning.
28. (d) is correct. (a), (b), and (c) do not involve replacement of maladaptive behaviors with more adaptive responses.
29. (b) is correct. (a), (c), and (d) are not associated with Parkinson's disease, but with other disorders.
30. (c) is correct. (a) may help Judy get over an attack; (b) may help her predict an attack; and (d) is a form of treatment used for severe psychological disorders, not asthma.

CHAPTER 5
PERSONALITY DISORDERS

CHAPTER AT A GLANCE

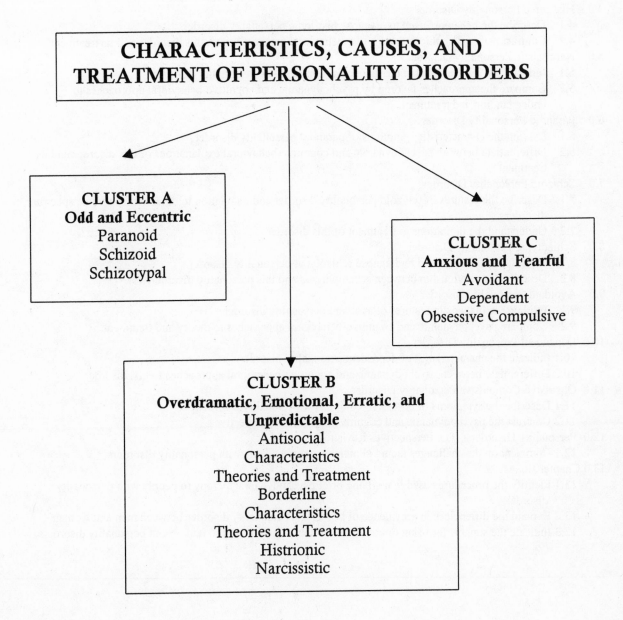

CHARACTERISTICS, CAUSES, AND
TREATMENT OF PERSONALITY DISORDERS

CLUSTER A
Odd and Eccentric
Paranoid
Schizoid
Schizotypal

CLUSTER C
Anxious and Fearful
Avoidant
Dependent
Obsessive Compulsive

CLUSTER B
Overdramatic, Emotional, Erratic, and
Unpredictable
Antisocial
Characteristics
Theories and Treatment
Borderline
Characteristics
Theories and Treatment
Histrionic
Narcissistic

Learning Objectives

1.0 The Nature of Personality Disorders
    1.1   Describe the general features of a personality disorder as diagnosed in *DSM-IV*.
2.0   Antisocial Personality Disorder
    2.1   Indicate the behaviors that are used to diagnose antisocial personality disorder.
    2.2   Contrast the biological, psychological, and sociocultural perspectives on understanding and treating antisocial personality disorder.
3.0   Borderline Personality Disorder
    3.1   Explain the characteristic features of borderline personality disorder.
    3.2   Compare the biological, psychological, and sociocultural theories and treatment of borderline personality disorder.
4.0   Histrionic Personality Disorder
    4.1   Describe the behaviors used to diagnose histrionic personality disorder.
    4.2   Contrast psychodynamic and cognitive-behavioral perspectives on this disorder and its treatment.
5.0   Narcissistic Personality Disorder
    5.1   Indicate the features used in the diagnosis of narcissistic personality disorder.
    5.2   Compare the approaches favored by psychodynamic and cognitive-behavioral approaches to understanding and treatment.
6.0   Paranoid Personality Disorder
    6.1   Explain the characteristic symptoms of paranoid personality disorder.
    6.2   Differentiate between psychodynamic and cognitive-behavioral explanations of this disorder and its treatment.
7.0   Schizoid Personality Disorder
    7.1   Describe the features of schizoid personality disorder and its relation to other schizophrenia spectrum disorders.
    7.2   Understand the limitations to treatment of this disorder.
8.0   Schizotypal Personality Disorder
    8.1   Indicate the features used to diagnose schizotypal personality disorder.
    8.2   Describe the relationship between schizophrenia and this personality disorder.
9.0   Avoidant Personality Disorder
    9.1   Explain the diagnostic features of avoidant personality disorder.
    9.2   Compare psychodynamic and cognitive-behavioral approaches to theory and treatment.
10.0 Dependent Personality Disorder
    10.1 Indicate the characteristics of dependent personality disorder.
    10.2 Differentiate between psychodynamic and cognitive-behavioral approaches to this disorder.
11.0 Obsessive-Compulsive Personality Disorder
    11.1 Describe the symptoms of obsessive-compulsive personality disorder.
    11.2 Contrast the psychodynamic and cognitive-behavioral perspectives.
12.0 Personality Disorders: The Perspectives Revisited
    12.1 Comment on the challenges facing clinicians treating clients with personality disorders.
13.0 Chapter Boxes
    13.1 Identify the procedures used in applying brief psychodynamic therapy to people with personality disorders.
    13.2 Explain the differences in prevalence of borderline personality disorder between men and women.
    12.3 Indicate the support for using dimensional models of personality to understand personality disorders.

Identifying the Disorder

Write the name of the personality disorder in the blank next to the symptoms listed.

1. _____ Lack of regard for the legal or moral standards of society, often leading the individual to commit criminal or malicious acts.

2. _____ Unusual suspiciousness of others and constant attempts to guard oneself from harm.

3. _____ Eccentricities of thought, behavior, appearance, and ways of relating to others, often accompanied by peculiar beliefs.

4. _____ Chronic pattern of unstable mood, relationships, and identity.

5. _____ Excessive reliance on others, leading the individual to become incapable of making decisions or acting autonomously.

6. _____ Lack of interest in social relationships accompanied by emotional coldness and restrictiveness.

7. _____ Unrealistic, inflated sense of one's own importance.

8. _____ Overly dramatic emotionality in various realms of everyday behavior.

9. _____ Fear of closeness to others and being terrified by the prospect of being publicly embarrassed.

10. _____ Unusual levels of perfectionism and rigidity.

Matching

Put the letter from the right-hand column corresponding to the correct match in the blank next to each item in the left-hand column.

1. ___ Exaggerated sense of self-importance seen in individuals with narcissistic personality disorder.
2. ___ Childhood disorder involving criminality that often precedes the development in adulthood of antisocial personality disorder.
3. ___ Term used to refer to the continuum of disorders including schizophrenia, schizotypal personality disorder, and schizoid personality disorder.
4. ___ Frequently the goal of treating antisocial personality disorder.
5. ___ Researcher who proposed that people with antisocial personality disorder are relatively insensitive to anxiety-provoking situations.
6. ___ Ability to restrain one's immediate urge to act; often lacking in children who later develop antisocial personality disorder.
7. ___ Term once used for what is now known as schizotypal personality disorder.
8. ___ Therapeutic approach in which the clinician presents some harsh realities to a client.
9. ___ Suicidal gesture used to gain attention from others.
10. ___ Cognitive-behavioral theorist who developed a dialectical method of therapy for borderline personality.

a. confrontation
b. Marsha Linehan
c. impulse control
d. latent schizophrenia
e. stimulating feelings of remorse
f. grandiosity
g. conduct disorder
h. schizophrenia spectrum
i. Hervey Cleckley
j. Parasuicide

Short Answer

1. Contrast the psychodynamic and cognitive-behavioral explanations of each of the following personality disorders:

Personality disorder	Psychodynamic view	Cognitive-behavioral view
Borderline		
Paranoid		
Histrionic		
Narcissistic		
Avoidant		
Dependent		
Obsessive-compulsive		

2. Summarize the evidence for biological causes of the following personality disorders:

Disorder	Biological explanations
Antisocial personality disorder	
Borderline personality disorder	
Schizoid personality disorder	
Schizotypal personality disorder	

3. Answer the following questions concerning the nature of personality disorders and their diagnosis and treatment.
   a. What is the difference between a personality trait and a personality disorder?

_____

_____

b. What factors do clinicians look for in making diagnoses of personality disorders?

_____

_____

c. What are two major problems involved in diagnosing these disorders?

_____

_____

d. How do clinicians attempt to set goals for treating clients with these disorders?

_____

_____

e. What is the role of a clinician's theoretical perspective in treating people with personality disorders?

_____

_____

4. For each of the following disorders, describe approaches to treatment and problems that are often encountered in implementing these treatments:

Disorder	Approach to treatment	Problems encountered in treatment
Antisocial personality disorder		
Borderline personality disorder		
Paranoid personality disorder		
Schizoid personality disorder		
Dependent personality disorder		
Obsessive-compulsive personality disorder		

5. Answer the following questions about brief psychodynamic treatment of personality disorders.

a. Why are clinicians attempting to develop shorter forms of therapy for personality disorders?

_____

_____

b. What specific techniques do clinicians use when doing brief therapy with personality disordered clients?

_____

_____

c. What does the research suggest about the effectiveness of time-limited or brief therapy for people with personality disorders?

_____

_____

d. Concerning the case of Harold Morrill, if Dr. Tobin were to use short-term therapy, what one theme or issue in his life do you think she might emphasize in order to maximize the benefits of their sessions?

_____

_____

From The Case Files of Dr. Sarah Tobin: Thinking About Harold's Case

Answer the following questions about the case of Harold Morrill.

1. What behaviors did Dr. Tobin observe during her first meeting with Harold that made her wary of her ability to work effectively with him?

_____

_____

_____

2. Briefly summarize the facts and conclusions that make up Dr. Tobin's formulation of Harold's case.

_____

_____

_____

3. What assessment instruments gave Dr. Tobin specific insight into the nature and extent of Harold's problems?

_____

_____

_____

4. Why was Dr. Tobin not surprised that her treatment plan was not successful with Harold?

_____

_____

_____

How Are We Different?

Answer the following questions about "How People Differ: Explaining the Prevalence of Borderline Personality Disorder Among Women."

1. What behaviors associated with borderline personality disorder are stereotypically female?

_____

_____

2. What possible explanations (other than bias in the diagnostic criteria) are there to account for why more women than men are diagnosed with borderline personality disorder?

_____

_____

3. Referring to the discussion of the feminist-relational perspective of abnormality that was the subject of a text box in Chapter 4, comment on what contribution this perspective might make to explaining the gender disparity between men and women who suffer from borderline personality disorder.

_____

_____

Review at a Glance

A (1)_____ involves a longlasting maladaptive pattern of inner experience and behavior, dating back to adolescence or young adulthood, that is manifested in at least two of the following areas: (2)_____, (3)_____, (4)_____, and (5)_____. This inflexible pattern is evident in various (6)_____ and (7)_____ situations, and cause (8)_____ or (9)_____. Personality disorders cause major (10)_____ and (11)_____difficulty, leading to longlasting impairment. The DSM-IV separates personality disorders into three clusters based on shared characteristics. Cluster A comprises (12)_____, (13)_____, and (14)_____ personality disorders, which share the features of (15)_____ and (16)_____ behavior. Cluster B includes (17)_____, (18)_____, (19)_____, and (20)_____ personality disorders. People with these disorders are (21)_____, (22)_____, and (23)_____ or (24)_____. In Cluster C are (25)_____, (26)_____, and (27)_____ personality disorders, characterized by (28)_____and (29)_____ behaviors.

People with (30)_____ have a lack of regard for society's moral or legal standards. This diagnosis has its origins in Cleckley's notion of (31)_____, a personality type characterized by features such as (32)_____, (33)_____, (34)_____, (35)_____, and (36)_____. The DSM-IV criteria added (37)_____and (38)_____behaviors. Biological theories suggest that this disorder has roots in (39)_____. Psychological theories focus on the notion that these individuals are unable to feel (40)_____or_____ and to (41)_____. Sociocultural perspectives focus on (42)_____, (43)_____, and (44)_____experiences. Experts recommend (45)_____ in treatment, especially in (46)_____therapy.

Borderline personality disorder is characterized by (47)_____, (48)_____, and unstable (49)_____ and (50)_____. Many people with this condition engage in (51)_____ and (52)_____behavior. Biological theory focuses on (53)_____ that may have evolved as a result of early (54)_____. Psychological theories have dwelled on (55)_____ and (56)_____as predisposing factors. Sociocultural views focus on the possibility that many people develop this disorder as a result of (57)_____ in contemporary society. In terms of treatment, clinicians try to balance levels of (58)_____ and (59)_____, giving special attention to issues of (60)_____ and (61)_____. Linehan's (62)_____ involves components of (63)_____ and (64)_____.

(65)_____ personality disorder is characterized by excesses in emotionality and attention seeking. People with (66)_____personality disorder show a pattern of detachment from relationships and restricted range of emotional expression. Those with (67)_____ personality disorder show a pattern of social and interpersonal deficits marked by acute discomfort with and reduced capacity for close relationships. They also experience (68)_____ or _____ distortions and (69)_____. People with (70)_____ personality disorder show pervasive patterns of grandiosity, need for admiration, and lack of empathy. Avoidant personality disorder is characterized by a pattern of (71)_____, (72)_____, and (73)_____to negative evaluation. People with (74)_____personality disorder have an excessive need to be taken care of. The diagnosis of obsessive-compulsive personality disorder is characterized by a preoccupation with (75)_____, (76)_____, and (77)_____ and _____ control.

Given the lack of certainty about the causes of personality disorders, clinicians tend to focus on efforts to (78)_____ rather than attempt to bring about total change. Consequently, most therapists (79)_____treatment in response to the particular needs and difficulties of each client.

Multiple Choice

1. Dr. Tobin noted Harold's turbulent relationships, unpredictable emotions, self-destructive behaviors, and identity disturbance and diagnosed him with which personality disorder?
   a. antisocial
   b. paranoid
   c. schizoid
   d. borderline

2. In treating people with antisocial personality disorder, it is recommended that the clinician
   a. adopt a confrontational approach.
   b. adopt a supportive approach.
   c. supplement psychotherapy with medication.
   d. bring the client's family into treatment.

3. Those who know Lisa have difficulty with her unpredictable vacillation between idealizing and devaluing other people, a symptom known as
   a. volatility.
   b. splitting.
   c. lability.
   d. ambivalence.

4. Psychodynamic explanations of paranoid personality disorder see it as rooted in the defense mechanism of
   a. rationalization.
   b. denial.
   c. projection.
   d. reaction formation

5. Compared with people with avoidant personality disorder, those with schizoid personality disorder
   a. do not wish to have relationships.
   b. wish to have relationships.
   c. often suffer from a mood disorder.
   d. often are diagnosed with an Axis I disorder.

6. Researchers studying narcissistic and histrionic personality disorders have reported that
   a. the disorders can be easily differentiated.
   b. features of these two disorders overlap.
   c. both are genetically determined.
   d. they share the feature of hidden paranoia.

7. Cognitive-behavior theorists propose that people with obsessive-compulsive personality disorder
   a. have a hidden wish to be sloppy and disorderly.
   b. displace sexual energy into obsessional thinking and compulsive behavior.
   c. struggle with seemingly uncontrollable aggressive impulses.
   d. have their self-worth depend on conforming to an ideal abstract of perfectionism.

8. The higher prevalence of borderline personality disorder among women is explained by researchers as due to
   a. gender bias in the diagnostic criteria.
   b. disturbed family relationships.
   c. biological gender differences.
   d. higher sexual abuse during childhood.

9. A psychologist notes that a client's TAT stories are filled with themes of rage, intense feelings, identity confusion, and fears of abandonment. These themes correspond to which personality disorder?
   a. borderline
   b. antisocial
   c. schizotypal
   d. paranoid

10. When they were children, many adults who are diagnosed with antisocial personality disorder would have met the diagnostic criteria for
    a. dependent disorder.
    b. conduct disorder.
    c. antisocial disorder.
    d. histrionic disorder.

11. A core feature of people with narcissistic personality disorder is
    a. depression.
    b. mania.
    c. grandiosity.
    d. splitting.

12. Object relations theorists view people with dependent personality disorder as being
    a. insecurely attached.
    b. frustrated and hostile.
    c. self-defeating.
    d. passive-aggressive.

13. Diagnosis of a personality disorder is difficult because
    a. there may be a more specific problem for which the client seeks treatment.
    b. the disorders have such rigid diagnostic criteria.
    c. it is so difficult to detect the disorder in a person's behavior.
    d. these individuals are often aware that they have a problem but avoid seeking treatment.

14. A common developmental factor in the psychological environment of individuals with antisocial personality disorder is
    a. parental drug abuse.
    b. parental disharmony.
    c. abusive siblings.
    d. lack of schooling.

15. An inability to distinguish between one's own identity and the identities of others is characteristic of which personality disorder?
    a. schizoid
    b. self-defeating
    c. borderline
    d. narcissistic

16. In therapy, clients with borderline personality disorder are particularly likely to
    a. become aloof and distant from the therapist.
    b. describe their problems in vague and ambiguous terms.
    c. become pathologically dependent on the therapist.
    d. show narcissistic behavior.

17. It is difficult to treat people with schizoid and schizotypal personality disorder because
    a. they are emotionally unstable.
    b. they tend to view their therapist with suspicion.
    c. their treatment is often mandated by the courts.
    d. they are cognitively and emotionally out of touch.

18. According to current psychoanalytic theorists, parental failure to provide reassurance and positive responses to accomplishments may lead to the development of this personality disorder
    a. histrionic
    b. schizoid
    c. schizotypal
    d. narcissistic

19. Brief psychodynamic treatment of personality disorders is most likely to be effective when
    a. the client is resistant to establishing a working relationship.
    b. therapy takes an unfocused and global approach.
    c. there is a prominent interpersonal theme in the client's symptoms.
    d. the therapist avoids confrontation with the client on specific issues.

20. Which of the following is the one of the most significant factors in determining whether or not an individual has a personality disorder?
    a. if they are experiencing personal distress because of their behavior pattern
    b. if they have been convicted of crime related to their behavior
    c. if their problem has played a long-term role throughout their lives
    d. if they are having serious difficulty holding down a job

21. Which personality disorder is characterized by a lack of regard for society's moral and legal standards?
    a. antisocial
    b. borderline
    c. narcissistic
    d. passive-aggressive

22. Studies on family inheritance of criminal behavior have demonstrated that
    a. fraternal twins have a higher concordance rate for this type of behavior than do identical twins.
    b. sons are more likely to receive the extra Y chromosome from their mothers than from their fathers.
    c. identical twins have a higher concordance rate for this type of behavior than do fraternal twins.
    d. there is no set pattern that might indicate a genetic component.

23. The formation of intense and demanding relationships with others is characteristic of
    a. antisocial personality disorder.
    b. schizoid personality disorder.
    c. avoidant personality disorder.
    d. borderline personality disorder.

24. The personality disorder in which the primary symptom is constant efforts by the individual to attract attention with exaggerated displays of emotion is called
    a. histrionic personality disorder.
    b. borderline personality disorder.
    c. antisocial personality disorder.
    d. paranoid personality disorder.

25. Which personality disorder is characterized by an unrealistic, inflated sense of self-importance and an inability to see the perspectives of other people?
    a. borderline personality disorder
    b. obsessive-compulsive personality disorder
    c. passive-aggressive personality disorder
    d. narcissistic personality disorder

26. People with paranoid personality disorder tend to
    a. become overly dependent on others.
    b. engage in criminal acts.
    c. be impulsive.
    d. keep their distance from people.

27. What does the expression "schizophrenia spectrum disorders" mean?
   a. Schizophrenia, schizoid, and schizotypal personality disorders all involve visual hallucinations.
   b. Most of the personality disorders are related to schizophrenia.
   c. Borderline personality disorder is related to schizotypal personality disorder.
   d. Schizophrenia, schizoid, and schizotypal personality disorders may be on the same continuum.

28. Chris is a very shy 30-year-old woman who usually stays home and doesn't interact with other people. At work she strays away from the other people in the office as if she were afraid to talk to anyone. Chris might be diagnosed as suffering from
   a. avoidant personality disorder.
   b. antisocial personality disorder.
   c. dependent personality disorder.
   d. passive-aggressive personality disorder.

29. A serial killer would most likely be diagnosed with
   a. avoidant personality disorder.
   b. dependent personality disorder.
   c. histrionic personality disorder.
   d. antisocial personality disorder.

30. Lorraine always needs to be the center of attention. She talks loudly, gesturing wildly in hopes of gaining an audience. Everything in her life is, to hear her tell it, either far better or far worse than events in the lives of her friends. Lorraine may be suffering from
   a. dependent personality disorder.
   b. histrionic personality disorder.
   c. borderline personality disorder.
   d. schizoid personality disorder.

Answers

IDENTIFYING THE DISORDER

1. antisocial	4. borderline	7. narcissistic	10. obsessive-compulsive
2. paranoid	5. dependent	8. histrionic	
3. schizotypal	6. schizoid	9. avoidant	

MATCHING

1. f	3. h	5. i	7. d	9. j
2. g	4. e	6. c	8. a	10. b

SHORT ANSWER

1.

Personality disorder	Psychodynamic view	Cognitive-behavioral view
Borderline	Problems in the early development of the self due to parents who either do not allow the child to achieve an independent identity or who are physically, emotionally, or sexually abusive	Dichotomous thinking about the self and others and low sense of self-efficacy leading to lack of confidence, low motivation, and inability to seek long-term goals
Paranoid	Heavy reliance on the defense mechanism of projection	Mistaken assumptions that people will harm if they get the chance and that one needs to be wary of the malicious motives of others
Histrionic	Traditional view is that histrionic personality disorder is a variant of hysteria, the product of unresolved Oedipal conflicts and overreliance on the defense mechanism of repression. Other psychoanalytic theorists propose that the disorder is the result of a global cognitive style that cannot focus on details in life situations.	Mistaken assumption that one is unable to handle life on one's own, causing the individual to seek someone else to make up for this deficit; the global nature of the individual's cognitive style leads to diffuse and exaggerated emotional states and unstable evaluations of others
Narcissistic	Traditional explanation is that the disorder is due to failure to progress beyond early psychosexual stages of development. Object relations theorists propose that the individual develops the disorder in response to faulty parenting, in which the child is made to feel insecure and inadequate. This type of parenting leads the child to develop a false grandiose view of the self.	Faulty belief that one is special and deserves to be treated better than other people; problems result when these grandiose ideas about the self clash with experiences in the real world
Avoidant	Horney's theory proposes that avoidant personality represents a "turning away from others" due to expectations that one will be criticized and rejected.	Hypersensitivity to rejection occurs due to childhood experiences of extreme criticism by parents. This leads to the faulty belief that one is flawed, unworthy, and undeserving of the attention and friendship of others. Avoidance develops as a means of protection from this anticipated rejection.
Dependent	Traditional view is that the disorder reflects regression to or fixation at the oral stage of development due to overindulgence or neglect by parents of dependency needs. Object relations theorists view the disorder as the result of insecure attachment and low self-esteem.	Unassertiveness and anxiety over making independent decisions result from doubts about one's adequacy and ability to solve problems. Assertiveness with others would threaten the security of relationships.

Personality disorder	Psychodynamic view	Cognitive-behavioral view
Obsessive-compulsive	Traditional view is that the disorder is due to fixation at or regression to the anal stage of psychosexual development. More recent views emphasize an overly narrow and rigid cognitive style.	Unrealistic concern about being perfect and avoiding mistakes

2.

Disorder	Biological explanations
Antisocial personality disorder	Extra chromosome (XYY pattern) Excess testosterone Defects in frontal lobes of cortex and/or limbic system Neuropsychological deficits in learning and attention Genetic inheritance
Borderline personality disorder	Genetic inheritance Abnormal neuroendocrine functions Electrophysiological functions
Schizoid personality disorder	Genetic inheritance, possibly linked to schizophrenia
Schizotypal personality disorder	Genetic inheritance, possibly reflecting a latent form of schizophrenia

3.
a. A personality trait is an enduring pattern, as is a personality disorder, but a personality disorder is specifically identified as creating difficulties in the individual's life or feelings of personal distress.
b. The clinician looks at the client's overall life history to determine whether the current problems have been present on a long-standing basis.
c. The client often seeks treatment for other problems, such as depression.
   Many personality disorders share similar features.
d. Rather than seek complete personality change, clinicians tend to focus their work on achieving a set of more limited but realizable goals that will help alleviate the client's current distress.
e. Most clinicians tend to individualize their treatment for the client's particular disorder and to integrate relevant theoretical perspectives that are most appropriate for the client's disorder.

4.

Disorder	Approach to treatment	Problems encountered in treatment
Antisocial personality disorder	Stimulate realization that client's behavior has caused harm to others. Reflect the selfish and self-defeating nature of the client's behavior.	Individuals with this disorder often do not seek help voluntarily and, when in treatment, do not change easily.
Borderline personality disorder	Combine an approach that uses confrontation of client's maladaptive thoughts and defenses with providing a sense of stability and predictability. Help client recognize self-destructive nature of certain high-risk or harmful behaviors. Medication may also be used to alleviate symptoms of depression and anxiety.	Their volatility, inconsistency, and intensity make it difficult for these clients to remain in therapy. At the same time, clients may become pathologically dependent on their therapists.
Paranoid personality disorder	Cognitive-behavioral approach suggests countering client's mistaken assumptions and increasing client's self-efficacy. Generally, it is important to collaborate with client, increase client's awareness of other points of view, and help client become more assertive.	Client is likely to be distrustful of therapist and the therapy process.
Schizoid personality disorders	Help client clarify communication skills and modify isolated and eccentric behaviors.	Clients tend to be cognitively and emotionally inaccessible. Progress is likely to be slow and limited in scope.
Obsessive-compulsive personality disorder	Focus on client's maladaptive thoughts, possibly combining this approach with paradoxical instructions to become more symptomatic.	Obsessive-compulsive client tends to ruminate excessively, and therapy might feed into this process.

5.
   a. Traditionally, therapies for people with personality disorders have been lengthy endeavors, often resulting in only limited change in their patterns of relating with others. Though not explicitly stated in the text box, insurance companies and managed care providers are also demanding short-term treatment.
   b. Steering the therapy sessions toward a central, maladaptive theme and confronting clients about styles of relating by calling attention to such behaviors as they arise in therapy; both are designed to heighten the client's emotional involvement in therapy
   c. Research suggests that time-limited therapies are as effective as other forms of therapy, but even the typical "brief" therapy for personality disorders (6 to 12 months) is longer than brief therapy for other disorders.

d. She would likely confront him about his manner of relating to her, his splitting (putting her on a pedestal at one point, criticizing her at another), and his problem with respecting the boundaries of therapy.

FROM THE CASE FILES OF DR. SARAH TOBIN: THINKING ABOUT HAROLD'S CASE

1. He idealized her, and he did not even know her. His appearance was unkempt and shaggy, and he looked immature for his age. He voiced intensity about his interactions with others, most of which ended in anger. He voiced no responsibility for any of the failures in his relationships.
2. The facts of Harold's past fit a pattern commonly seen in those with borderline personality disorder. His family was highly dysfunctional, his mother overprotective and his father emotionally unavailable. His mother's control contributed to his inability to find a life for himself. He patterned his relationships after those of his parents. His mother's criticism left him with a lack of confidence about himself.
3. The WAIS-III subtest scores showed unevenness in his cognitive functioning. He showed deficits in comprehending tasks, yet he understood the issues. His MMPI-2 profile revealed serious personality disorganization with some psychotic-like features. His responses to the Rorschach test contained many unusual responses, with many references to sadistic human destruction, fire, and explosions. His TAT stories revealed themes of rage brought on by feelings of abandonment, characters were described as having sudden and chaotic mood changes, and his plots were disorganized.
4. Dr. Tobin has a lot of experience with borderline clients, with whom it is usually difficult to create and maintain a trusting therapeutic relationship. She was not surprised that her work with Harold came to an unsuccessful and frustrating end.

HOW ARE WE DIFFERENT?

1. Intensity of relationships and affective instability are stereotypical female traits.
2. Though differing biology (hormonal differences, sensitivity to endorphins) may play a role, history of sexual abuse appears to be a significant factor in the development of borderline personality disorder in girls (girls are more likely to be sexually abused than boys).
3. Inasmuch as women are more relationally oriented and more emotionally expressive, the feminist-relational approach would take that into account as a major factor in the development of borderline personality disorder in women whose childhood's are characterized by neglect, abuse, and trauma. Since relationships are so salient in the lives of most women, it stands to reason that their childhood experiences would leave them feeling frightened and insecure in their relations with others and would have provided a very bad model for their adult relationships.

REVIEW AT A GLANCE

1. personality disorder
2. cognition
3. affectivity
4. interpersonal functioning
5. impulse control
6. personal
7. social
8. distress
9. impairment
10. intrapsychic
11. interpersonal
12. paranoid
13. schizoid
14. schizotypal
15. odd
16. eccentric
17. antisocial
18. borderline
19. histrionic
20. narcissistic
21. overdramatic
22. emotional
23. erratic
24. unpredictable
25. avoidant
26. dependent

27. obsessive-compulsive
28. anxious
29. fearful
30. antisocial personality disorder
31. psychopathy
32. lack of remorse
33. extreme egocentricity
34. lack of emotional expressiveness
35. impulsivity
36. untruthfulness
37. disreputable
38. manipulative
39. brain abnormalities
40. fear or anxiety
41. process information not relevant to their immediate goals
42. family
43. early environment
44. socialization
45. confrontation
46. group
47. poor impulse control
48. fluctuating self-image
49. mood
50. interpersonal relationships
51. splitting
52. parasuicidal
53. brain differences
54. trauma
55. trauma
56. abuse
57. diminished cohesion
58. support
59. confrontation
60. stability
61. boundaries
62. dialectical behavior therapy
63. acceptance
64. confrontation
65. Histrionic
66. schizoid
67. schizotypal
68. cognitive; perceptual
69. behavioral eccentricities
70. narcissistic
71. social inhibition
72. feelings of inadequacy
73. hypersensitivity
74. dependent
75. orderliness
76. perfectionism
77. mental; interpersonal
78. improve the client's current life experiences
79. individualize

MULTIPLE CHOICE

1. (d) is correct. (a), (b), and (c) are not characterized by the described behaviors.
2. (a) is correct. (b), (c), and (d) would not be effective techniques for an antisocial client.
3. (b) is correct. (a), (c), and (d) do not characterize moving from devaluation to idealization.
4. (c) is correct. (a), (b), and (d) do not typify a paranoid personality.
5. (a) is correct. (b) is true of those with avoidant disorder; there is no reason to expect that (c) and (d) would be true.
6. (b) is correct. (a) , (c) , and (d) are not correct statements.
7. (d) is correct. There is no evidence that (a), (b), and (c) would be correct statements.
8. (d) is correct. There is no evidence that (a) and (c) are relevant; (b) is a fact in many homes.
9. (a) is correct. (b), (c), and (d) are not characterized by the described behaviors.
10. (b) is correct. (a) and (d) are not related to antisocial disorder and (c) is not diagnosed before the age of 18.
11. (c) is correct. (a), (b), and (d) are not associated with narcissistic personality disorder.
12. (a) is correct. (b), (c), and (d) are not associated with dependent personality disorder.
13. (a) is correct. (b) , (c), and (d) are not true. In fact the opposite of these statements is more likely.
14. (b) is correct. (a), (c), and (d) are not known to be related to the development of antisocial personality disorder.
15. (c) is correct. (a), (b), and (d) are not characterized by this problem with boundaries.
16. (c) is correct. (a), (b), and (c) would not be behaviors expected of a borderline client.
17. (d) is correct. (a), (b), or (c) would not necessarily characterize these clients.
18. (d) is correct. This factor is not generally related to the development of (a), (b), or (c).
19. (c) is correct. (a), (b), and (d) would make it likely that brief therapy would not be successful.

20. (c) is correct. (a), (b), and (d) may be indicated in several types of disorders. disorders, not just personality disorders.
21. (a) is correct. (b), (c), and (d) are not associated with the described behaviors.
22. (c) is correct. (a), (b), and (d) are not supported by current research.
23. (d) is correct. (b) and (c) would be unlikely to form intense relationships; relationship style has not been a focus of study with (a).
24. (a) is correct. (b), (c), and (d) are not characterized by this type of behavior.
25. (d) is correct. (a), (b), and (c) are not typified by this behavior.
26. (d) is correct. (a) is the virtual opposite of (d); (b) and (c) are not consistent with paranoid personality disorder.
27. (d) is correct. There is no basis for the statements in (a), (b), and (c).
28. (a) is correct. The behaviors described are not associated with (b), (c), or (d).
29. (d) is correct. The behaviors described are not associated with (b), (c), or (d).
30. (b) is correct. The behaviors described are not associated with (a), (c), or (d).

CHAPTER **6**
ANXIETY DISORDERS

CHAPTER AT A GLANCE

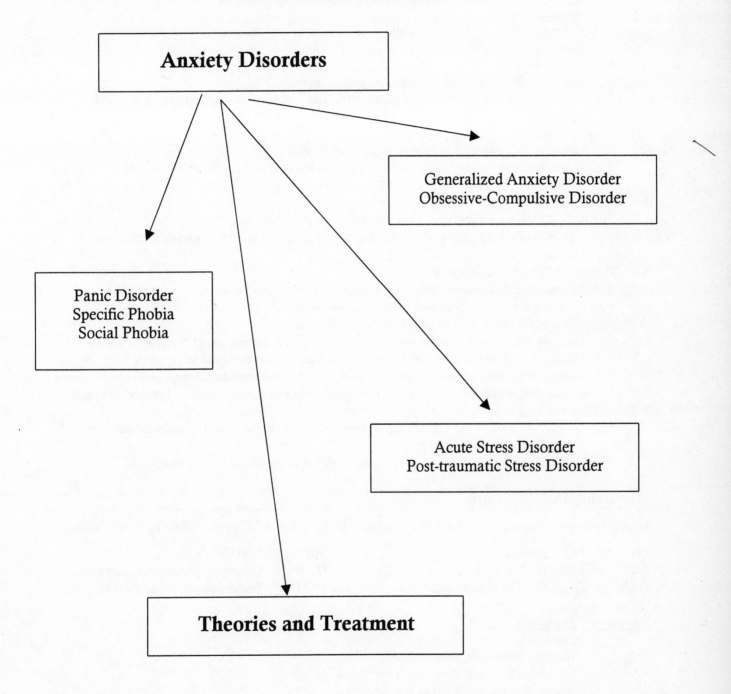

Anxiety Disorders

Generalized Anxiety Disorder
Obsessive-Compulsive Disorder

Panic Disorder
Specific Phobia
Social Phobia

Acute Stress Disorder
Post-traumatic Stress Disorder

Theories and Treatment

Learning Objectives

1.0 The Nature of Anxiety Disorders
    1.1 Describe the characteristics of anxiety symptoms.
    1.2 Differentiate between fear and anxiety.

2.0 Panic Disorder
    2.1 Explain the characteristic features of panic disorder and the symptoms of the related disorder, agoraphobia.
    2.2 Contrast biological, behavioral, and cognitive-behavioral approaches to understanding and treating panic disorder.

3.0 Specific Phobias
    3.1 Indicate the features used to diagnose specific phobias.
    3.2 Discuss the cognitive-behavioral, behavioral, and biological perspectives on theory and treatment.

4.0 Social Phobia
    4.1 Describe the symptoms of people with social phobia.
    4.2 Explain how social phobia develops and how behavioral and cognitive-behavioral methods can be used in treatment.

5.0 Generalized Anxiety Disorder
    5.1 Indicate the symptoms used in the diagnosis of generalized anxiety disorder.
    5.2 Describe how biological and life stress approaches can contribute to understanding and treatment.

6.0 Obsessive-Compulsive Disorder
    6.1 Enumerate the diagnostic criteria of obsessive-compulsive disorder.
    6.2 Compare behavioral, cognitive-behavioral, and biological perspectives.

7.0 Acute Stress Disorder and Post-Traumatic Stress Disorder
    7.1 Describe the features of acute stress disorder and post-traumatic stress disorder.
    7.2 Discuss the relationship between severity of symptoms and exposure to stressors.
    7.3 Indicate the issues involved in understanding the role of trauma in psychological disorders and approaches to treatment that involve biological, behavioral, and cognitive-behavioral methods.

8.0 Chapter Boxes
    8.1 Explain the controversy regarding psychosurgery for extreme treatment-resistant cases of obsessive-compulsive disorder.
    8.2 Describe research concerning the long-term effects of psychological trauma.

Identifying the Disorders

Put the name of the anxiety disorder in the blank next to the symptom using the following abbreviations:

PD	= Panic disorder		**SpP**	= Specific phobia
SoP	= Social phobia		**OCD**	= Obsessive-compulsive disorder
GAD	= Generalized anxiety disorder		**PTSD**	= Post-traumatic stress disorder

Disorder	**Symptom**
1. ____	Flashbacks.
2. ____	Inability to perform tasks in public.
3. ____	Excessive worrying about minor problems.
4. ____	Intense fear accompanied by loss of control.
5. ____	Repetitive thoughts and behaviors that cannot be controlled.

6. ____ Fear of particular objects, activities, or situations.
7. ____ Avoidance of places where one might be trapped and have an anxiety attack.
8. ____ Chronic sense of edginess, worry, dread, and irritability.
9. ____ Time-consuming, unnecessary rituals that cannot be controlled.
10. ____ Avoidance of feared objects, activities, or situations.
11. ____ Fear of public embarrassment or humiliation.
12. ____ Denial of an unpleasant, disastrous event.

Matching

Put the letter from the right-hand column corresponding to the correct match in the blank next to each item in the left-hand column.

1. ___ Behavioral treatment in which the client is trained to substitute a new response to anxiety in the presence of a feared stimulus.
2. ___ Anxiety disorder involving extreme fear of public humiliation.
3. ___ Type of panic attack that arises without a situational cue.
4. ___ Heightened sensitivity to stimuli in the environment.
5. ___ Most effective medication for treating anxiety symptoms.
6. ___ Type of panic attack that does not occur with every exposure in every instance of exposure to a possible threat.
7. ___ Learned associations between internal or external cues and feelings of anxiety.
8. ___ Fear of being trapped or stranded without help.
9. ___ Type of panic attack that occurs with each exposure to a stimulus or cue.
10. ___ Behavioral treatment involving reduction of muscular tension.
11. ___ Medication used in treating obsessive compulsive disorder.
12. ___ Cognitive-behavioral treatment of anxiety disorders in which client learns to discontinue anxiety-related ideas
13. ___ Anxiety disorder involving repetitive, uncontrollable thoughts and behaviors.
14. ___ Explanation of panic disorder with agoraphobia based on cognitive-behavioral theory.
15. ___ Behavioral treatment in which the therapist subjects the client to feared stimuli until anxiety diminishes.

a. conditioned fear reactions
b. situationally predisposed
c. agoraphobia
d. counterconditioning
e. situationally bound
f. social phobia
g. flooding
h. hypervigilance
i. unexpected
j. clomipramine
k. relaxation training
l. obsessive-compulsive disorder
m. fear of fear
n. thought stopping
o. benzodiazepines

Short Answer

1. Describe the role of the following neurotransmitters in anxiety disorders:

Neurotransmitter	Role in anxiety disorders
Serotonin	
GABA	
Norepinephrine	

2. A behavior therapist is working with a client who has a spider phobia. Describe what treatment approach would be involved in each of the following methods:

Method	Treatment approach
Systematic desensitization	
Graded *in vivo* exposure	
Imaginal flooding	
Flooded *in vivo* exposure	

3. For each of the three approaches used in treating obsessive-compulsive disorder, indicate the mechanism of action and specify a limitation or disadvantage of each approach:

Method	Mechanism of action	Limitation or problem
Behavioral		
Medications		
Psychosurgery		

4. Summarize three forms of evidence used to support the role of biology in obsessive-compulsive disorder:

_____

_____

_____

_____

_____

5. Indicate the main differences between social phobia and panic disorder with agoraphobia:

Social phobia	Panic disorder with agoraphobia

6. Summarize the cognitive-behavioral perspective as applied to each of the following anxiety disorders:

Disorder	Cognitive-behavioral explanation
Panic disorder with agoraphobia	
Specific phobia	
Social phobia	
Generalized anxiety disorder	
Post-traumatic stress disorder	

Acrostic

Fill in the boxes with the term that identifies what is written below the box (or which correctly fits the blank space). When you have completed all of them, place the letter with the number below it in the same numbered space at top of puzzle; when the puzzle is correctly solved, you will have the name of a condition related to anxiety disorders.

Period of intense fear accompanied by feeling a loss of control.

Medication most effective in treating symptoms of anxiety.

Extreme somatic treatment used to treat obsessive-compulsive disorder.

Systematic desensitization and flooding are behavioral methods that involve _____ to the threatening situation.

Phase in PTSD in which flashbacks occur.

Phobia characterized by anxiety over public performance.

According to one theory, panic attacks are caused by an excess of this chemical in the blood.

Live presentation of a feared stimulus is used in this form of behavioral therapy.

_____stopping is used in this form of behavioral therapy.

The trade name of fluoxetine, a medication that alters serotonin levels in the brain.

Focusing on Research: The Enduring Effects of Psychological Trauma

Answer the following questions concerning the Research Focus, "The Enduring Effects of Psychological Trauma."

1. What are six possible long-term effects on women of sexual or physical abuse?
_____
_____

2. What eight factors are likely to increase the chances that a person exposed to trauma will suffer symptoms of PTSD?

_____   _____
_____   _____
_____   _____
_____   _____

3. List five types of treatments that are used for PTSD:
_____
_____
_____
_____

From The Case Files of Dr. Sarah Tobin: Thinking About Barbara's Case

Answer the following questions about the case of Barbara Wilder.

1. What symptoms did Dr. Tobin observe on first meeting Barbara?
_____
_____
_____

2. Describe how Dr. Tobin assessed Barbara.
_____
_____
_____

3. Summarize the facts and conclusions that made up Dr. Tobin's formulation of Barbara's case.
_____
_____
_____

4. Describe the nature and course of Barbara's treatment.
_____
_____
_____

Review at a Glance

Anxiety disorders are characterized by experiences of (1)_____,
(2)_____or _____, (3)_____,
(4)_____, and occasionally a (5)_____or _____.
(6)_____ is characterized by frequent and recurrent (7)_____, intense
sensations of fear and physical discomfort. This disorder is often found in association with
(8)_____, the fear of being trapped or unable to escape if a panic attack occurs.
(9)_____ and (10)_____ perspectives have been particularly useful for
understanding and treating this disorder. Treatment based on the cognitive-behavioral perspective involve
(11)_____ training and (12)_____ or _____ flooding as ways of
breaking the cycle of fear of having a panic attack. The most commonly prescribed medications are
(13)_____ and (14)_____ medications.

(15)_____ are irrational fears of particular objects or situations. Cognitive-
behaviorists believe that specific phobias are caused by (16)_____ and
(17)_____. Cognitive-behavioral treatments include (18)_____,
(19)_____, (20)_____, (21)_____,
(22)_____, (23)_____, (24)_____,
(25)_____, and (26)_____.

A (27)_____ is a fear of being observed by others so as to feel humiliated or
embarrassed. Cognitive-behavioral approaches explain this disorder as stemming from an
(28)_____. Behavioral treatment methods include (29)_____,
(30)_____, and (31)_____.

People with (32)_____ have a number of unrealistic worries that spread
to various spheres of life. The cognitive-behavioral approach to this disorder emphasizes the
(33)_____nature of these worries. Treatment is geared toward (34)_____.

In (35)_____, individuals develop (36)_____, thoughts they
cannot get rid of, and (37)_____, irresistible and repetitive behaviors. The cognitive-
behavioral approach sees these symptoms as the product of a (38)_____ between anxiety and
the thoughts and acts, which temporarily can produce relief from (39)_____. The biological
explanation for the disorder suggests that it may be associated with an excess of the neurotransmitter
(40)_____. Treatment with medications such as (41)_____ seems to be
effective. Cognitive-behavioral treatment methods include (42)_____ and
(43)_____.

In (44)_____, the individual is unable to recover from anxiety associated with
a traumatic life event, such as a tragedy, a disaster, an accident, or combat experience. The aftereffects of
the traumatic event include (45)_____, (46)_____, and
(47)_____ that alternate with (48)_____. A briefer form of the disorder
is known as (49)_____. Cognitive-behavioral approaches regard the disorder as a result
of (50)_____ thoughts, feelings of (51)_____,
(52)_____ from others, and a (53)_____outlook on life. Treatment
includes combinations of covering techniques, such as (54)_____therapy and
(55)_____. (56)_____ techniques include imaginal flooding and
(57)_____.

Multiple Choice

1. Which anxiety disorder is most common in young children?
    a. separation anxiety disorder
    b. obsessive-compulsive disorder
    c. generalized anxiety disorder
    d. panic disorder with agoraphobia

2. In people with panic disorder, the association of uncomfortable bodily sensations with memories of the previous panic attack can lead to a full-blown panic attack, a phenomenon known as
    a. unconditioned response.
    b. anticipatory response.
    c. conditioned fear reaction.
    d. prepanic aura.

3. Henri's job involves taking an elevator to the 35th floor, but his claustrophobia is creating serious problems. His therapist vividly describes people trapped in elevators, and asks Henri to imagine the scenes, an approach called
    a. imaginal flooding.
    b. systematic desensitization.
    c. *in vivo* desensitization.
    d. decompensation.

4. What antidepressant medication might be prescribed for obsessive-compulsive disorder?
    a. chlorpromazine
    b. chlorazepam
    c. clozapine
    d. clomipramine

5. Following a traumatic life event, people go through a series of characteristic responses. The initial reaction, involving a sense of alarm and strong emotion, is called the
    a. outcry phase.
    b. denial/intrusion phase.
    c. traumatic phase.
    d. intrusion phase.

6. The surgical treatment used in extreme cases of obsessive-compulsive disorder is known as
    a. cingulotomy.
    b. hyperthyroidism.
    c. uncovering.
    d. lactate infusion.

7. Treatment of Barbara Wilder began in her home, in which she was guided step-by-step through situations that approximated situations that had terrified her in the past, techniques known as
    a. flooding and medication.
    b. hypnosis and age regression.
    c. symptom mastery and cognitive structuring.
    d. *in vivo* techniques and graded exposure.

8. Marlene told her therapist that since her rape she has been terrorized by experiences that seem like hallucinations, similar to those she once had following LSD use. These experiences are called
    a. flashbacks.
    b. intrusions.
    c. delusions.
    d. obsessions.

9. Which neurotransmitter is activated when an individual is placed under stress or in a dangerous situation?
    a. GABA
    b   norepinephrine
    c. serotonin
    d. acetylcholine

10. Every time that Jonathan sees a spider, he experiences extreme fear and anxiety. Jonathan would be diagnosed as having
    a. generalized anxiety disorder.
    b. aversion disorder.
    c. obsessive-compulsive disorder
    d. specific phobia

11. A woman feels that she must scrub her hands for exactly ten minutes after eating any food. This behavior is called
    a. an obsession.
    b. a compulsion.
    c. a delusion.
    d. a specific phobia.

12. What type of panic attack is an essential element of the diagnosis of panic disorder?
    a. situationally bound
    b. situationally predisposed
    c. agoraphobic
    d. unexpected (uncued)

13. To which chemical in the blood do individuals with panic disorder seem hypersensitive?
    a. insulin
    b. norepinephrine
    c. progesterone
    d. lactate

14. The most effective antianxiety medications are called
    a. neuroleptics.
    b. amphetamines.
    c. benzodiazepines.
    d. narcotics.

15. Which behavioral technique is often successful in the treatment of panic disorder with agoraphobia?
    a. lactate therapy
    b. modeling
    c. relaxation training
    d. flooding

16. Which theoretical perspective views the causes of phobias to be based on the individual's faulty inferences and generalizations?
    a. cognitive
    b. humanistic
    c. existential
    d. psychoanalytic

17. The cognitive-behavioral method in which the client is taught not to have anxiety provoking thoughts is called
    a. imaginal flooding.
    b. thought stopping.
    c. graded thinking.
    d. *in vivo* desensitization.

18. A cognitive-behavioral therapist would treat an individual with generalized anxiety disorder by
    a. teaching the client to recognize and change anxiety-producing thoughts.
    b. using free association to illuminate unconscious conflicts.
    c. actively and empathically listening to the client's concerns.
    d. urging the client to develop an enhanced sense of self.

19. Panic disorder in women is associated with what early childhood experience?
    a. parental illness and substance abuse
    b. overachieving school performance
    c. overindulgence by parental figures
    d. supportive family environment

20. In the treatment of PTSD, clinicians may administer medication to control
    a. impulsivity.
    b. appetite disturbance.
    c. high level of sociability.
    d. anxiety, depression, or nightmares.

21. Shelly experiences intense periods of fear and physical discomfort that interfere with her daily living. Shelly may have a(n)
    a. somatoform disorder.
    b. anxiety disorder.
    c. dissociative disorder.
    d. mood disorder.

22. Which of the following statements about the experience of panic attacks in the general population is true?
    a. Many people have had at least one panic attack by the time they reach adulthood.
    b. Many people experience panic attacks more frequently than they think.
    c. Most people have had panic attacks by the time they were ten years old.
    d. Very few individuals in our society have had a panic attack.

23. The fear of being stranded without help available if a panic attack occurs is called
    a. hydrophobia.
    b. simple phobia.
    c. agoraphobia.
    d. social phobia.

103

24. Wendy encounters test anxiety in Professor Carey's and Professor Burke's classes, but not in Professor Hart's class? Which of the following best characterizes Wendy's panic attacks?
   a. uncued
   b. situation-bound
   c. cued
   d. situationally predisposed

25. According to the cognitive-behavioral perspective, a full-blown panic attack may be triggered even before the appropriate bodily changes have taken place because of the association of certain bodily sensations with
   a. memories of the last panic attack.
   b. unconscious conflicts.
   c. memories of poor attachments in childhood.
   d. increased lactate levels.

26. An irrational and unabating fear of a particular object, activity, or situation is defined as
   a. agoraphobia.
   b. social phobia.
   c. an aversion.
   e. a specific phobia.

27. The behavioral approach to treating phobias, which involves gradually exposing the client to the feared stimulus while the client practices relaxation exercises is called
   a. systematic desensitization.
   b. flooding.
   c. aversive conditioning.
   d. systematic relaxation.

28. Tom, a 50-year-old man, feels anxious most of the time. His symptoms include dizziness, nausea, trembling, and heart palpitations. He is constantly fidgeting and cannot sit still for a minute. Tom would be diagnosed as having
   a. panic disorder.
   b. generalized anxiety disorder.
   c. attention deficit disorder.
   d. hyperactivity.

29. An urge or drive toward action that leads to the performance of repetitive, ritualistic behaviors is called a(an)
   a. habit.
   b. obsession.
   c. compulsion.
   d. delusion.

30. In general, an increased risk of developing PTSD is correlated with
   a. the severity of the trauma.
   b. the individual's genetic predisposition to other psychological disorders.
   c. how rapidly treatment follows.
   d. drug use.

Answers

IDENTIFYING THE DISORDERS

1. PTSD	5. OCD	9. OCD
2. SoP	6. SpP	10. SpP
3. GAD	7. PD	11. SoP
4. PD	8. GAD	12. PTSD

MATCHING

1. d	4. h	7. a	10. k	13. l
2. f	5. o	8. c	11. j	14. m
3. i	6. b	9. e	12. n	15. g

SHORT ANSWER

1.

Neurotransmitter	Role in anxiety disorders
Serotonin	Deficiency of serotonin may be involved in panic disorders, as indicated by efficacy of treatment by fluoxetine, which increases availability of serotonin in the brain.
GABA	It is proposed that panic disorder is due to GABA deficiency; neurons in subcortical brain areas involved in panic attacks become more active with less GABA to inhibit them.
Norepinephrine	There is some evidence that panic disorder is caused by heightened levels of norepinephrine when the individual is placed under stress.

2.

Method	Treatment approach
Systematic desensitization	Teaching the client to relax while imagining coming closer and closer to touching a spider.
Graded *in vivo* exposure	Exposing the client in steps to an actual spider
Imaginal flooding	Instructing the client to imagine touching and holding a spider
Flooded *in vivo* exposure	Giving the client a spider to touch and hold until the client no longer feels anxiety

3.

Method	Mechanism of action	Limitation or problem
Behavioral	Thought-stopping to reduce obsessional thinking; exposure to situations that provoke the compulsions or obsessions	Successful in 75 percent of cases but does not reduce symptoms in the remaining 25 percent who enter treatment
Medications	May compensate for serotonin deficiencies in certain individuals with the disorder	Not effective for all individuals with the disorder
Psychosurgery	Cutting neuronal tracts between the frontal lobe and a part of the limbic system	A radical intervention reserved only for clients who are resistant to other treatment methods

4.

There is a higher concordance rate in monozygotic compared to dizygotic twins.

Symptoms of obsessive-compulsive disorder have been observed in people with neurological disorders that affect the basal ganglia.

Brain imaging studies suggest that there is increased metabolic activity in the basal ganglia and frontal lobes.

5.

Social phobia	Panic disorder with agoraphobia
Anxiety is specific to potentially embarrassing contexts in which one's behavior might be observed by others	The individual fears going out of a safe place due to a concern that a panic attack may strike
No unusual response to lactate injection	Lactate injection can provoke the experience of a panic attack.
Equally common in men and women	More common in women than men

6.

Disorder	Cognitive-behavioral explanation
Panic disorder with agoraphobia	Fear of fear
Specific phobia	Faulty inferences and overgeneralizations
Social phobia	Focus attention on imagined criticism
Generalized anxiety disorder	Focus on worries, which leads to a vicious cycle
Post-traumatic stress disorder	Excessive guilt and self-blame for traumatic events

ACROSTIC

panic attack	exposure	lactate	Prozac
benzodiazepines	intrusion	*in vivo*	traumatic
psychosurgery	social	thought	

ACROSTIC ANSWER: Agoraphobia

FOCUSING ON RESEARCH

a.
depression
anxiety
substance abuse
sexual dysfunction
dissociation
interpersonal problems

b.
dissociative symptoms
loss of autonomy
stressful life experiences
greater extent of trauma
prior psychological symptoms
demographic factors
childhood exposure to trauma
genetic predisposition

c.
pharmacological
conditioning
improved coping
"covering" techniques
"uncovering" technique

FROM THE CASE FILES OF DR. SARAH TOBIN: THINKING ABOUT BARBARA'S CASE

1. Barbara was writhing on the floor in what appeared to be a convulsion. She was gasping for breath, and had the appearance of a frightened child. Her body moved rigidly, she shuffled her feet, and she looked worried.
2. Dr. Tobin conducted an unstructured interview about her childhood, adolescence, and adult life to date. Dr. Tobin then referred Barbara to Dr. Herter for a comprehensive behavioral assessment, that included a focused interview, administration of the Body Sensations Questionnaire and Agoraphobia Cognitions Questionnaire, and Barbara's self-monitoring by means of a Panic Attack Record.
3. Barbara's mother and grandmother may have had similar symptoms, leading Dr. Tobin to hypothesize that Barbara had inherited a biological propensity to develop panic attacks. Barbara's relationship with her parents was stressful. Her mother was overcontrolling and her father unreliable and unpredictable. Barbara felt unable to please either parent, and when she left home she felt guilty about leaving her mother. Barbara's early panic attacks were all connected with some kind of emotional conflict—the unresolved conflict about leaving home and separating from a roommate with whom she had formed attachment. Later attacks generalized to all places outside Barbara's apartment.
4. Based upon the referral by Dr. Tobin, Dr. Herter employed behavioral and cognitive-behavioral techniques., including *in vivo* techniques, graded exposure training, cognitive restructuring, and assertiveness training. Dr. Herter began with home-based therapy. Eventually they progressed to a near-by convenience store, then a mall. Barbara learned new ways to think about panic-arousing situations. She also gained some insight into the connection between her interpersonal conflicts and her panic attacks. She stared calling her mother more frequently. Barbara had a relapse when her mother was pressuring her to return home, but she recovered quickly and continued in individual therapy for an additional six months. She eventually overcame her panic attacks and said that she had developed new ways of solving problems related to the possible attacks and her relationship with her mother.

REVIEW AT A GLANCE

1. physiological arousal
2. apprehension; or feelings of dread
3. hypervigilance
4. avoidance
5. specific fear; phobia
6. Panic disorder
7. panic attacks
8. agoraphobia
9. Biological
10. cognitive
11. relaxation training
12. *in vivo;* imaginal
13. antianxiety
14. antidepressant

107

15. Specific phobias
16. previous learning experiences
17. a cycle of negative, maladaptive thoughts
18. flooding
19. systematic desensitization
20. imagery
21. _in vivo_ exposure
22. participant modelingcognitive restructuring
24. coping self-statementsthought stopping
26. increasing the sense of self-efficacysocial phobia
28. unrealistic fear of criticism_in vivo_ exposure
30. cognitive restructuringsocial skills training
32. generalized anxiety disorderunrealistic
34. breaking the negative cycle of worryobsessive-

compulsive disorder
36. obsessionscompulsions
38. learned associationanxiety
40. serotoninclomipramine
42. exposure
43. thought stoppingpost-traumatic stress disorder
45. flashbacksnightmares
47. intrusive thoughtsdenial
49. acute stress disordernegative and maladaptive
51. ineffectivenessisolation
53. pessimisticsupportive
55. stress management
56. Uncovering
57. desensitization

MULTIPLE CHOICE

1. (a) is correct. (c) and (d) are not generally seen in young children; (b) may sometimes be manifest in children.
2. (c) is correct. (a) and (b) are not the correct terms for the described behavior; there is no such condition as (d).
3. (a) is correct. (b) and (c) would not involve imagining, and (d) is not associated with phobia therapy.4. (d) is correct. (a), (b), and (c) are not normally prescribed for obsessive-compulsive disorder.
5. (a) is correct. (c) is the trauma itself; (b) and (d) occur later.
6. (a) is correct. (b) is a condition, not a treatment; (c) and (d) are other types of therapeutic measures.
7. (d) is correct. (a) is not a step-by-step process; (b) and (c) do not fit the described procedures.
8. (a) is correct. (b) is not a term specific to treatment; (c) and (d) involve thoughts, not sensory experiences.
9. (b) is correct. (a), (c), (d) are not activated by stress.10. (d) is correct. (a), (b), and (c) do not describe specific phobias.
11. (b) is correct. (a) is a thought that gives rise to (b); (c) is a thought that has no basis in reality; (d) is an irrational fear about something specific.
12. (d) is correct. (a) and (b) arise in certain situations; (c) is experienced by some who have panic disorders.
13. (d) is correct. (a), (b), and (c) are not known to be involved in panic disorder.14. (c) is correct. (a) is used to treat schizophrenia; (b) is a stimulant; (d) a painkiller.
15. (c) is correct. (a), (b), and (d) are not normally used to treat agoraphobia.
16. (a) is correct. (b), (c), and (d) do not address an individual's thought processes as causes of disorders.
17. (b) is correct. (a) involves imagining; (c) is not a known technique; (d) involves therapy in a life-like situation.
18. (a) is correct. (b) and (d) are not the main focus of cognitive-behavioral treatment; (c) is a method used in humanistic therapy.
19. (a) is correct. (b), (c), and (d) are not implicated in women's experiencing of panic disorder.
20. (d) is correct. (a) and (b) are not associated with PTSD; (c) is not a problem that needs treatment.
21. (b) is correct. (a), (c), and (d) are not associated with fear and physical discomfort.
22. (a) is correct. (b), (c), and (d) are not supported by theory or empirical evidence.
23. (c) is correct. (a) is fear of water; (b) is not a recognized disorder; (d) involves fear of social situations.

24. (d) is correct. (a) involves a panic attack unassociated with any situation; (b) is incorrect because Wendy does not encounter panic in all test-taking situations; (c) does not fit the fact pattern described.

25. (a) is correct. (b), (c), and (d) involve perspectives other than cognitive-behavioral.

26. (d) is correct. (a) is a fear of leaving home and being exposed to the threat of panic attacks; (b) is a fear about social settings and situations; (c) is something unpleasant, not necessarily feared.

27. (a) is correct. (b) is the opposite of (a); (c) would be counter-indicated in treating phobias; and (d) involves relaxation of the body, not exposure to the feared stimulus.

28. (b) is correct. (a) is time-limited; (c) and (d) are children's behavioral disorders, not an adult anxiety disorder. disorders.

29. (c) is correct. (a) is not necessarily associated with an urge or drive; (b) is the thought leading to (c); (d) is an unrealistic thought or idea.

30. (a) is correct. (b), (c), and (d) are not associated with onset of PTSD

CHAPTER 7
SOMATOFORM DISORDERS, PSYCHOLOGICAL FACTORS AFFECTING MEDICAL CONDITIONS, AND DISSOCIATIVE DISORDERS

CHAPTER AT A GLANCE

Dissociative Disorders
Dissociative Identity Disorder
Dissociative Amnesia
Dissociative Fugue
Depersonalization Disorder
Theories and Treatment

Somatoform Disorders
Conversion Disorder
Somatization Disorder
Body Dysmorphic Disorder
Hypochondriasis
Conditions Related to Somatoform
Disorders
Theories and Treatment

Psychological Factors Affecting Medical Conditions
Axis I Disorders
Psychological Symptoms
Personality Traits
Maladaptive Health Behaviors
Stress-Related Responses
Specific Psychological Factors

Learning Objectives

1.0 Somatoform Disorders
    1.1 Describe somatoform disorders as the translation of psychological conflicts into physical symptoms.
    1.2 Indicate the symptoms of conversion disorder.
    1.3 Enumerate the diagnostic features of somatization disorder.
    1.4 Describe the characteristics of body dysmorphic disorder.
    1.5 Indicate the symptoms used to diagnose hypochondriasis.
    1.6 Contrast the theories and treatment of somatoform disorders.

2.0 Psychological Factors Affecting Medical Conditions
    2.1 Explain the basis of the DSM-IV category of psychological factors affecting physical conditions, including psychophysiological disorders and sleep disorders.
    2.2 Discuss the theories and treatments of the DSM-IV category psychological factors affecting medical conditions.

3.0 Dissociative Disorders
    3.1 Indicate the symptoms used in the diagnosis of dissociative identity disorder, explanations of this disorder as due to trauma, and the use of hypnotherapy and cognitive-behavioral treatment methods.
    3.2 Describe the symptoms of dissociative amnesia.
    3.3 Enumerate the diagnostic criteria for dissociative fugue.
    3.4 Indicate the symptoms used to diagnose depersonalization disorder.
    3.5 Discuss the role of trauma as a cause of dissociative disorders.
    3.6 Explain the theories and treatment of dissociative amnesia, dissociative fugue, and depersonalization disorders.

4.0 Somatoform Disorders, Psychological Factors Affecting Medical Conditions, and Dissociative Disorders: The Perspectives Revisited
    4.1 Describe how various perspectives enhance our understanding of the causes and treatment of somatoform and dissociative disorders, as well as psychological factors affecting medical conditions.

5.0 Chapter Boxes
    5.1 Discuss the difficulty involved in distinguishing a medical illness from a somatoform disorder.
    5.2 Indicate the nature of the research evidence supporting dissociative identity disorder as a legal defense.

Identifying the Disorders

Write the name of the disorder in the blank next to the symptoms listed.

1. _____ Misinterpretation of normal bodily signs as indicators of disease.
2. _____ State of confusion about personal identity accompanied by a flight from home.
3. _____ Translation of psychological conflict into a set of specific physical symptoms.
4. _____ Disturbance in sleep and daytime functioning due to disrupted sleep-wake schedule.
5. _____ Complaints of physical pain that have no physiological basis.
6. _____ Exaggerated and unrealistic dissatisfaction with a part of one's body.
7. _____ Continued experiences of waking up suddenly and in a panic from sound sleep.
8. _____ Development of more than one self within the same individual.
9. _____ Chronic form of factitious disorder in which the person's life becomes consumed with pursuit of medical care.
10. _____ Chronic difficulty with getting to sleep.
11. _____ Psychological issues expressed through multiple and recurrent physical symptoms.
12. _____ Recurrent and persistent episodes of feeling disconnected from one's own body.
13. _____ Continuous feeling of a need for sleep and of never being fully rested.
14. _____ Deliberate fabrication of physical or psychological symptoms for an ulterior motive.
15. _____ Inability to remember personal details and experiences not due to brain damage.
16. _____ Feigning of symptoms due to inner need to maintain a sick role.

Matching

Put the letter from the right-hand column corresponding to the correct match in the blank next to each Multiple Choice item in the left-hand column.

1. ___ Field that focuses on study of connections among stress, the nervous system, and the immune system.
2. ___ Treatment shown to be effective for dissociative identity disorder.
3. ___ Condition in which individual feigns signs of physical illness for an ulterior motive.
4. ___ Condition in which normal bodily signs are interpreted as symptoms of disease.
5. ___ A fully developed personality in dissociative identity disorder that is separate from the main personality.
6. ___ Disorders in which a person's physical problems are temporally linked to a stressful event.
7. ___ Disorder in which person induces symptoms in another who is under the individual's care.
8. ___ The primary personality in multiple personality disorder.
9. ___ A method of coping in which a person reduces stress by trying to feel better about the situation.
10. ___ Personality type characterized by impatience, irritability, competitiveness, and time pressure.
11. ___ Interdisciplinary approach to psychophysiological disorders in which clients are taught to gain control over physical problems.
12. ___ Coping style that involves taking action to address the situation.
13. ___ Inability to remember events occurring in a specific time period.
14. ___ Personality type characterized by suppressed emotions, compliance, and conformity.
15. ___ Condition in which a person feeling distressed and unhappy seeks therapy for a physical disorder.

a. psychoneuroimmunology
b. behavioral medicine
c. localized amnesia
d. host
e. masked depression
f. Type C personality
g. malingering
h. hypnotherapy
i. alter
j. emotion-focused coping
k. Type A personality
l. psychophysiological
m. factitious disorder by proxy
n. .hypochondriasis
o. problem-focused coping

Anagrams

Rearrange the letters for each item so that they form a word that fits the definition. When you have completed each item, arrange the large bold letters so that they form another term.

1. I N V E C N R S O   A somatoform disorder in which unacceptable drives or conflicts are translated into physical symptoms.

2. R A P R Y M I   A kind of gain involving relief from anxiety or responsibility due to the development of physical or psychological symptoms.

3. S P O S I H N Y   Technique used in therapy for dissociative identity disorder.

4. G U F E U   Condition in which an individual becomes confused about personal identity and travels unexpectedly away from home.

5. S O P H M I R C D Y   In body _____ disorder, the individual is intensely dissatisfied with a part of his or her own body.

6. M U A R T A   Type of experience commonly in the backgrounds of people with dissociative identity disorder.

Syndrome in which the individual's life becomes consumed with the pursuit of medical care:

_ _ _ _ _ _ _ _ _ _ _ ' _

Short Answer

1. List five reasons for the misdiagnosis of dissociative identity disorder:

    _____

    _____

2. Explain how each of the following contributes to the way an individual responds to stressful situations:

Context	
Internal or personal qualities	
External or situational resources	

115

3. Specify the type of amnesia that applies to each of the following cases (assume the amnesia applied only to the period or memory loss described):

	A man forgets everything that happened during the month while his wife was dying of cancer.
	A young woman has no recall of events in her past life following her duty in the Persian Gulf war.
	A man forgets the type of car he drove before a hurricane hit his community.
	An incest victim remembers her childhood only through the time when she was abused.

4. Place an "X" next to the term or name that does not belong with the others:

a. Motor disturbances
   Localized amnesia
   Sensory disturbances
   Symptoms simulating physical illness

d. Briquet
   Charcot
   Janet
   Kluft

b. Malingering
   Factitious disorder
   Hypochondriasis
   Munchausen syndrome

e. Primary gain
   Trauma
   Secondary gain
   Unconscious guilt

c. Dissociative identity disorder
   Pain disorder
   Depersonalization disorder
   Dissociative amnesia

5. Contrast the relationship between psychological and physical aspects of functioning represented in each of the following disorders:

Disorder	Nature of physical complaint	Presence of actual physical symptoms	Theorized role of psychological factors
Conversion disorder			
Somatization disorder			
Somatoform pain disorder			
Body dysmorphic disorder			
Hypochondriasis			
Factitious disorder			
Psychophysiologi cal conditions			

6. Answer the following questions regarding the relationship between psychological factors and physical health.

a. What is the relationship between the terms "psychological factors affecting physical condition" and "psychosomatic illness"?

_____

_____

b. What is the relationship between the terms "psychological factors affecting physical condition" and "psychophysiological disorders"?

_____

_____

c. How is stress thought to lead to the development of physical symptoms?

_____

_____

d. What does research indicate about the effects of emotional expression on a person's ability to recover from stress?

_____

_____

e. What is the explanation of the relationship between the Type C personality and cancer?

_____

_____

f. How is Type A personality thought to be related to heart disease?

_____

_____

7. Describe one positive aspect and one negative aspect of primary and secondary gain from the point of view of the individual with a somatoform disorder:

Type of gain	Positive aspect	Negative aspect
Primary		
Secondary		

8. Describe one problem involved in the treatment of somatoform disorder, dissociative identity disorder, and other dissociative disorders:

Disorder	Problem involved in treatment
Somatoform disorder	
Dissociative identity disorder	
Other dissociative disorders	

9. A woman has just been told that her daughter is in trouble at school, an event that she perceives as stressful. Contrast the emotion-focused and problem-focused ways of coping with this stress in terms of the categories below:

Coping method	Example	Possible positive outcome	Possible negative outcome
Emotion-focused			
Problem-focused			

10.

a. Sam exercises for half an hour before he goes to bed, because it is the only chance he has. He drinks coffee continuously throughout the day, with his last cup after dinner. Since his room is fairly small, he does all his studying on his bed. His unpredictable work hours lead Sam to sleep at different times on different days. Lately, Sam has been feeling exhausted and that he has not been able to sleep enough, and is very worried about this. What are Sam's bad sleep habits?

_____

_____

b. What psychological treatments might a clinician recommend for Sam to improve his sleep?

_____

_____

Focusing on Research

Answer the following questions concerning "Research Focus: Dissociative Identity Disorder as a Legal Defense."

1. In what two ways might a defendant use a claim of dissociative identity disorder as a defense in a criminal trial?

_____

_____

2. What assessment instrument can help clinicians detect malingering of multiple personalities?

_____

_____

3. What facts in the client's history and aspects of current functioning might a clinician look for in an effort to distinguish malingering from real dissociative disorder?

_____

_____

From The Case Files of Dr. Sarah Tobin: Thinking About Rose's Case

1. Describe the sequence of events that led to Dr. Tobin's contact with Rose.

_____

_____

2. Discuss how Dr. Tobin assessed Rose.

_____

_____

3. What were the facts and conclusions that made up Dr. Tobin's formulation of Rose's case?

_____

_____

4. Describe the course and outcome of Rose's treatment.

_____

_____

Review at a Glance

In somatoform disorders, conditions in which psychological factors affect medical condition, and dissociative disorders, the (1)_____ expresses (2)_____conflict and (3)_____ in unusual ways.(4)_____disorders include a variety of conditions in which psychological conflicts become translated into physical problems or complaints that cause (5)_____ or (6)_____ in a person's life. (7)_____ disorder involves the translation of unacceptable drives or troubling conflicts into (8)_____ or (9)_____ symptoms that suggest some kind of (10)_____ or (11)_____condition. (12)_____involves the expression of psychological issues through bodily problems that have no basis in physiological dysfunction. In (13)_____, some kind of pain, which causes intense personal distress or impairment, is the predominant focus of the client's medical complaint. People with (14)_____ disorder are preoccupied, almost to the point of being delusional, with the idea that a part of their body is ugly or defective. Individuals with (15)_____ believe or fear that they have a serious illness, when, in fact, they are experiencing normal bodily reactions. (16)_____ and (17)_____ are associated with somatoform disorders. (18)_____ involves deliberately faking the symptoms of physical illness or psychological disorder for an ulterior motive. In (19)_____, people fake symptoms or disorders, not for the purpose of any particular gain but because of an inner need to maintain a sick role. In (20)_____, a person induces physical symptoms in another person who is under the individual's care. Theorists consider (21)_____ and (22)_____ gain as the basis for the development of somatoform disorders. Somatoform disorders are best viewed as an interplay of (23)_____, (24)_____, (25)_____, and (26)_____. According to the *DSM-IV* diagnostic criteria, the psychological factors that may affect medical conditions include (27)_____, (28)_____, (29)_____, (30)_____, (31)_____, and (32)_____. Researchers and clinicians have focused on the process by which people learn to deal with (33)_____ and have developed sophisticated theories and techniques pertaining to (34)_____. Experts in the field of (35)_____ are finding answers to complex questions regarding the nature of the (36)_____relationship.

In (37)_____, the person develops more than one self or personality. The *DSM-IV* criteria capture the essence of what many clients report, namely, (38)_____, (39)_____, and (40)_____. In (41)_____, the individual is unable to remember important personal details and experiences, usually associated with traumatic or very stressful events. (42)_____ is a condition in which a person who is confused about personal identity suddenly and unexpectedly travels to another place. In (43)_____, distortions of mind-body perceptions happen repeatedly and without provocation. Experts agree that dissociative disorders commonly arise as a result of (44)_____, usually associated with experiences of childhood (45)_____. Treatment depends on the nature of the dissociative disorder, but the goal is (46)_____ of the fragmented components of the individual's (47)_____ and (48)_____. (49)_____ and other therapeutic techniques are commonly used to attain this goal.

Multiple Choice

1. Rose Marston had no motive for feigning illness and truly believed she had a physical disorder. These factors led to the diagnosis of:
   a. factitious disorder.
   b. malingering.
   c. somatization disorder.
   d. body dysmorphic disorder

2. Job stress often causes Ralph's ulcer to flare up. Ralph seems to have a
   a. psychophysiological condition.
   b. somatoform disorder.
   c. factitious disorder.
   d. dissociative disorder.

3. The behavior characterized by being hard driving, competitive, and impatient, associated with heart disease is called Type
   a. Z pattern.
   b. B pattern.
   c. C pattern.
   d. A pattern.

4. Researchers urge caution before diagnosing a conversion disorder, because as many as half of those diagnosed as having conversion disorder turn out years later to have had
   a. a true physical illness.
   b. a true psychological disorder.
   c. hypochondriacal symptoms.
   d. dissociative symptoms.

5. People with somatization rarely seek out psychotherapy voluntarily because they
   a. lack the financial resources to pay for therapy.
   b. fear that the clinician might detect their motive for feigning illness.
   c. do not consider their physical difficulties to have an emotional cause.
   d. are too embarrassed to talk about their physical problems.

6. Each of the following disorders involves unexplainable medical symptoms except
   a. hypochondriasis.
   b. somatization disorder.
   c. somatoform pain disorder.
   d. conversion disorder.

7. Marlene has repeatedly tried to make her 11-month-old son physically ill, so that she can rush him to the emergency room and receive medical attention. Her condition is called
   a. factitious substitution.
   b. Munchausen's syndrome.
   c. malingering.
   d. factitious disorder by proxy.

8. Which of the following questions is not part of the Dissociative Disorders Interview Schedule?
   a. Were you physically abused as a child or adolescent?
   b. Do you feel physical pain that lacks a physical basis?
   c. Do you ever speak about yourself as "we" or "us"?
   d. Do you ever feel that there is another person or persons inside you?

9. Disturbances in the amount, quality, or timing of sleep are referred to as
   a. hyposomnias.
   b. nocturnal dysfunctions.
   c. dyssomnias.
   d. parasomnias.

10. People with depersonalization disorder
    a. have more than one personality.
    b. feel as though they are not real.
    c. forget details about personal identity.
    d. fabricate disturbance to get secondary gain.

11. The higher rate of hypertension in African-Americans compared to Whites is thought by researchers to be due to
    a. lower physiological reactivity to stress.
    b. a tendency to express strong emotions.
    c. lower levels of Type A behavior.
    d. patterns of poverty and discrimination.

12. The inability to recall past events from a particular date up to and including the present time is called
    a. continuous amnesia.
    b. generalized amnesia.
    c. selective amnesia.
    d. psychogenic amnesia.

13. Disorders in which psychological conflicts are translated into physical complaints are the
    a. anxiety disorders.
    b. dissociative disorders.
    c. personality disorders.
    d. somatoform disorders.

14. Legal experts and psychologists have found this reaction to be indicative of a true diagnosis of dissociative identity disorder in forensic cases.
    a. extreme distress and interference of symptoms in daily life
    b. emergence of new personalities during therapy
    c. stereotypical criminal personalities as alters
    d. moderate or little distress over symptoms

15. Mr. Warren has seen many physicians, complaining of difficulty swallowing, chest pain, and blurred vision. Medical examination yields no basis for his claims. Mr. Warren seems to have this somatoform disorder.
    a. factitious disorder
    b. psychalgia
    c. pain disorder
    d. somatization disorder

16. Which somatoform disorder is characterized by dissatisfaction and delusional preoccupation with the idea that some part of the body is ugly or defective?
    a. Briquet's syndrome
    b. psychalgia
    c. body dysmorphic disorder
    d. hypochondriasis

17. A man persistently views his mild headaches as an indication he has a brain tumor despite lack of evidence in support of his claim. This individual may be suffering from
    a. conversion disorder.
    b. psychogenic pain disorder.
    c. somatization disorder.
    d. hypochondriasis.

18. In contrast to individuals with dream anxiety disorder, people with sleep terror disorder
    a. have pleasant dreams that cause them to wake up.
    b. do not recall any dream or any unusual occurrences during the night.
    c. move and walk about in their sleep.
    d. usually experience the terror during REM sleep.

19. The central or core personality in dissociative identity disorder is referred to as the
    a. cardinal personality.
    b. nuclear personality.
    c. alter ego.
    d. host personality.

20. The coping style that involves trying to improve one's feelings about the situation is referred to as
    a. emotion-focused coping.
    b. problem-focused coping.
    c. cognitive coping.
    d. confrontive coping.

21. Disorders involving conditions in which psychological conflicts are translated into physical complaints are the
    a. anxiety disorders.
    b. dissociative disorders.
    c. personality disorders.
    d. somatoform disorders.

22. Connie is relatively unconcerned about the fact that she has suddenly lost all sensation in her left hand. This bizarre lack of concern is referred to as
    a. psychalgia.
    b. hysteria.
    c. la belle indifference.
    d. Briquet's syndrome.

23. If an individual suffering from a somatoform disorder only complains of pain that has no physiological basis, he or she may receive a specific diagnosis of
    a. pain conversion disorder.
    b. psychic neuralgia.
    c. somatoform pain disorder.
    d. hypochondriasis.

24. Which somatoform disorder is characterized by the client's dissatisfaction and delusional preoccupation with the idea that some part of his or her body is ugly or defective?
    a. Briquet's syndrome
    b. psychalgia
    c. body dysmorphic disorder
    d. hypochondriasis

25. The fabrication of physical symptoms for the purpose of gaining material rewards or money is referred to as
    a. malingering.
    b. somaticizing.
    c. masking.
    d. catastrophizing.

26. The avoidance of burdensome responsibilities because one is disabled is a
    a. primary gain.
    b. secondary gain.
    c. positive reinforcement.
    d. avoidance reward.

27. Ralph has an ulcer. More often than not, the stress related to his job as an executive gets so bad that his ulcer flares up. Which of the following best describes his condition?
    a. psychological factor affecting a medical condition
    b. somatoform disorder
    c. factitious disorder
    d. adjustment disorder

28. In which dissociative disorder does an individual develop more than one self, typically in response to some psychological trauma?
    a. dissociative identity disorder
    b. schizophrenia
    c. schizoid personality disorder.
    d. dissociative fugue

29. An overwhelming majority of people who suffer from dissociative identity disorder have experienced
    a. heavy drug and alcohol usage in adolescence.
    b. a sudden schizophrenic break during late adolescence.
    c. a difficult Oedipus complex resolution in the phallic stage.
    d. some form of severe sexual or physical abuse in childhood.

30. A dissociative experience in which the individual experiences alterations of mind-body perception ranging from detachment from one's experiences to the feeling that one has stepped out of one's body is called.
    a. fugue state.
    b. depersonalization.
    c. dissonance.
    d. dissociative amnesia.

ANSWERS

IDENTIFYING THE DISORDERS

1. Hypochondriasis
2. Dissociative fugue
3. Conversion disorder
4. Circadian rhythm sleep disorder
5. Pain disorder
6. Body dysmorphic disorder
7. Sleep terror disorder
8. Dissociative identity disorder
9. Munchausen's syndrome
10. Primary insomnia
11. Somatization Disorder
12. Depersonalization disorder
13. Primary hypersomnia
14. Malingering
15. Dissociative amnesia
16. Factitious disorder

MATCHING

1. a
2. h
3. g
4. n
5. i
6. l
7. m
8. d
9. j
10. k
11. b
12. o
13. c
14. f
15. e

ANAGRAMS

1. CONVERSION
2. PRIMARY
3. HYPNOSIS
4. FUGUE
5. DYSMORPHIC
6. TRAUMA

Final word= MUNCHAUSEN'S

SHORT ANSWER

1. Dissociative identity disorder is linked to epilepsy, schizophrenia, and somatoform disorder.
   The symptoms of dissociative identity disorder are not consistent over time.
   The individual may try to cover up symptoms.
   Dissociative symptoms may be mixed with mood disturbance or personality disorder.
   The individual may be functioning at a high level and not appear to have a disorder.

2.

Context	What precedes an event can influence its effects; an unexpected stress (such as a loss) may be more stressful than one that follows a long period of preparation.
Internal or personal Qualities	Internal or personal qualities such as biological, personality, and cognitive vulnerabilities can influence a person's coping resources.
External or situational resources	External or situational resources such as a social network and material resources can help buffer the impact of a stressful event.

3.
Localized
Generalized
Selective
Continuous

4.
a. Localized amnesia
b. Hypochondriasis
c. Pain disorder
d. Kluft
e. Trauma

5.

Disorder	Nature of physical complaint	Physical symptoms	Theorized role of psychological factors
Conversion disorder	Involuntary loss or alteration of bodily functioning.	No	Caused by underlying conflict.
Somatization disorder	Multiple and recurrent bodily symptoms.	No	Caused by underlying conflict.
Somatoform Pain disorder	Pain.	No	Caused by underlying conflict.
Body dysmorphic disorder	Preoccupied with dissatisfaction over appearance of bodily part.	No	Unrealistic perception of appearance.
Hypo-Chondriasis	Exaggerated concern over normal bodily reactions.	No	Acceptable way for finding help for other problems such as depression.
Factitious disorder	Physical or psychological symptoms are feigned.	No	Desire to be center of attention, nurtured, masochistic wish to experience pain.
Psycho-physological conditions	Asthma, headaches, ulcer.	Yes	Psychological factors can initiate, aggravate, or prolong medical problems.

6.
a. The term "psychological factors affecting physical condition" replaces "psychosomatic" based on evidence that such disorders are not "in the person's head."
b. These conditions include situations when a person's physical symptoms are temporally linked to a stressful event. The simpler term "psychophysiological" has traditionally been used to refer to these conditions.
c. A stressful event can lower resistance to disease. Such an event can also aggravate symptoms of a chronic stress-related disorder. Current explanations propose that stress stimulates lowers immune activity, leaving the body vulnerable to conditions such as gastroenterological problems, infection, cancer, allergic reactions, and arthritis.
d. Research by McClelland suggests that the suppression of emotions can lead to harmful physical reactions and research by Pennebaker suggests that it can be physically beneficial to put emotions into words.
e. The Type C personality is a proposed personality type identified in cancer victims who cannot express their negative feelings toward others. This activation may lead to chronic arousal of the sympathetic nervous system and lowered efficiency of the immune system, which is involved in the body's natural protection against cancer.
f. People with a Type A personality are thought to be in a state of heightened activation, leading to high blood pressure and risk of heart and arterial disease.

7.

Type of gain	Positive aspect	Negative aspect
Primary	Avoidance of burdensome responsibilities.	Lost wages.
Secondary	Sympathy and attention from others.	Annoyance and anger from others.

8.

Disorder	Problem involved in treatment
Somatoform disorder	Avoid reinforcing the client's adoption of the sick role, but also provide support so that client accepts psychological treatment.
Dissociative identity disorder	Avoid inadvertent reinforcement of other personalities.
Other dissociative disorders	Avoid provoking a dissociative episode in the client by moving too fast through the uncovering of traumatic memories.

9.

Coping method	Example	Possible positive outcome	Possible negative outcome
Emotion-focused	Try to look at the event in positive terms, such as it will help the daughter "grow as a person."	The mother will feel better about the situation.	The mother will fail to intervene on the daughter's behalf, and she may get into more serious trouble.
Problem-focused	Talk to the daughter's teachers and guidance counselors to get at the root of the problem.	Changes may be implemented that help improve the daughter's behavior.	The mother may feel frustrated if she finds that no one at school can really help.

10.
a.
Exercising before bedtime.
Drinking coffee within six hours of bedtime.
Using his bed for activities other than sleeping.
No regular sleep schedule.
Worrying about his sleep problems.
b.
Simple educational intervention to improve his sleep habits.
Behavioral strategies such as relaxation, biofeedback, and cognitive self-control.
Stress management.

FOCUSING ON RESEARCH

1. They may claim that they are not competent to stand trial or that the disorder precluded them from appreciating and understanding their criminal actions.

2. The Structured Clinical Interview for DSM-IV Dissociative Disorders (SCID-D) has been particularly useful in evaluating the severity of dissociative symptoms and in diagnosing dissociative disorders in both psychiatric and legal contexts.
3. Evidence of periods of amnesia, personality change, and other aspects of fragmented experience in the client's current functioning that are interfering in everyday life, as well as evidence that the client suffered extreme abuse in childhood; the malingerer would not show emotional scars or abuse and would find it difficult to maintain a consistent façade of dissociated feelings, thoughts, and memories that he or she could associate with different personality traits.

FROM THE CASE FILES OF DR. SARAH TOBIN: THINKING ABOUT ROSE'S CASE

1. The hospital emergency room physician referred Rose to Dr. Tobin. Rose had gone to the emergency room on 15 occasions in the past year complaining about what seemed to be serious medical problems (vomiting; nausea; and chest, back and joint pain and neurological symptoms), yet doctors could make no diagnosis.
2. Dr. Tobin conducted an interview and administered the WAIS-III, MMPI-2, TAT, and Rorschach.
3. The most important fact was that Rose had a younger sister who was born with severe abnormalities. Emily got all the attention in the family, until Emily died as a teenager. Rose dropped out of college due to a series of unexplainable illnesses and ailments. She could not keep a job due to incapacitating physical symptoms, and she had recently applied for disability benefits. Rose's physical symptoms began after Emily died, suggesting that Rose identified with her sister and took on her symptoms, in part to punish herself for unconscious guilt about being healthy and to keep her from living up to her potential. Rose's symptoms also gave her parents something to focus on after Emily's death. This kept them from dealing with the dysfunctions in their marriage.
4. Therapy had to address the emotional and psychological problems that were underlying the physical symptoms. Dr. Tobin recommended individual, group, and family therapy. Rose rejected family therapy, saying her father would never agree to it. She stayed in individual therapy for only a few weeks before she stopped, saying she had found a cure for her physical problems. Several months later, she was admitted to the emergency room following a suicide attempt through an overdose of pain medication. She resumed therapy with Dr. Tobin, yet she never seemed to make the connection between her physical problems and the difficulties in her emotional life. After she was involved in a car accident and had several minor operations, she phoned Dr. Tobin and said that she would not be returning to therapy because of her need for intensive medical care and rehabilitation.

REVIEW AT A GLANCE

1. body
2. psychological stress
3. stressSomatoform
5. distress
6. impairment
7. Conversion
8. bodily motor
9. sensory symptoms
10. neurological
11. medical
12. Somatization disorder
13. pain disorder
14. body dysmorphic
15. hypochondriasis
16. Malingering
17. factitious disorders
18. Malingering
19. factitious disorder
20. factitious disorder by proxy
21. primary
22. secondary
23. biological factors
24. learning experiences
25. emotional factors
26. faulty cognitions
27. Axis I disorders
28. psychological symptoms
29. personality traits
30. maladaptive health behaviors
31. stress-related physiological responses
32. less specific psychological factors
33. emotional experiences
34. coping
35. psychoneuroimmunology
36. mind-body
37. dissociative disorders
38. intense detachment
39. disorganization
40. amnesia
41. dissociative amnesia
42. Dissociative fugue
43. depersonalization disorder
44. intense trauma
45. abuse
46. integration
47. personality
48. cognition
49. Hypnotherapy

MULTIPLE CHOICE

1. (c) is correct. (a) and (b) involve feigning; (d) concerns body image.
2. (a) is correct. (b), (c), and (d) concern disorders for which there is no physical basis.
3. (d) is correct. (a), (b), and (c) are not associated with the described behaviors.
4. (a) is correct. (b), (c), and (d) would not involve actual physical illness.
5. (c) is correct. They are not feigning (b), and there is no reason to think that (a) and (d) are accurate statements.
6. (a) is correct. (b), (c), and (d) involve manifestations of disorders; people with (a) do not normally manifest physical symptoms.
7. (d) is correct. (a) is not a disorder; (b) involves making one's self ill; (c) involves feigning illness.
8. (b) is correct. (a), (c), and (d) are part of the interview schedule.
9. (c) is correct. (a), (b) and (d) are not generally used terms for sleep disorders.
10. (b) is correct. (a), (c), and (d) are not associated with the described behaviors.
11. (d) is correct. Evidence does not support (a), (b), and (c).
12. (a) is correct. (b) is more global; (c) is limited to certain memories; and (d) involves amnesia associated with leaving one's home.
13. (d) is correct; (a), (b), and (c) does not involve physical complaints.
14. (a) is correct. (b) and (c) would indicate a false diagnosis; (d) is not related to dissociative identity disorder.
15. (d) is correct. (a) involves feigning; (b) is not a disorder; (c) involves wide-spread bodily pain.
16. (c) is correct. (b) is not a disorder; (a) and (d) do not involve body image.
17. (d) is correct. (a) and (c) concern disorders for which there is no physical basis; (b) is not a known disorder.
18. (b) is correct. (a) is not a disorder; (c) may indicate sleepwalking or REM disorder; terrors are not experienced in (d), nightmares are.
19. (d) is correct. (a) and (b) are not accepted psychological terms; (c) refers to a psychodynamic theory.
20. (a) is correct. (b) involves focusing on the situation; (c) and (d) are not terms used for dealing with feelings about situations.
21. (d) is correct. (a), (b), and (c) do not involve physical complaints caused by psychological conflicts.
22. (c) is correct. (a) is not a psychological term; (b) is the former term for conversion disorder; (d) is the former name for somatization disorder.
23. (c) is correct. (a) and (b) are not terms used to describe disorders; (d) involves a fear of having a disorder, but with no apparent symptoms.
24. (c) is correct. (a) is the former term for somatization disorder; (b) is not a term used to refer to disorders; and (d) involves a fear of having a disorder with no apparent symptoms.
25. (a) is correct. (b) and (c) are not terms that describe psychological disorders; (d) is a term used to describe a cognitive process.
26. (a) is correct. (b) refers to the attention and sympathy one may gain when disable; (c) is a term used in operant conditioning; (d) is not a term used to describe a psychological process.
27. (a) is correct. (b), (c), and (d) involve disorders without a physical basis.
28. (a) is correct. (b) is a psychotic disorder; (c) is a personality disorder; and (d) is an anxiety disorder in which a person may wander away from home and develop and temporarily develop a new identity.
29. (d) is correct. (a), (b), and (c) are not associated with development of dissociative identity disorder.
30. (b) is correct. (a) involves wandering away from one's home; (d) involves a loss of memory; and (c) is a cognitive process.

CHAPTER 8
SEXUAL DISORDERS

CHAPTER AT A GLANCE

WHAT ARE ABNORMAL SEXUAL BEHAVIORS?

Paraphilias
Pedophilia
Exhibitionism
Fetishism
Frotteurism
Sexual Masochism
Sexual Sadism
Transvestic Fetishism
Voyeurism

Gender Identity Disorders

Sexual Dysfunctions
Hypoactive Sexual Desire
Sexual Aversion Disorder
Female Sexual Arousal Disorder
Male Erectile Disorder
Female Orgasmic Disorder
Male Orgasmic Disorder
Premature Ejaculation
Sexual Pain Disorders

Learning Objectives

1.0 What Is Abnormal Sexual Behavior?
    1.1 Discuss the issues involved in defining abnormal sexual behavior.
2.0 Paraphilias
    2.1 Explain the characteristic features of paraphilias, including pedophilia, exhibitionism, fetishism, frotteurism, sexual masochism, sexual sadism, transvestic fetishism, and voyeurism.
    2.2 Contrast biological and behavioral explanations of the paraphilias, including the concept of "lovemap."
    2.3 Discuss the treatments of paraphilias.
3.0 Gender Identity Disorders
    3.1 Describe the features of gender identity disorders.
    3.2 Discuss the possible causes of and treatments for gender identity disorders.
4.0 Sexual Dysfunctions
    4.1 Indicate the nature of sexual dysfunctions and their relationship to the human sexual response cycle.
    4.2 Outline the diagnostic criteria for sexual dysfunctions, including hypoactive sexual desire disorder, sexual aversion disorder, female sexual arousal disorder, male erectile disorder, female and male orgasmic disorders, premature ejaculation, and sexual pain disorders.
    4.3 Discuss the roles of biological and psychological factors in the cause and treatment of sexual dysfunctions.
5.0 Sexual Disorders: The Perspectives Revisited
    5.1 Identify the perspectives that have the most promise for understanding and treating sexual disorders.
6.0 Chapter Boxes
    6.1 Explain the nature of the relationship between pedophilia and childhood sexual victimization.
    6.2 Discuss the issues concerning the use of Viagra as treatment for male sexual dysfunction.

Identifying Disorders

Write the name of the sexual disorder in the blank at the left that fits the symptom described at the right.

1. _____ Intense urges and fantasies involving exposure of genitals to a stranger.
2. _____ A woman is unable to experience orgasm during sexual activity.
3. _____ A man cannot attain or maintain an erection during sexual activity.
4. _____ Strong recurrent sexual attraction to an object.
5. _____ Recurrent or persistent pain in the genitals during intercourse.
6. _____ A man reaches orgasm before he wishes during a sexual encounter.
7. _____ Active dislike of intercourse and other sexual activities.
8. _____ Sexual gratification derived from rubbing against unsuspecting strangers.
9. _____ Attraction to sexual situations in which satisfaction is derived from having painful stimulation applied to oneself.
10. _____ A man has an uncontrollable urge to dress as a woman to achieve sexual gratification.
11. _____ A woman is convinced that she is a man trapped in the body of woman.
12. _____ Uncontrollable attraction to children to the point that sexual gratification can be achieved only in their presence or while fantasizing about them.
13. _____ Attraction to sexual situations in which the individual dominates the partner to the point of causing the partner physical and/or emotional pain.
14. _____ A man cannot experience orgasm during sexual activity.

Matching

Put the letter from the right-hand column corresponding to the correct match in the blank next to each item in the left-hand column.

1. ___ Behavior or attitudes associated with society's definition of maleness or femaleness.

2. ___ Condition in which a person is interested solely in deriving sexual gratification from a specific part of another person's body.

3. ___ One of the pair of researchers who first studied the human sexual response in the laboratory.

4. ___ Paraphilic behavior in which the individual derives pleasure from dominating or being dominated by a sexual partner.

5. ___ Representation of an individual's sexual fantasies and preferences.

6. ___ Sexual dysfunction in which the man is unable to attain or maintain an erection.

7. ___ Paraphilia in which the individual attains sexual gratification from exposing his genitals to others.

8. ___ Anxiety experienced by a person during sexual intercourse due to preoccupation with his or her performance.

9. ___ Type of pedophilia in which an individual with a normal history of sexual development becomes sexual with a child in certain contexts.

10. ___ Disorder in which the individual feels trapped in the body of the other sex.

11. ___ Individual's attraction to members of the same and/or the other sex.

12. ___ Type of pedophilia in which the individual maintains a continuous interest in children as sexual partners.

13. ___ Sexual dysfunction in which the man reaches orgasm in a sexual encounter before he wishes to.

14. ___ Paraphilia in which a man derives sexual gratification from dressing as a woman.

15. ___ Clinician who developed an integrative approach to treating sexual dysfunctions.

a. preference molester
b. sexual orientation
c. male erectile disorder
d. gender identity disorder
e. Helen Singer Kaplan
f. spectatoring
g. situational molester
h. transvestic fetishism
i. premature ejaculation
j. partialism
k. Virginia Johnson
l. gender role
m. sadomasochism
n. lovemap
o. exhibitionism

Short Answer

1. Indicate the contributions and limitations of Masters and Johnson's research on human sexual functioning:

Contributions	Limitations

2. A client is distressed over the fetish he has about baby's diapers. Describe the following behavioral methods that could be used in treating this client:

Type of method	Description of method
Counterconditioning	
Aversive conditioning	
Covert conditioning	
Orgasmic reconditioning	

3. Describe what is considered "abnormal" about coercing a partner to have sex while tied down, compared with having sex in an exotic place that both partners enjoy:

_____

_____

_____

4.

a. Describe the four subtypes of sexual aggressors identified by Hall and colleagues, and summarize the descriptions and treatments recommended for each type:

Type				
Description				
Treatment				

b. Contrast the argument put forth by Nicholas Groth that pedophilia is motivated by a desire for power, compared with David Finkelhor's position that sexuality is the primary motivation for the pedophilia:

Power explanation	
Sexuality explanation	

5. For each of the following somatic treatments for sexual dysfunctions, identify the disorder it is intended to treat, the intended mechanism of action, and problems or disadvantages associated with each:

Somatic treatment	Disorder	Mechanism of action	Problems/Disadvantages
Administer progesterone			
Surgical implant of penile prosthesis			
Castration			
Sex reassignment surgery			
Hypothalamotomy			

6. Anne is living with her long-term partner, Mary. Describing herself as a "traditional woman," Anne is interested in domestic activities and works as a manicurist. She and Mary have a sexual relationship, and this relationship is consistent with Anne's sense of herself as a woman. Based on this information, answer the following questions:

a. Is Anne's gender role masculine or feminine? Why?

_____

_____

b. Is her gender identity that of a male or female? Why?

_____

_____

c. What is Anne's sexual orientation? Is this consistent with her gender identity? Why or why not?

_____

_____

133

7. Contrast physical and psychological causes of sexual dysfunctions:

Physical	Psychological

8. Identify which sexual disorder or problem is treated by each of the following methods:

Method of treatment	Sexual disorder or problem
Dilators	
Squeeze technique	
Stop-start technique	

9. Delineate childhood experiences that might result in the development of sexual disorders:

Disorder	Childhood experiences
Paraphilias	
Sexual dysfunctions	
Gender identity disorder	

Word Find

Circle the words defined below in this puzzle.

```
W L B T M F C I L E T O H C T
V O Y E U R A A P H R K V O B
A V U R E O H E R K A O A V Q
R E R E C T I L E R N E R E U
E M G C E T N S M A S T E R S
S A S F I E U T A D V O D T Y
A P D I E U L O T R E Y S G E
D O I N M R C A U O S A E H Z
I B C I H I D I R C T H C V W
S M F A K S D F E T I S H I R
T S C R N M B D I S C N I O Q
M O A O A L E W I N E S M N J
```

1. According to John Money, a disturbance in an individual's _____ is responsible for the development of a paraphilia.
2. In _____ sensitization, the individual learns to associate unpleasant emotional states with the paraphilic behavior.
3. A sexual dysfunction in which a man is unable to achieve or maintain sexual arousal is called male _____ disorder.

4. Researcher who, along with Johnson, brought the study of human sexuality into the laboratory: _____
5. The paraphilia in which the individual derives sexual pleasure from rubbing his genitals against an unwitting stranger: _____
6. In the paraphilia called _____ fetishism, a person derives sexual gratification from dressing as a member of the other sex.
7. Individual who derives pleasure from inflicting pain on another person: _____
8. A person who derives sexual pleasure from secretly watching other people in a nude or partially clothed state, or having sex: _____
9. In _____ ejaculation, a man is unable to control his orgasmic response until the time in sexual relations that he desires.
10. Strong and recurrent sexual attraction to an object, without which an individual cannot achieve sexual gratification: _____

135

Focusing on Research

Answer the following questions about "Research Focus: A Relationship between Pedophilia and a History of Being Sexually Victimized"

1. Summarize the research about the link between child sexual abuse and pedophilia.

    _____

    _____

2. What is the relationship among serious family disturbance, sexual victimization, and victim offending in later life?

    _____

    _____

3. Why is it important to understand the causes of pedophilia?

    _____

    _____

From The Case Files of Dr. Sarah Tobin: Thinking About Shaun's Case

Answer the following questions about the case of Shaun Boyden.

1. Describe Dr. Tobin's impressions of Shaun when she met him for the first time, pursuant to court referral.

    _____

    _____

2. How did Dr. Tobin assess Shaun and what was her diagnosis?

    _____

    _____

3. What aspects of Shaun's psychosocial history were important for Dr. Tobin's case formulation?

    _____

    _____

4. Indicate the nature and outcome of Shaun's treatment.

    _____

    _____

Review at a Glance

Sexual behavior is considered a psychological disorder if it (1)_____ or causes an individual to experience (2)_____ or _____. (3)_____ are disorders, lasting at least (4)_____ months, in which an individual has recurrent, intense sexual arousing fantasies, urges, or behaviors involving (5)_____, (6)_____, or (7)_____. (8)_____ is a disorder in which an adult (9)_____ years of age or over has uncontrollable sexual urges toward (10)_____. In (11)_____, a person has (12)_____ and _____ involving (13)_____. People with (14)_____ are preoccupied with an (15)_____ in order to achieve (16)_____. A (17)_____ has recurrent sexual urges and fantasies of

136

(18)_____ or (19)_____ another person. (20)_____ is a disorder marked by an attraction to achieving sexual gratification by having (21)_____.
(22)_____ involves deriving sexual gratification from activities that (23)_____.
(24)_____ is a disorder in which a man has an uncontrollable urge to
(25)_____(also known as _____) as his primary means of achieving sexual gratification. (26)_____ is a sexual disorder involving (27)_____. Most paraphilias emerge during (28)_____. Although biological factors play a role in some paraphilias,
(29)_____ seem to be central. In most cases, one or more (30)_____ have taken place in childhood involving a (31)_____that results in a paraphilia. Treatments include
(32)_____, (33)_____, and (34)_____ or _____ therapy.
        (35)_____ is a condition involving a discrepancy between an individual's
(36)_____ and _____ and a sense of inappropriateness about his or her assigned gender. The biological explanation focuses on the effects of (37)_____ that affect
(38)_____. Psychological theories focus on factors such as (39)_____,
(40)_____, and the (41)_____. Various factors influence choice of intervention. The most extreme method is (42)_____.(43)_____ involve abnormalities in an individual's sexual (44)_____ and (45)_____. The individual with (46)_____ has an abnormally low level of interest in sexual activity.
(47)_____ is characterized by an active dislike and avoidance of genital contact with a sexual partner. A woman with (48)_____ experiences persistent or recurrent inability to attain or maintain normal responses of sexual excitement during sexual activity. (49)_____ involves recurrent partial or complete failure to attain or maintain an erection during sexual activity.
(50)_____ is the inability for a woman to achieve orgasm, and
(51)_____involves a man having specific difficulty in the orgasm stage. The man with
(52)_____ reaches orgasm in a sexual encounter long before he wishes to.
(53)_____, which involve the experience of pain associated with intercourse, are diagnosed as either(54)_____ or (55)_____. (56)_____, which affects both males and females, involves recurrent or persistent (57)_____ before, during, or after sexual intercourse. (58)_____, which affects only females, involves (59)_____ or
_____ involuntary spasms of the outer muscles of the vagina. Sexual dysfunctions can be caused by (60)_____ or (61)_____ problems or by an interaction of both.
Treatment of sexual dysfunctions includes (62)_____ and psychological interventions, such as (63)_____, (64)_____, and (65)_____therapy techniques.

Multiple Choice

1. Researchers have noted that this factor may increase the likelihood of sexual offenses in adulthood.
   a. early family conflict and abuse
   b. secure patterns of attachment
   c. highly consistent parenting patterns
   d. lack of physical or sexual abuse

2. Fetishism appears to develop in a way similar to exhibitionism in that
   a. most people with fetishism were sexually abused as children.
   b. early life experiences result in a connection between sexual arousal and the behavior.
   c. brain damage early in life appears to cause certain paraphilias.
   d. these paraphilias are commonly associated with sexual dysfunction.

3. An individual who has recurrent, intense sexual urges and sexually arousing fantasies of rubbing against another person is referred to as a(n)
   a. voyeur.
   b. sadist.
   c. frotteur.
   d. fetishist.

4. Jackson has a normal sexual history; however, following the financial collapse of his company, he sexually molested the young daughter of his business partner. Jackson is considered a
   a. preference molester.
   b. child rapist.
   c. paraphiliac.
   d. situational molester.

5. The most common physiological intervention for treating pedophilia involves
   a. administering the female hormone progesterone.
   b. administering the male hormone testosterone.
   c. psychosurgery called hypothalamotomy.
   d. administering electroconvulsive therapy.

6. Bondage is a term associated with
   a. sexual sadism.
   b. sexual dysfunction.
   c. fetishism.
   d. transvestic fetishism.

7. The phenomenon in which a man derives sexual excitement from the thought or image of himself as having a female anatomy or biological characteristics such as menstruation or the ability to breast-feed is called
   a. transvestic fetishism.
   b. autogynephilia.
   c. inorgasmia.
   d. autoeroticism.

8. Which of the following factors has a positive influence on the postoperative readjustment of people who have had sex reassignment surgery?
   a. the quality of the surgery itself
   b. the individual's marital status
   c. uncertainty about the decision
   d. poor adjustment prior to surgery

9. The term that refers to the degree to which a person is erotically attracted to members of the same or other sex is
   a. sexual orientation.
   b. gender identity.
   c. gender role.
   d. transsexualism.

10. The disorder involving an abnormally low level of interest in sexual activity is called
    a. a paraphilia.
    b. sexual arousal disorder.
    c. hypoactive sexual desire disorder.
    d. orgasmic disorder.

11. The condition in which a man develops erection problems after a period of normal functioning is referred to as
    a. primary erectile dysfunction.
    b. secondary erectile dysfunction.
    c. hypoactive sexual desire disorder.
    d. sexual aversion disorder.

12. Dyspareunia is a condition that involves
    a. psychological distress associated with a paraphilia.
    b. depression that accompanies a sexual dysfunction.
    c. involuntary spasms of the outer muscles of the vagina.
    d. pain associated with sexual intercourse.

13. A sexual behavior is considered a psychological disorder if it
    a. is forbidden by state, local, or federal law.
    b. is viewed as unacceptable by society or an individual's culture.
    c. causes harm to others or distress to the individual.
    d. involves unconventional sexual practices.

14. Biological theorists contend that exhibitionistic behavior may be the result of:
    a. damage to the ventromedial hypothalamus.
    b. unconscious desires for the parent of the opposite sex.
    c. loss of nervous system control of sexual inhibition.
    d. a cultural emphasis on male dominance.

15. A woman is erotically obsessed with men's ankles to the point of exclusion of all other erotic stimuli. This woman's desires are illustrative of
    a. partialism.
    b. sadism.
    c. frotteurism.
    d. voyeurism.

16. The behavioral intervention geared toward a relearning process in which the individual associates sexual gratification with appropriate stimuli is called
    a. aversion therapy.
    b. orgasmic reconditioning.
    c. cognitive restructuring.
    d. sensate focus.

17. A radical surgical procedure designed to treat individuals with pedophilia involves the destruction of areas of which brain structure?
    a. the pituitary gland
    b. the frontal lobe
    c. the hippocampus
    d. the hypothalamus

18. Research regarding the "conversion" of gays and lesbians has shown that these treatments are
    a. are ineffective and may be harmful.
    b. more effective for lesbians than gay men.
    c. successful when used with medication.
    d. recommended by most therapists.

19. An active dislike of intercourse or related sexual activities is the main symptom of which sexual dysfunction?
    a. male erectile disorder
    b. sexual arousal disorder
    c. sexual aversion disorder
    d. hypoactive sexual desire disorder

20. Based on what you have read about Masters and Johnson's technique of sensate focus, in which perspective does this technique seem to be rooted?
    a. psychodynamic
    b. cognitive
    c. humanistic
    d. behavioral

21. Which of the following is the key feature of paraphilias?
    a. The object of desire must be an inanimate object.
    b. They must involve abnormal physiological functioning.
    c. They must be short-term conditions.
    d. There must be a dependence on the sexual target for arousal.

22. Which of the following best describes a preference molester?
   a. an individual who prefers children, especially boys, as his sexual partners
   b. a violent child abuser whose behavior is an expression of hostile sexual drives
   c. an individual who has a normal history of sexual development but is occasionally overcome by pedophilic impulses
   d. a person with normal impulses who occasionally has sex with children

23. Bob has intense recurrent fantasies in which he is walking along the beach and a woman approaches. As she gets near, he unbuttons his pants and exposes his genitals to her. At that instant, she falls madly in love with him and they make love in the sand. Bob occasionally acts out these fantasies, and might be given the diagnosis of
   a. sexual sadism.
   b. exhibitionism.
   c. transvestic fetishism.
   d. frotteurism.

24. Wendy has just purchased a vibrator in order to enhance her sexual arousal when she makes love to her husband. Which of the following statements best describes this situation?
   a. Wendy would be considered a fetishist.
   b. Wendy's husband might be diagnosed with erectile disorder.
   c. Wendy might be diagnosed with hypoactive sexual desire disorder.
   d. Wendy's behavior would not necessarily be considered fetishistic.

25. In which paraphilia does the individual masturbate by rubbing up against an unsuspecting stranger?
   a. pedophilia
   b. voyeurism
   c. transvestic fetishism
   d. frotteurism

26. Which disorder is characterized by a discrepancy between an individual's assigned sex and his or her gender identity?
   a. sexual aversion disorder
   b. hypoactive desire disorder
   c. homosexuality
   d. gender identity disorder

27. Katie is not interested in sexual activity and reports no desire for it, nor does she fantasize about having sex. Katie might be diagnosed as having
   a. hypoactive sexual desire disorder.
   b. sexual arousal disorder.
   c. inhibited female orgasm disorder.
   d. sexual aversion disorder.

28. Dwayne is very interested in sex but his penis remains flaccid despite erotic stimulation. Dwayne has
   a. sexual arousal disorder.
   b. sexual aversion disorder.
   c. male erectile disorder.
   d. inhibited male orgasm disorder.

29. Karen and Mark are being treated for a sexual dysfunction and their therapist is urging them to take turns stimulating each in nonsexual ways for a few weeks. Their therapist is using which of the following methods?
   a. the squeeze technique
   b. the start-stop procedure
   c. systematic resensitization
   d. sensate focus

30. Katasha, 13, likes to wear boy's clothing and play softball. She also likes to wear her hair short and is not interested in makeup or jewelry. Her mother is unnecessarily worried that she might have which of the following disorders?
   a. oppositional defiant disorder
   b. conduct disorder
   c. sexual behavior disorder
   d. gender identity disorder

Answers

IDENTIFYING DISORDERS

1. Exhibitionism
2. Female orgasmic disorder
3. Male erectile disorder
4. Fetishism
5. Dyspareunia
6. Premature ejaculation
7. Sexual aversion disorder
8. Frotteurism
9. Sexual masochism
10. Transvestic fetishism
11. Gender identity disorder
12. Pedophilia
13. Sexual sadism
14. Male orgasmic disorder

MATCHING

1. l
2. j
3. k
4. m
5. n
6. c
7. o
8. f
9. g
10. d
11. b
12. a
13. i
14. h
15. e

SHORT ANSWER

1.

Contributions	Limitations
Dispelled myths about sexuality	Laboratory setting was artificial
Provided a scientific basis for understanding sex	Samples studied were non-random
Gave a humanistic orientation to sexual functioning	An implicit sex bias which pathologized women

2.

Type of method	Description of method
Counterconditioning	Substitute relaxation for arousal in the presence of baby's diapers.
Aversive conditioning	Present a punishing stimulus every time the client touches baby's diapers.
Covert conditioning	Teach the client to imagine being humiliated while masturbating with baby's diapers.
Orgasmic reconditioning	Have the client experience orgasm while in the presence of appropriate sexual stimuli.

3. "Abnormal" sexual behavior involves sexual activity that causes harm to another person or that causes the individual to experience distress. Coercing a partner causes harm to that person; two consenting individuals having sex in an out-of-the-way place is distressing to neither person, even though it may be atypical.

4.a.

Type	Physiological	Cognitive	Affective	Sexual
Description	Experiences deviant sexual arousal patterns. Victims likely to be male children.	Plans sexual aggression. Victims likely to be acquaintances or relatives.	Lacks affective control, sexual aggression likely to be impulsive. Depressed victimizes children, and angry victimizes adults.	Long history of personality and adjustment difficulties. Use violence toward victims.
Treatment	Castration, hormonal treatment, and aversion therapy.	Victim empathy training and relapse prevention.	Cognitive therapy for depression or anger.	Cognitive therapy, social skills training, behavior therapy, and prevention in adolescence.

b.

Power explanation	A desire to over-power children. Need to overcome loneliness. Act out aggressive impulses.
Sexuality explanation	Emotional congruence. Sexual arousal. Emotional blockage with adults. Poor socialization.

5.

Somatic treatment	Disorder	Mechanism of action	Problems/Disadvantages
Administer progesterone	Pedophilia	Reduce sex drive by reducing testosterone.	Potentially damaging side effects. Lowers ability to respond to appropriate stimuli. May lead to false belief of cure. No change in object of sexual desire.
Surgical implant of penile prosthesis	Erectile disorder	Permits erection.	Invasive, possible psychological impact.
Castration	Pedophilia and other dangerous sex offenses	Reduces sex drive by eliminating production of testosterone.	Arousal still possible. Radical intervention. May not eradicate deviant fantasies and wishes.
Sex reassignment surgery	Gender identity disorder	Changes body to be consistent with gender identity.	Results not perfect and hormones still needed. Childbearing potential is lost. Psychological benefits are mixed.

Somatic treatment	Disorder	Mechanism of action	Problems/Disadvantages
Hypothalamotomy	Pedophilia	Change arousal patterns by targeting source of these patterns in the hypothalamus.	Ethical issues. Destruction of brain tissue can have unintended side effects. May decrease sex drive but not preference for children.

6.
a. Anne's gender role is feminine because she defines herself as "traditional," and has "feminine" interests and job.
b. Her gender identity is that of a female because she views herself as a woman.
c. Her sexual orientation is homosexual. Sexual orientation is independent of gender identity, so there is no basis for an inconsistency between her gender identity as a woman and her sexual orientation as a homosexual.

7.

Physical	Psychological
Illness and disease. Anatomical abnormalities or problems with sex organs. Medications. Drugs.	Misinformation about sex. Spectatoring. Cultural expectations. Relationship problems.

8.

Method of treatment	Sexual disorder or problem
Dilators	Vaginismus
Squeeze technique	Premature ejaculation
Stop-start technique	Premature ejaculation

9.

Disorder	Childhood experiences
Paraphilias	Early associations between sex and inappropriate stimuli.
Sexual dysfunctions	Traumatization and abuse. Learning of negative attitudes toward sexuality.
Gender identity disorder	Reinforcement of cross-gender behaviors..

WORD FIND

1. lovemap
2. covert
3. erectile
4. masters
5. frotteurism
6. transvestite
7. sadist
8. voyeur
9. premature
10. fetish

FOCUSING ON RESEARCH

1. Some studies have found that many pedophiles were sexually abused as children. Others have observed that the rate of childhood sexual abuse among pedophiles is only slightly higher than that of individuals who commit other sexual offenses. However, men who had been victims of more than one instance of sexual abuse and had also suffered emotional abuse were much more likely to engage in sexual activities with minors, perhaps out of identification with their abusers.

2. Early relationship disturbances with caregivers and sexual abuse within the family are characteristic of the most violent sexual offenders. Because offenders lack adequate models for relationships and for controlling aggressive and sexual impulses, sexual offenses become acceptable outlets for the feelings of isolation, anger, and sexual arousal that these individuals experienced as children.

3. With improved understanding, more effective treatments can be formulated and prevention programs developed in which those at greatest risk of perpetuating the cycle of abuse can be helped before they act on their fantasies and inclinations.

FROM THE CASE FILES OF DR. SARAH TOBIN: THINKING ABOUT SHAUN'S CASE

1. Shaun was 46 years old but he dressed like a teenager, and the harshness of his face made him look a decade older. He appeared uncomfortable and was emotional, weeping as he talked about his sexual urges and the possibility that he might lose his daughters. He denied ever having molested a child before this incident and said his wife knew nothing about his problem.

2. Dr. Tobin administered the WAIS-III, the MMPI-2, the Rorschach, and the TAT, as well as specialized sexual assessment inventories. His IQ was average, his MMPI-2 scales indicated that he was guarded and suspicious, and his Rorschach responses indicated impulsivity and restricted ability to fantasize. This led Dr. Tobin to believe that he could be counted on acting out his immediate impulses without considering the consequences of his actions. His TAT stories contained themes of victimization. The sexual assessment inventories confirmed Shaun's preference for sex with young boys, almost to the exclusion of any other sexual act. He had sex with his wife, but only to please her. Dr. Tobin diagnosed him with severe pedophilia.

3. As a young boy, Shawn was treated harshly by his father and neglected by his mother. He longed for his father's approval and felt outraged at having been made to feel so worthless. He suppressed his feelings of powerlessness. He may have been sexually abused. His volunteer work with young boys was, to him, a way of helping boys in need. He identified with the young boys and did not see them as different from himself, though he was many years older than they were.

4. Dr. Tobin got Shaun admitted into an outpatient treatment program, which consisted of intensive individual and group therapy, as well as aversion therapy aimed at reducing and eventually eliminating his sexual responsiveness to children. He responded well to aversion therapy but was slower to come to terms with his problems in group and individual therapy. When he finally admitted that a neighbor had sexually abused him when he was 12, he started to gain some insight into his own behavior as repetitive of what he had experienced. He continued in therapy for years and then left the state to start a new life.

REVIEW AT A GLANCE

1. causes harm to others
2. persistent or recurrent distress; impairment in important areas of functioning
3. Paraphilias
4. six
5. nonhuman objects
6. children or other nonconsenting persons
7. the suffering or humiliation of self or partner
8. Pedophilia
9. sixteen
10. sexually immature children
11. exhibitionism
12. intense sexual urges; arousing fantasies
13. genital exposure to strangers
14. fetishism
15. object
16. sexual gratification
17. frotteur
18. rubbing against
19. fondling
20. Sexual masochism
21. painful stimulation applied to one's own body
22. Sexual sadism
23. harm another person
24. Transvestic fetishism
25. wear a woman's clothing; cross-dressing
26. Voyeurism
27. observing the nudity or sexual activity of others

28. adolescence
29. psychological factors
30. learning events
31. conditioned response
32. medication
33. psychotherapy
34. group; family
35. Gender identity disorder
36. assigned sex; gender identity
37. hormones
38. fetal development
39. a parent's preference for a child of the other gender
40. early attachment experiences
41. unintentional reinforcement of cross-gender behavior by parents
42. sex reassignment surgery
43. Sexual dysfunctions
44. responsiveness
45. reactions

46. hypoactive sexual desire disorder
47. Sexual aversion disorder
48. female sexual arousal disorder
49. Male erectile disorder
50. Female orgasmic disorder
51. male orgasmic disorder
52. premature ejaculation
53. Sexual pain disorders
54. dyspareunia
55. vaginismus
56. Dyspareunia
57. pain
58. Vaginismus
59. recurrent; persistent
60. physical
61. psychological
62. medication
63. behavioral
64. cognitive-behavioral
65. couples

MULTIPLE CHOICE

1. (a) is correct. (b). (c), and (d) would decrease the likelihood of sexual offending.
2. (b) is correct. There is no evidence for (a), (c), and (d).
3. (c) is correct. (a) involves looking at others; (b) the infliction of pain; and (d) objects or particular body parts.
4. (d) is correct. (a) involves preferring sex with children; (b) is forced sexual intercourse; (c) is a general term, not a diagnosis itself.
5. (a) is correct. (b) would be counterindicated; (c) and (d) are not used to treat this disorder.
6. (a) is correct. (b), (c), and (d) do not involve tying up a sexual partner.
7. (b) is correct. (a) involves dressing in women's clothing; (c) the inability to experience orgasm; and (c) sexual acts performed on one's self.
8. (a) is correct. (b), (c), and (d) are not necessarily related to postsurgical adjustment.
9. (a) is correct. (b) involves the extent to which one's behavior matches one's assigned sex; (c) the gender-based behavior itself; and (d) involves dressing and living as the opposite of your assigned sex.
10. (c) is correct. (b) does specifically describe low interest level; (a) involves sexual satisfaction through abnormal means; and (d) is the inability to achieve orgasm.
11. (b) is correct. (a) means the problem is more general; (c) and (d) involve lack of interest or distaste for sex.
12. (d) is correct. (c) describes vaginismus; (a) and (b) are psychological, not physical, states.
13. (c) is correct. (a) involves legal issues; (b) and (d) involve cultural and social standards.
14. (c) is correct. (a), (b), and (d) are not known to be associated with exhibitionism.
15. (a) is correct. (b), (c), and (d) describe other sexual disorders.
16. (b) is correct. (a) involves reconditioning by pairing sexual response with pain or discomfort; (c) is a cognitive method; and (d) is a form of couple's therapy.
17. (d) is correct. (a), (b), and (c) are not directly associated with abnormal sexual behaviors.
18. (a) is correct. There is no clear evidence in support of (b), (c), and (d).
19. (c) is correct. (a) involves male dysfunction; (b) and(c) have to do with level of desire.
20. (d) is correct. (a), (b), and (c) are not contributors to this therapeutic approach.
21. (d) is correct. (a), (b), and (c) are not required for paraphilias.
22. (d) is correct. (a), (b), and (c) do not fit the description of the person preferring children.
23. (b) is correct. (a) involves utilizing pain for the purposes of pleasure; (b) exposing one's self; and (c) dressing as the opposite sex.
24. (d) is correct. (a), (b), and (c) do not fit the described behavior, trying to enhance normal sexual performance.
25. (d) is correct. (a) involves sex with children; (b) looking at others in the sex act; and (c) sexual arousal from dressing as the opposite sex.

26. (d) is correct. (a) and (b) have to do with sexual desire; (c) is not a disorder.
27. (a) is correct. (b) and (c) involve problems in arousal and performance; (d) is a dislike for sex.
28. (c) is correct. (a) and (b) are not indicated by a flaccid penis and (d) involves orgasm, not penile erection.
29. (d) is correct. (a) and (b) involve manipulating and prolonging sexual performance; (c) is a behavioral method used to treat some sexual disorders.
30. (d) is correct. (a), (b), and (c) do not match the described behaviors.

CHAPTER 9
MOOD DISORDERS

CHAPTER AT A GLANCE

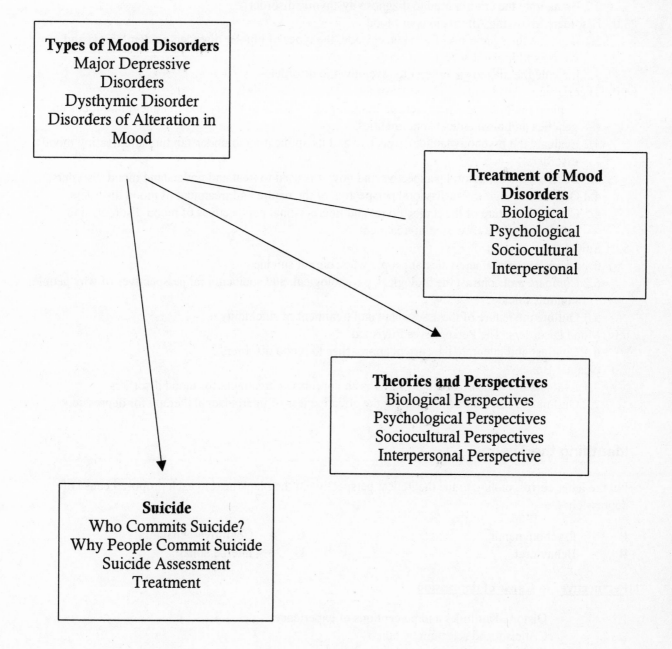

Types of Mood Disorders
Major Depressive Disorders
Dysthymic Disorder
Disorders of Alteration in Mood

Treatment of Mood Disorders
Biological
Psychological
Sociocultural
Interpersonal

Theories and Perspectives
Biological Perspectives
Psychological Perspectives
Sociocultural Perspectives
Interpersonal Perspective

Suicide
Who Commits Suicide?
Why People Commit Suicide
Suicide Assessment
Treatment

Learning Objectives

1.0 General Characteristics of Mood Disorders
    1.1 Define the nature of an episode as used to diagnose a mood disorder.
2.0 Depressive Disorders
    2.1 Indicate the diagnostic characteristics of a major depressive episode, types of depression, epidemiology, and course of major depressive disorder.
    2.2 Enumerate the criteria used to diagnose dysthymic disorder.
3.0 Disorders Involving Alternations in Mood
    3.1 Describe the symptoms of a manic episode, the types of bipolar disorder, epidemiology, and course of bipolar disorder.
    3.2 Indicate the diagnostic criteria for cyclothymic disorder.
4.0 Theories and Treatments of Mood Disorders
    4.1 Explain the biological perspective, including approaches to theory and treatment that focus on genetics and biochemical abnormalities.
    4.2 Evaluate the psychodynamic perspective and its application to understanding and treating mood disorders.
    4.3 Describe the behavioral perspective and how it is used to treat and understand mood disorders.
    4.4 Outline the cognitive-behavioral perspective of the nature and treatment of mood disorders.
    4.5 Clarify the nature of the sociocultural and interpersonal perspectives of mood disorders and indicate how they are used in treatment.
5.0 Suicide
    5.1 Describe the characteristics of people who commit suicide.
    5.2 Compare and contrast the biological, psychological, and sociocultural perspectives of why people commit suicide.
    5.3 Outline the nature of the assessment and treatment of suicidality.
6.0 Mood Disorders: The Perspectives Revisited
    6.1 Contrast and integrate the current approaches to mood disorders.
7.0 Chapter Boxes
    7.1 Evaluate the issue of whether Prozac is an appropriate treatment for mood disorders.
    7.2 Outline the research demonstrating the effectiveness of interpersonal therapy for depression.

Identifing the Theory

Put the letter corresponding to the theoretical perspective in the blank next to each proposed cause of depression:

P	=	Psychodynamic	**C**	= Cognitive-behavioral
B	=	Behavioral	**I**	= Interpersonal

Perspective	**Cause of depression**
1. _____	Distorted attitudes and perceptions of experiences.
2. _____	Criticism and rejection by others.
3. _____	Feelings of guilt and abandonment.
4. _____	Negative view of self, world, and future.
5. _____	Lack of intimate relationships
6. _____	Attributions of helplessness.

7. _____ Loss of loved object.
8. _____ Lack of positive reinforcement.
9. _____ Perceived loss, which diminishes self-esteem.
10. _____ Disruption of customary routines or scripts.

Matching

Put the letter from the right-hand column corresponding to the correct match in the blank next to each item in the left-hand column.

1. ___ Wonder drug of the 1990s.
2. ___ Lethargic and listless behavior.
3. ___ Medication most effective in treating bipolar disorder.
4. ___ Relatives with identical genetic makeup.
5. ___ Taking excessive responsibility for failures.
6. ___ Symptom of major depressive disorder.
7. ___ Treatment of depression that involves working through conflicts related to particular life concerns.
8. ___ Measurement of cortisol levels.
9. ___ Treatment of depression that involves changing dysfunctional thoughts.
10. ___ Response to ECT.
11. ___ Chronic and less intense form of depression.
12. ___ Explanations that people make of the things that happen to them.
13. ___ Period of elevated and expansive mood.
14. ___ Chronic vacillation between states of euphoria and dysphoria.
15. ___ Variant of depression that has no external causes.

a. endogenous
b. attributions
c. cognitive restructuring
d. lithium
e. psychomotor retardation
f. manic episode
g. dysthymic disorder
h. monozygotic twins
i. DST
j. short-term dynamic psychotherapy
k. clonic phase
l. example of cognitive distortion
m. Prozac
n. dysphoria
o. cyclothymic disorder

Short Answer

1. What are five factors that predispose a person to recurrent depression?

   _____   _____

   _____   _____

   _____

2. From the point of view of the person experiencing a manic episode, what are two appealing and two disturbing features of such an experience?

Appealing features	Disturbing features

3. What are three reasons for the Amish being considered especially suitable to study for research on bipolar disorder?

_____

4. What three lines of specific evidence are used to support genetic theories of mood disorders?

_____

_____

5. Describe the evidence indicating an interaction of genetic and environmental contributions to mood disorders, as indicated by research on adult female twins:

_____

_____

6. What two facts challenge the monoamine deficit hypothesis of depression?

_____

7. People with major depressive disorder show what altered biological rhythms?

_____

_____

_____

8. List two experimental methods for treating depression that involve altering biological rhythms, and explain the proposed method of action for each:

Treatment	Proposed method of action

9. Fill in the information in the following chart with the proposed mechanism of action, disorder for which it is applied, and problems involved in the use of each somatic treatment listed:

Treatment	Mechanism of action	Disorder	Problems
Tricyclic antidepressants			
MAOIs			
Prozac			
Lithium			

Treatment	Mechanism of action	Disorder	Problems
Electroconvulsive therapy			

10. Describe the following theories of suicide and the theorist who proposed the theory or the basis of support for the theory:

Theory	Description	Theorist or basis of support for theory
Anomie		
Communication		
Hopelessness		
Genetic		
Neurotransmitter		

Letterbox Puzzle

Find the words that fit the definitions below each of the puzzles. The words may be formed by choosing one block from each column. You may cross out squares as you solve, because each box is used only once.

DE	OS	ST	O	N	VE
E	R	I	S	MI	DE
S	E	AN	S	OL	UM
D	P	RE	HY	RT	C
R	Y	AS	PA	SI	IC
M	EL	T	CH	O	AL

Clues:

- Period in which specific intense symptoms are present.
- Type of depression involving loss of interest in activities, symptoms in the morning, significant disturbance of appetite, and extreme feelings of guilt.

- In major _____ disorder, the individual feels extreme dysphoria, has physical symptoms, experiences low self-esteem, and may be suicidal.
- Depressive disorder involving chronic sadness without a period of intense symptoms.
- Pattern of depression in which symptoms are worst during the fall or winter.
- Specifier used to indicate that a woman, depression follows the birth of a child.

E	CL	R	Z	A	I
C	U	R	O	A	A
C	OG	PH	TH	RI	IC
P	O	O	TI	YM	VE
B	I	O	Q	SO	C
CY	R	NI	T	I	AR

Clues:
- Disorder involving intense alternations in mood involving manic and/or depressive episodes.
- Hormone involved in mobilizing the body's resources in times of stress.
- Medication used to treat depression by altering the serotonin system; considered the "wonder drug" of the 1990s.
- According to one theory, people who are depressed experience a _____ triad of negative feelings about the self, the world, and the future.
- Feelings of intense elation or positive mood.
- Disorder involving chronic alternations in mood from mild depression to hypomania.

Focusing on Research

Answer the following questions from "Research Focus: Interpersonal Therapy for Depression."

1. Summarize the common research question shared by the studies

_____

_____

2. What are the most reasonable conclusions that can be drawn from the studies concerning the relative effectiveness of medication, cognitive-behavioral therapy, and interpersonal therapy to treat depression?

_____

_____

From The Case Files of Dr. Sarah Tobin: Thinking About Janice's Case

Answer the following questions about the case of Janice Butterfield.

1. Outline the history of Janice's illness and treatment as reported to Dr. Tobin by Dr. Hampden.

_____

_____

2. Describe Dr. Tobin's assessment of Janice and her diagnosis.

_____

_____

3. What was Dr. Tobin's formulation of Janice's case?

_____

_____

4. Describe the course and outcome of Janice's treatment.

_____

_____

A mood disorder involves a disturbance in a person's (1)_____ or (2)_____. People can experience this disturbance in the form of (3)_____, (4)_____, or a (5)_____. An (6)_____ is a time-limited period during which specific intense symptoms of a disorder are evident. (7)_____ involves acute but time-limited episodes of depressive symptoms, such as feelings of (8)_____, a loss of interest in (9)_____, (10)_____ symptoms, and disturbances in (11)_____ and _____ behavior. Individuals with major depressive disorder also have cognitive symptoms, such as a negative (12)_____, feelings of (13)_____, an inability to (14)_____, and (15)_____. Depressive episodes are either (16)_____ or (17)_____. People with (18)_____ disorder have, for at least (19)_____ years, depressive symptoms such as low (20)_____, low (21)_____, poor (22)_____, (23)_____ difficulty, feelings of (24)_____, and disturbances of (25)_____ and _____.

(26)_____ disorder involves intense experiences of elation or euphoria called a (27)_____, characterized by heightened levels of (28)_____, (29)_____, and (30)_____. A mixed episode consists of symptoms of both a (31)_____episode and a (32)_____ episode, which alternate rapidly. (33)_____ disorder involves a vacillation between (34)_____ and (35)_____ episodes. (36)_____ disorder involves one or more manic episodes sometimes (but not always) with one or more (37)_____ episodes. In bipolar II disorder, the individual has had (38)_____ major depressive episodes and at least (39)_____ hypomanic episode.

Biological theories explaining mood disorders focus on (40)_____ and (41)_____ functioning. Psychological theories emphasize the (42)_____, (43)_____ and (44)_____, aspects of mood disturbance. From the behavioral viewpoint, depression is the result of a reduction in (45)_____, deficient (46)_____, or (47)_____. According to the cognitive perspective, depressed people react to stressful experiences with a way of thinking called the (48)_____, a negative view of (49)_____, (50)_____, and (51)_____. (52)_____ are errors in the way people draw conclusions from their experiences, applying illogical rules such as (53)_____ or (54)_____. (55)_____ theory emphasizes disturbed social functioning.

Biological treatments for depression include mostly (56)_____ and, for extreme cases, (57)_____. (58)_____ is the most widely used medication for bipolar disorder. Psychological interventions involve the (59)_____ and (60)_____.

Sociocultural and interpersonal interventions focus on treatment within the context of an (61)_____ system, such as an (62)_____relationship.

Many suicidal people have a (63)_____ disorder, and some suffer from other serious (64)_____ disorders. Most interventions incorporate (65)_____ and (66)_____ methods.

Multiple Choice

1. Suicide hot lines may not be effective because
   a. they are often poorly funded and staffed.
   b. callers do not divulge their identity.
   c. they are staffed by undertrained people.
   d. people do not call when at highest risk.

2. A diagnosis of bipolar disorder requires
   a. the experience of a depressive episode.
   b. the experience of a manic episode.
   c. a family history of mood disorder.
   d. normal premorbid personality.

3. The suicide rate is highest among white males aged
   a. 15 to 24.
   b. 30 to 40.
   c. 50 to 65.
   d. 85 or older.

4. Which of the following factors indicates that a suicide case should be viewed as high-risk?
   a. an elaborate suicide plan
   b. low suicidal lethality
   c. low suicidal intention
   d. parasuicidal intent

5. People with cyclothymic disorder experience chronic
   a. episodes of depression.
   b. episodes of mania.
   c. alterations from dysphoria to hypomania.
   d. unrelenting hypomania.

6. Which statement is true regarding the role of genetics in mood disorders?
   a. In families in which one parent has a mood disorder, between 60 percent and 70 percent of offspring are likely to develop a mood disorder.
   b. Among dizygotic twins, the concordance rate is between 45 percent and 50 percent.
   c. Among monozygotic twins, the concordance rate is between 65 percent and 70 percent.
   d. In families in which both parents have mood disorders, between 90 percent and 95 percent of their offspring are likely to develop a mood disorder.

7. A psychiatrist has determined that a client has bipolar disorder. Of the following, which kind of medication is most likely to be prescribed?
   a. lithium carbonate
   b. tricyclics
   c. MAOIs
   d. anticonvulsants

8. The popularity of fluoxetine (Prozac) as a treatment of depression is due to the fact that Prozac is
   a. economical.
   b. impressively effective with few side effects.
   c. so aggressively marketed.
   d. targeted to a wide range of neurotransmitters.

9. According to Seligman's learned helplessness model, depressed people
   a. view themselves as incapable of having an effect on their environment.
   b. take comfort in the attention they receive from others.
   c. tend to exaggerate their symptoms in order to get out of undesirable responsibilities.
   d. have negative views of self, world, and future.

10. Dr. Charney is a cognitive-behavioral therapist. She is least likely to use which approach?
    a. cognitive restructuring
    b. didactic work
    c. graded task assignments
    d. aversive conditioning

11. Catecholamine is to _____ as indolamine is to _____.
    a. serotonin; norepinephrine.
    b. GABA; serotonin.
    c. norepinephrine; serotonin.
    d. dopamine; norepinephrine.

12. In an important NIMH study comparing the relative effectiveness of medications and psychotherapy, Elkin and his colleagues concluded that people with
    a. severe depression benefited most from cognitive behavioral therapy alone.
    b. mild depression benefited most from small doses of antidepressant medication.
    c. severe depression benefited from neither medication nor psychotherapy.
    d. mild depression benefited nearly equally from medication, cognitive-behavioral therapy, and interpersonal psychotherapy.

13. In the textbook case of Janice Butterfield, Dr. Tobin noted that Janice's WAIS-R scores reflected her serious depression. Which of the following would have led Dr. Tobin to draw this conclusion?
    a. Lethargy caused Janice to receive a Performance IQ substantially below her Verbal IQ.
    b. Janice's vocabulary definitions were not particularly creative, thus causing her to receive a below average Verbal IQ.
    c. There was a negative correlation between Janice's IQ score and her MMPI-2 scores.
    d. Most of Janice's responses contained aspects of delusional thinking and bizarre associations.

14. Researchers find that there is a sizeable percentage of individuals suffering from depression who also have the symptoms of another psychological disorder. Which disorder is it?
    a. somatization disorder
    b. post-traumatic stress disorder
    c. anxiety disorder
    d. dissociative disorder

15. Researchers have proposed that the seasonal type of depression may be caused by alterations in biological rhythms due to seasonal variations in
    a. caloric intake.
    b. temperature.
    c. norepinephrine production.
    d. light.

16. Central to early psychodynamic explanations of depression is the notion of
    a. "loss" at an unconscious level.
    b. disordered thinking patterns.
    c. lack of positive reinforcement.
    d. regression to an egoless state.

17. Which of the following statements is true regarding the rate of depression in African Americans?
    a. It is generally higher than is found for Whites.
    b. The rates are highest for those in their twenties.
    c. The rates are highest for those in their forties.
    d. The rates of seasonal depression are higher than in Whites.

18. That depressed people may be hypersensitive to norepinephrine levels and that biochemical changes in their brains may have decreased their abnormal sensitivity to norepinephrine is related to the process of
    a. synergism.
    b. down-regulation.
    c. catecholamine deregulation.
    d. up-regulation.

19. An alternate somatic treatment for individuals suffering from severe depression who are not helped by medications is
    a. dexamethasone therapy.
    b. acetylcholamine therapy.
    c. electroconvulsive therapy.
    d. tricyclic antidepressant therapy.

20. The therapy derived from interpersonal theory follows a set of guidelines derived from
    a. case studies.
    b. empirical research.
    c. naturalistic observations.
    d. laboratory studies.

21. Terms such as mild, severe, in remission, and recurrent as they apply to mood disorders are referred to as
    a. designators.
    b. denoters.
    c. ppliers.
    d. specifiers.

22. The theory that depression stems from a negative view of one's self, the world, and the future comes from which perspective?
    a. psychodynamic
    b. behavioral
    c. interpersonal
    d. cognitive-behavioral

23. Joe has a mood disorder in which he experiences alternating episodes of severe depression and mild bouts of mania. Which of the following diagnoses would best describe Joe's condition?
    a. bipolar I disorder
    b. bipolar II disorder
    c. manic depression
    d. cyclothymia

24. Major depression is to _____ as bipolar disorder is to _____.
    a. dysthymia; cyclothymia
    b. dysphoria; euphoria
    c. depression; mania
    d. dysphoria; hypothymia

25. The notion that low levels of norepinephrine cause depression and high levels cause mania is the basis of what is called the _____ hypothesis.
    a. catecholamine
    b. GABA
    c. adrenaline
    d. serotonin

26. Dr. Jaspers feels that Rhonda's manic episode is an unconscious defense that she is using to guard against sinking into a state of gloom and despair. Based on this information Dr. Jaspers' orientation is most likely
    a. humanistic.
    b. behavioral.
    c. existential.
    d. psychodynamic.

27. The phenomenon that Seligman observed in dogs that were subjected to inescapable shock is referred to as
    a. cognitive distortion.
    b. volitional apathy.
    c. learned helplessness.
    d. conditioned hopelessness.

28. According to Aaron Beck's cognitive theory, errors that depressed people make in the way that they draw conclusions from their experiences are called
    a. attribution errors.
    b. delusions.
    c. cognitive distortions.
    d. cognitive misattributions.

29. Which theory connects the ideas of psychoanalytic theorists with the ideas of behavioral and cognitive theorists?
    a. interpersonal theory
    b. psychodynamic theory
    c. family/systems theory
    d. person-centered theory

30. Which of the following medications is LEAST likely to be prescribed to treat depression because of the possibility of addiction?
    a. Prozac
    b. Lithium
    c. Ritalin
    d. Elavil

Answers

IDENTIFYING THE THEORY
1. C   3. P   5. I   7. P   9. C
2. I   4. C   6. C   8. B   10. B

MATCHING
1. m   4. h   7. j   10. k   13. f
2. e   5. l   8. i   11. g   14. o
3. d   6. n   9. c   12. b   15. a

SHORT ANSWERS
1. History of past depressive episodes;
    recent stress;
    minimal social support;
    family history of depression;
    lifestyle, personality, and health behaviors.
2. Appealing features - Heightened energy; heightened creativity.
    Disturbing features - Irritability; lack of judgment.
3. They have restricted lineage.
    Careful genealogical records are kept.
    Their religion prohibits drug and alcohol use.
4. Higher concordance based on proximity of biological relationship, including clustering of disorders among families of probands.
    Family lineage studies that identify specific chromosomal abnormalities.
    Adoption studies showing higher concordance among biological than adoptive relatives.
5. Female twins with a genetic predisposition to depression who suffered a traumatic life event had a much higher rate of depression (15 percent) than female twins with no genetic predisposition to depression (6 percent). Female twins who did not experience a traumatic event had an equal rate of depression (about 1 percent) regardless of genetic predisposition.
6. Medications take at least 2 weeks to have effects.
    There is no evidence of a relationship between antihypertensive medication use (which reduces catecholamine activity) and depression.
7. Altered REM patterns, decreased time between falling asleep and REM sleep, earlier awakenings, seasonal variations in symptoms

8.

Treatment	Proposed method of action
Light therapy	Exposure to bright light reduces melatonin production by the pineal gland; this may relieve depression in some people.
Sleep deprivation	Altering a person's biological rhythm through sleep deprivation may alleviate depression and in some cases may increase the effects of antidepressant medication.

9.

Treatment	Mechanism of action	Disorder	Problems
Tricyclic antidepressants	Increase monoamine activity	Depression	Take at least 2 weeks to have effect. Not effective for all depressions.
MAOI's	Inhibit MAO	Depression	Take at least 2 weeks to have effect. Potentially dangerous side effects.
Prozac	Increase serotonin activity	Depression	Possible risks of suicidality and increased impulsivity.
Lithium	Decreased catecholamine activity	Bipolar disorder	Potentially dangerous side effects. From client's perspective, interferes with "high."
Electroconvulsive therapy	Not known	Depression	Short-term memory loss. Adverse connotations.

10.

Theory	Description	Theorist or basis of support for theory
Anomie	Feeling of alienation from society leads individual to experience suicidal wishes.	Emil Durkheim
Communication	Suicide is an attempt at interpersonal communication.	Edwin Shneidman
Hopelessness	Depression leads to unresolvable feelings of stress and hopelessness.	Aaron Beck
Genetic	Suicidality has an inherited component.	Higher rates of concordance of suicidality in identical compared with fraternal twins; adoption studies support the role of heredity.
Neurotransmitter	Physiological differences exist between suicidal completers and controls.	Suicide victims found to have lower GABA levels in hypothalamus, lower serotonin levels.

LETTERBOX PUZZLE

Episode   Dysthymic   Bipolar   Cognitive
Melancholic   Seasonal   Cortisol   Euphoria
Depressive   Postpartum   Prozac   Cyclothymic

FOCUSING ON RESEARCH

1. The studies were designed to determine the relative effectiveness of interpersonal psychotherapy, cognitive behavioral psychotherapy, and medication for treating depression.
2. Generally, interpersonal psychotherapy and medication are equally as effective for treating all kinds of depression, while cognitive-behavioral therapy is not as effective as medication.
3. We need to know specifically how interpersonal therapy and medication interact and how many sessions are needed to achieve optimal therapeutic results.

FROM THE CASE FILES OF DR. SARAH TOBIN: THINKING ABOUT JANICE'S CASE

1. Janice had been seeing Dr. Hampden for 2 months. She appeared with complaints of exhaustion, sleep disturbance, lack of appetite, feelings of sadness and gloom, and interpersonal problems with her husband. Dr. Hampden prescribed Prozac, but Janice felt no better. The morning she was referred to Dr. Tobin, she attempted suicide by asphyxiating herself in the car. Her husband found her and intervened.

2. Dr. Tobin conducted an interview, administered the MMPI-2, Rorschach, TAT, WAIS-III, and Beck Depression Inventory-II. Dr. Tobin diagnosed Janice with major depressive disorder.

3. Janice had unresolved conflicts over her mother's death, about which she felt relief and grief. Janice had stayed close to her mother long after her father's death when Janice was 14. Janice took care of her mother until she died, but she also felt resentment about doing so. As Janice's daughter reached toddlerhood, her issues with her mother were reactivated. Being a mother also thwarted her career goals, and Janice felt resentment toward her husband.

4. Janice agreed to admit herself to the hospital, where she remained for 3 weeks. Since she was so deeply depressed, she continued on antidepressant medication and had individual therapy with Dr. Tobin (who used cognitive-behavioral and psychodynamic techniques) and couples therapy with one of Dr. Tobin's colleagues. Janice gained insight into the sources of her depression (which were biological, psychodynamic, and cognitive in origin), learned new ways of thinking about herself and her relationships, and improved communication with her husband. Her husband learned to relate differently to Janice and to understand the impact of his behavior on Janice and the family.

REVIEW AT A GLANCE

1. emotional state
2. mood
3. extreme depression
4. excessive elation
5. combination of depression and elation
6. episode
7. Major depressive disorder
8. extreme dejection
9. previously pleasurable aspects of life
10. bodily
11. eating; sleeping
12. self-view
13. guilt
14. concentrate
15. indecisiveness
16. melancholic
17. seasonal
18. dysthymic
19. two
20. energy
21. self-esteem

22. concentration
23. decision-making
24. hopelessness
25. appetite; sleep
26. Bipolar
27. manic episode
28. thinking
29. behavior
30. emotionality
31. manic
32. major depressive
33. Cyclothymic
34. dysphoria
35. hypomanic
36. Bipolar I
37. major depressive
38. one or more
39. one
40. neurotransmitter
41. hormonal
42. behavioral
43. cognitive
44. interpersonal

45. positive reinforcements
46. social skills
47. stressful life experiences
48. cognitive triad
49. the self
50. the world
51. the future
52. Cognitive distortions
53. arbitrary inferences
54. overgeneralizing
55. Interpersonal
56. antidepressant medication
57. electroconvulsive therapy
58. Lithium carbonate
59. behavioral
60. cognitive
61. interpersonal
62. intimate
63. mood
64. psychological
65. support
66. directive

MULTIPLE CHOICE

1. (d) is correct. While (b) may be true, that does not decrease their effectiveness; (a) and (c) are not true.
2. (b) is correct. (a), (c), and (d) are not required .
3. (d) is correct. (a) is the next highest rate, followed by (b) and (c).
4. (a) is correct. (b) and (c) mitigate against risk; (d) is also significant, but not as much so as (a).
5. (c) is correct. (a), (b), and (d) are incorrect because cyclothymia involves alterations in mood.
6. (c) is correct. There is no empirical evidence to support (a), (b), and (d).
7. (a) is correct. (b) and (c) are used for depression; (d) may sometimes be used with lithium to treat bipolar.
8. (b) is correct. (a) and (d) are incorrect; (c) is true but that is not why it is a popular treatment.

9. (a) is correct. (b), (c), and (d) do not describe the disorder.
10. (d) is correct. (a) is a cognitive-behavioral methods; (b) and (c) are not therapeutic modalities.
11. (c) is correct. (a). (b), and (d) do not match the given analogy.
12. (d) is correct. The evidence did not support (a), (b), and (c).
13. (a) is correct. The assessment did not indicate (a), (b), or (d).
14. (c) is correct. (a), (b), (c) are not experienced by a sizeable number of people with depression.
15. (d) is correct. (a), (b) , and (c) are not supported by evidence.
16. (a) is correct. (b) is a cognitive perspective; (c) a behavioral perspective; (d) is not representative of the psychodynamic or other perspectives.
17. (b) is correct. There is no evidence to support (a), (c), and (d).
18. (b) is correct. (a), (c), and (d) do not fit the described process.
19. (c) is correct. (a) and (d) are medications; (c) is not a medication regimen for depression.
20. (b) is correct. (a), (c), and (d) are not research methods used to test interpersonal therapy.
21. (d) is correct. (a), (b), and (c) do not describe the indicated terms.
22. (d) is correct. (a) believes that the roots of depression is in conflicting psychological processes stemming from childhood; (b) believes that depression is learned; and (c) is an integrative theory combining cognitive, behavioral, and psychodynamic perspectives.
23. (b) is correct. (a), (c), and (d) do not necessarily include the described phases.
24. (a) is correct. (b), (c), and (d) do not fit the described analogy.
25. (a) is correct. (b), (c), and (d) are neurotransmitters, but not implicated in the catecholamine hypothesis.
26. (d) is correct. (a), (b), and (c) would not have this explanation for depression.
27. (c) is correct. (a) is a term used in the cognitive perspective; (b) and (d) are not terms describing a psychological process.
28. (c) is correct. (a) involves who and what people blame or credit for events in their lives; (d) is an irrational thought; (d) is not a term used to describe a psychological process.
29. (a) is correct. (b), (c), and (d) do not integrate theories.
30. (c) is correct. (a) is an antidepressant, but it is not addictive; (b) is prescribed for bipolar; (d) is a tricyclic antidepressant, and not commonly used today.

CHAPTER 10
SCHIZOPHRENIA
AND RELATED DISORDERS

CHAPTER AT A GLANCE

SCHIZOPHRENIA

Phases
Active
Prodromal
Residual

Types
Catatonic
Disorganized
Paranoid
Undifferentiated
Residual

Symptoms
Delusions
Hallucinations
Disorganized Speech
Disturbed Behavior
Negative Symptoms
Social and Occupational
Dysfunctions

Other Psychotic Disorders
Schizophreniform Disorder
Schizoaffective Disorder
Delusional Disorder
Shared Psychotic Disorder

Theories and Treatment

Learning Objectives

1.0 Characteristics of Schizophrenia
    1.1 Identify the phases of schizophrenia.
    1.2 Describe the symptoms of schizophrenia including disturbance of thought content, perception, thinking, language, communication, speech, behavior, negative symptoms, and social and occupational dysfunction.
    1.3 Enumerate the types of schizophrenia, including catatonic, disorganized, paranoid, undifferentiated, and residual.
    1.4 Contrast the proposed dimensions of schizophrenia, including positive-negative and process-reactive.
    1.5 Describe the course of schizophrenia.
2.0 Other Psychotic Disorders
    2.1 Identity the characteristics of a brief psychotic disorder.
    2.2 Compare and contrast schizophreniform disorder and schizoaffective disorder.
    2.3 Describe delusional disorders
    2.4 Explain shared psychotic disorder.
3.0 Theories and Treatments of Schizophrenia
    3.1 Explain the biological perspectives on schizophrenia, including research and treatment that focus on brain structure and function, genetics, and biological stressors and vulnerability.
    3.2 Identify the psychological perspectives of schizophrenia.
    3.3 Describe the sociocultural perspective of schizophrenia, including the family systems perspective, behavioral perspective, and vulnerability models.
    3.4 Describe the course of schizophrenia.
    3.5 Compare and contrast biological, psychological, and sociocultural treatment interventions for schizophrenia.
4.0 Schizophrenia: The Perspectives Revisited
    4.1 Indicate the current status of research and theories on schizophrenia and the probable direction of future work in this area.
5.0 Chapter Boxes
    4.1 Explain the nature of the relationship between schizophrenia and social class.
    4.2 Evaluate the research about whether delusions can be modified through treatment.

Identifying the Disorders

Write the name of the disorder in which the symptoms described are the prominent features.

1. _____ Disturbances in thought content, style, perception, affect, psychomotor behavior, and interpersonal relating ability.

2. _____ Psychotic symptoms following a period of stress and lasting less than a month.

3. _____ False belief that one's partner is having an affair or in love with someone else.

4. _____ Delusions or hallucinations that others are trying to harm the individual.

5. _____ False belief that another person is in love with the individual.

6. _____ Mixed symptoms that do not meet the criteria for specific types of schizophrenia.

7. _____ Severe disturbances involving bizarre posturing or psychomotor behavior.

8. _____ False beliefs that one is being harassed or targeted by others.

9. _____ Psychotic symptoms that lack any particular theme or basis of organization.

10. _____ Psychotic disorder with symptoms of schizophrenia and mood disorder .
11. _____ Disorder with schizophrenia-like symptoms that lasts between 1 and 6 months.
12. _____ Disorder in which an individual is influenced by the delusion of a close one.

Matching

Put the letter from the right-hand column corresponding to the correct match in the blank next to each item in the left-hand column .

1. ___ Biological marker for schizophrenia involving visual tracking of a stimulus.
2. ___ Side effect of certain neuroleptics that involves uncontrollable shaking, muscle tightness, and eye twitches.
3. ___ A false perception involving one of the five senses.
4. ___ Treatment of schizophrenia in which individual is taught new ways of communicating and interacting with others.
5. ___ Behavioral treatment in which clients can earn rewards for engaging in appropriate social interactions and other daily routines.
6. ___ Term originally coined by Kraepelin to refer to the disorder that is now called schizophrenia.
7. ___ Swiss psychologist who defined the "Four A's" of schizophrenia.
8. ___ A deeply held false belief not consistent with an individual's cultural background.
9. ___ Model for explaining the inheritance of schizophrenia through contribution of several genes with varying influence.
10. ___ Parrotlike repetition of overheard words.
11. ___ German psychiatrist who developed a system for diagnosing schizophrenia based on "first rank" symptoms
12. ___ Period in the course of schizophrenia prior to the active phase of symptoms in which the individual□s functioning progressively deteriorates.
13. ___ Biological marker for schizophrenia in which the individual must make a response such as pushing a button when presented with a certain stimulus such as a specific letter.
14. ___ Period following the active phase of schizophrenia in which there are continuing signs of disturbance.
15. ___ Measure of the degree to which family members criticize, express hostility, and become overconcerned about a family member with schizophrenia.

a. Eugen Bleuler
b. sustained attention
c. prodromal phase
d. echolalia
e. Kurt Schneider
f. social skills training
g. multi-factorial polygenic threshold
h. token economy
i. hallucination
j. tardive dyskinesia
k. residual phase
l. expressed emotion
m. dementia praecox
n. smooth pursuit eye movements
o. delusion

165

Answer Game

This puzzle is like the popular television game in which contestants provide the question for answers within certain categories. To solve this puzzle, write in the question within each category that corresponds to each of the answers. The answers are arranged in approximately increasing order of difficulty so that a 100 point question is less difficult than a 400 point question. You may try playing this game with a friend, and see who receives the higher score.

Categories

Points	Theory	Treatment	Famous Person(s)	Research Design
100	A: An explanation of schizophrenia that focuses on altered neurotransmitter functioning. Q:	A: A somatic form of treatment that causes seizures. Q:	A: French physician who first identified schizophrenia as a disease. Q:	A: Design used to determine whether people with identical genetic endowment have the same risk for disorders. Q:
200	A: Explanation of schizophrenia that focuses on disturbed modes of communication within the home. Q:	A: Therapeutic environment in which staff and other clients work as a community. Q:	A: Quadruplets in NIMH study of genetic contributions to schizophrenia. Q:	A: Design in which people are studied who are born of biological parents with a disorder but raised by non-disordered parents. Q:
300	A: Behavioral explanation that schizophrenia results when an individual is designated as having the disorder and then acts accordingly. Q:	A: Behavioral intervention in which clients learn to interact appropriately with others. Q:	A: Introduced the idea of a vulnerability or diathesis model of schizophrenia. Q:	A: Design in which people are studied who are born of non-disordered parents but raised by disordered parents. Q:

166

Points	Theory	Treatment	Famous Person(s)	Research Design
400	A: Model of schizophrenia that proposes an interaction of genetic vulnerability and environmental stress. Q:	A: Medications that have antipsychotic properties. Q:	A: American psychiatrist who was one of the founders of the Danish adoption studies. Q:	A: Design in which people born of disordered parents are followed over their lives or assessed on certain key diagnostic tests. Q:

Short Answers

1. List Bleuler's "4 A's" and relate them to the current terms or concepts that are used to describe the same phenomena:

4 A's	Current diagnostic term or concept

2. Place a number next to the following ideas regarding the nature of schizophrenia indicating their historical order:

____ Restriction of criteria for diagnosing schizophrenia to a few critical symptoms that are clearly psychotic.

____ Distinction between Type I and Type II schizophrenia based on the nature of symptoms and other critical signs.

____ Schizophrenia defined as dementia praecox and regarded as due to premature brain degeneration.

____ Suggestion made that certain "first-rank" symptoms must be present for diagnosis of schizophrenia to be made.

____ Disorder labeled "schizophrenia" indicating that it was due to a split of psychic functions.

____ Schizophrenia identified as due to a form of disease.

3. List and define the symptoms of schizophrenia and summarize the potential impact on the individual of each:

Symptom	Potential impact

4. Three ways of classifying schizophrenia were described in the text. Describe the rationale and arguments against each basis of classification.

Basis of classification	Rationale in support of this classification	Arguments against this classification
Paranoid/catatonic/-disorganized/resid-ual/undifferentiated		
Positive-negative dimension		
Process-reactive dimension		

5. For each of the three disorders listed below, summarize the current explanations of the disorder and methods of treatment as described in the text:

Disorder	Current explanations	Treatment
Schizophreniform disorder		
Schizoaffective disorder		
Shared psychotic disorder		

6. For these biological explanations of schizophrenia, describe the proposed mechanism of action, original evidence to support the explanation, criticisms about it, and current understanding:

Explanation	Dopamine hypothesis	Chromosomal abnormality
Mechanism of action		
Supportive evidence		
Criticisms		
Current understanding		

7. For each of the following methods of studying genetic vs. environmental influences on schizophrenia, describe what it is intended to show and what the limitations of the method are:

Method	Purpose	Limitations
Family concordance		
Twin studies		
Discordant twin-offspring study		
Adoption study		
Cross-fostering study		

8. Place an "X" next to the term that does not belong with the others:

a. Transactional
Double-bind

Labeling
Expressed emotion

b. Cross-fostering
Increased ventricle size
Abnormal PET scans
Cortical atrophy

c. Token economy
Neuroleptics X
Social skills
Milieu therapy

d. Sustained attention
Smooth-pursuit eye movements
Event-related potential
Schizophrenia spectrum

e. High-risk
Diathesis stress
Dopamine hypothesis
Vulnerability

9. Answer the following questions regarding the case of the Genain quadruplets:

a. At what point in their lives did each of the sisters develop symptoms of schizophrenia?

_____
_____

b. What makes the study of the Genains so valuable in terms of understanding the causes of schizophrenia?

_____
_____
_____

c. What was the hypothesized role of Mrs. Genain in contributing to the illness of her daughters and why is it necessary to interpret her role with caution?

_____
_____
_____

d. How did the 1981 follow-up status of the four quadruplets compare with their status at the earlier testing?

_____
_____
_____

e. What are the implications of the results from the Genain study for the study of genetic and environmental contributions to schizophrenia?

_____
_____
_____

Focusing on Research

Answer the following questions from "Research Focus: Can Delusions Be Changed?"

1. What is the basis for the belief that people with schizophrenia can change the nature of their delusions?

_____

_____

2. Name and describe the techniques that cognitive therapists are using to help people modify their delusions.

_____

_____

From The Case Files of Dr. Sarah Tobin: Thinking About David's Case

Answer the following questions about the case of David Marshall.

1. Describe David as Dr. Tobin observed him in the emergency room.

_____

_____

2. Discuss Dr. Tobin's assessment and diagnosis of David.

_____

_____

3. Describe Dr. Tobin's formulation of David's case.

_____

_____

4. Discuss the nature of course of David's treatment.

_____

_____

How Are We Different?

Answer the following questions from the text box, "How People Differ: Schizophrenia and Social Class."
1. Compare the social causation and downward social drift hypothesis of schizophrenia.

_____

_____

2. How does the diathesis-stress model of mental illness contribute to the debate of the relationship between schizophrenia and social class?

_____

_____

3. What do we still need to know that might help explain the fact that these hypotheses may clarify the incidence of schizophrenia <u>within</u> a society, but not <u>between</u> societies?

_____

_____

171

Review at a Glance

Schizophrenia involves disturbances in (1)_____, (2)_____, (3)_____, (4)_____, (5)_____, (6)_____, and (7)_____ lasting at least (8)_____ months. Symptoms apparent during the active phase are (9)_____, (10)_____, (11)_____, (12)_____, and (13)_____. The active phase is often preceded by a (14)_____ phase and followed by a (15)_____ phase. The prodromal phase is characterized by maladaptive behaviors such as (16)_____, inability to (17)_____, (18)_____, (19)_____, (20)_____, (21)_____ and _____, (22)_____, odd (23)_____, and decreased (24)_____ and _____. The (25)_____ phase involves continuing indications of disturbance similar to the behaviors of the prodromal phase.

There are several types of schizophrenia. (26)_____ type is characterized by bizarre motor behaviors, while disorganized types consists of symptoms including disorganized (27)_____, disturbed (28)_____, and (29)_____ or (30)_____ affect. People with the paranoid type are preoccupied with one or more bizarre (31)_____ or have (32)_____ related to a theme of being persecuted or harassed. The diagnosis of (33)_____ type is used when a person does not meet the criteria for paranoid, catatonic, or disorganized type. (34)_____ type applies to people who have been diagnosed with schizophrenia and show lingering signs of the disorder without psychotic symptoms.

Schizophrenia is also characterized along two dimensions, distinguished by symptoms, for instance, (35)_____ (known as Type I) and (36)_____ symptoms, such as lack of motivation (known as Type II). The (37)_____ dimension differentiates a disorder that appears gradually over time from that provoked by a precipitant.

Disorders like those of schizophrenia include (38)_____, (39)_____, (40)_____, (41)_____, and (42)_____. Presumably, people who have schizophrenia have a (43)_____ determined (44)_____ to developing schizophrenia that develops when certain (45)_____ conditions are in place. Biological researchers have focused on abnormalities of brain (46)_____ and _____, (47)_____ predispositions, biological (48)_____, and (49_____ stressors. Current comprehensive models of care include (50)_____ treatments, psychological interventions primarily in the form of (51)_____ techniques, and sociocultural interventions that focus on (52)_____ therapy and (53)_____ involvement.

Multiple Choice

1. David Marshall's parents described to Dr. Tobin his gradual deterioration during late adolescence, suggesting that David was experiencing
   a. prodromal signs of schizophrenia.
   b. the residual phase of schizophrenia.
   c. schizoaffective disorder.
   d. a delusional disorder.

2. The "four A's" which Bleuler described as the fundamental features of schizophrenia are
   a. anomie, association, ambivalence, and autism.
   b. antagonism, affect, association, and autism.
   c. association, affect, ambivalence, and autism.
   d. affiliation, association, affect, and autism.

3. Smaller frontal lobes and limbic system structures are thought to relate to
   a. the negative subtype of schizophrenia.
   b. the positive subtype of schizophrenia.
   c. the presence of schizoaffective disorder.
   d. the reduced production of dopamine.

4. Edgar believes that his heart is being eaten away by worms, a delusion that fits into the category called
   a. somatic.
   b. persecutory.
   c. insertion.
   d. nihilistic.

5. Which of the following is not a recognized symptom of schizophrenia?
   a. disturbed interpersonal relating ability
   b. disturbed sleep patterns
   c. disturbance in sense of self
   d. disturbance of affect

6. Which term is used for a research design that studies children whose biological parents did not have schizophrenia but whose rearing parents did?
   a. index adoption
   b. schizophrenic spectrum
   c. multifactorial
   d. cross-fostering

7. The diathesis-stress model of vulnerability to schizophrenia proposes that
   a. some people have a predisposition that places them at risk for developing a disorder if exposed to certain stressful life experiences.
   b. trauma or stress may affect a person's interaction with offspring in such a way as to cause them to be vulnerable to developing a disorder.
   c. a disorder can only develop in individuals who have been exposed to stress.
   d. the closer the genetic relationship to a person with a disorder, the greater the likelihood of developing that disorder.

8. Soon after beginning a new and stressful job, Jason began to act in strange ways, such as sending e-mail messages to co-workers regarding life on other planets. After three months, Jason was given a medical leave and with treatment, returned to normal functioning. The most likely diagnosis for Jason would be
   a. brief psychotic disorder.
   b. schizophreniform disorder.
   c. reactive schizophrenia.
   d. schizoaffective disorder.

9. The symptoms of schizophrenia are associated with the overactivity of neurons that respond to which neurotransmitter?
   a. norepinephrine
   b. GABA
   c. serotonin
   d. dopamine

10. Janet and Jeannine have a close but extremely paranoid relationship. Over the years they have come to fuel each other's delusional thinking. This condition is called
    a. shared psychotic disorder.
    b. delusional disorder, jealous type.
    c. shared schizophrenia.
    d. delusional disorder, grandiose type.

11. Emil Kraepelin believed that "dementia praecox" resulted from
    a. lengthy institutionalization.
    b. deterioration of the brain.
    c. disturbed parent-child relationships.
    d. impaired cognitive capacity.

12. Disorders involving the single psychotic symptom of false beliefs are called
    a. shared psychotic disorders.
    b. schizophreniform disorders.
    c. delusional disorders.
    d. factitious disorders.

13. *DSM-I* and *DSM-II's* definitions of schizophrenia were
    a. very broad and resulted in overdiagnosis.
    b. too specific and narrow.
    c. stereotyped against minorities.
    d. not based on theory.

14. The case of the Genain quadruplets who developed schizophrenia provided evidence regarding the
    a. difference between Type 1 and Type 2 schizophrenia.
    b. role of dopamine in the development of schizophrenia.
    c. interaction of genetic and environmental factors in the development of schizophrenia.
    d. cross-fostering of schizophrenic traits among siblings.

15. Efforts by researchers to alter the nature and frequency of delusions in people with schizophrenia have shown that
    a. successful treatment required two to three years of intensive therapy.
    b. the greatest success resulted from reality testing exercises.
    c. although delusions decreased, subjects became more depressed and anxious.
    d. verbal challenges were most successful in promoting change.

16. According to the downward social drift hypothesis of schizophrenia,
    a. there is a decrease in the amount of brain processing of social input.
    b. people with schizophrenia develop the disorder because of low social class.
    c. after people develop schizophrenia, their social class declines.
    d. the friends of people with schizophrenia abandon them after they are diagnosed.

17. Which type of schizophrenia is characterized by incoherence, loose associations, inappropriate affect and haphazard behavior?
    a. paranoid type
    b. undifferentiated type
    c. catatonic type
    d. disorganized type

18. Researchers refer to the symptoms of schizophrenia that are exaggerations or distortions of normal thoughts, emotions, and behavior as
    a. positive symptoms.
    b. negative symptoms.
    c. anhedonic symptoms.
    d. hebephrenic symptoms.

19. Which dimension of schizophrenia provides a reliable basis for predicting the long-term outcome of the disorder?
    a. prodromal-residual
    b. paranoid-disorganized
    c. positive-negative
    d. catatonic-disorganized

20. The index of the degree that family members speak in ways that reflect criticism, hostile feelings, and emotional over-involvement or overconcern with regard to the individual with schizophrenia is referred to as
    a. event related potential.
    b. expressed emotion.
    c. expressive threshold.
    d. affective index.

21. The Swiss psychiatrist who abandoned the term "dementia praecox" for the current label schizophrenia was
    a. Emil Kraepelin.
    b. Eugen Bleuler.
    c. Adolf Meyer.
    d. Benedict Morel.

22. For the past three months, Tom's speech has been gradually deteriorating and becoming incoherent, and he has been exhibiting purposeless and stereotyped behaviors. His symptoms at this point are not extremely active. In what phase of schizophrenia might Tom be at this point?
    a. residual phase
    b. active phase
    c. remission phase
    d. prodromal phase

23. Lori has a constant sensation that she has snakes crawling through her intestines. Lori is experiencing a(n)
    a. hallucination.
    b. delusion.
    c. apparition.
    d. chimera.

24. Even while talking about the death of her husband a decade ago, Carol giggles almost uncontrollably. Many people in the hospital characterize her as being silly. What type of schizophrenia might she have?
    a. undifferentiated schizophrenia
    b. disorganized schizophrenia
    c. catatonic schizophrenia
    d. paranoid schizophrenia

25. The type of schizophrenia involving a complex of symptoms such as delusions, hallucinations, and incoherence, but in which no one symptom predominates is referred to as
    a. paranoid schizophrenia.
    b. undifferentiated schizophrenia.
    c. catatonic schizophrenia.
    d. disorganized schizophrenia.

26. Which term is used to refer to the gradual emergence of schizophrenia over time?
    a. process
    b. reactive
    c. acute
    d. chronic

27. Which of the following statements best characterize the current thinking regarding recovery from schizophrenia?
    a. No one actually ever recovers from schizophrenia; the best to hope for is long-term symptom management.
    b. Total recovery in all cases of schizophrenia is possible with the proper medication.
    c. Recovery rates vary widely based on how narrowly the researcher defines recovery.
    d. Long-term hospitalization is necessary in most cases; even then the prognosis is uncertain.

28. Jennifer recently experienced a brief psychotic episode soon after her miscarriage. The symptoms lasted only about a month. Jennifer had experienced
    a. schizophreniform disorder.
    b. schizoid personality disorder.
    c. brief psychotic disorder.
    d. disorganized schizophrenia.

29. The fact that antipsychotic drugs reduce the frequency of the symptoms of schizophrenia provides evidence for the
    a. dopamine hypothesis.
    b. hemispheric dominance hypothesis.
    c. frontal lobe atrophy hypothesis.
    d. serotonin hypothesis.

30. Which of the following is one of the biological markers for schizophrenia?
    a. smooth pursuit eye movements
    b. divided attention
    c. expressed emotion
    d. event related potential

Answers

IDENTIFYING DISORDERS

1. Schizophrenia
2. Brief psychotic disorder
3. Delusional disorder, jealous type
4. Schizophrenia, paranoid type
5. Delusional disorder, erotomanic type
6. Schizophrenia, undifferentiated type
7. Schizophrenia, catatonic type
8. Delusional disorder, persecutory type
9. Schizophrenia, disorganized type
10. Schizoaffective disorder
11. Schizophreniform disorder
12. Shared psychotic disorder

MATCHING

1. n
2. j
3. i
4. f
5. h
6. m
7. a
8. o
9. g
10. d
11. e
12. c
13. b
14. k
15. l

ANSWER GAME

Question Value	Theory	Treatment	Famous Person(s)	Research Design
			Categories	
100	What is the dopamine hypothesis?	What is ECT?	Who is Benjamin Morel?	What is a twin study?
200	What is family systems?	What is milieu therapy?	Who are the Genain sisters?	What is an adoption study?
300	What is labeling?	What is social skills training?	Who is Paul Meehl?	What is cross-fostering?
400	What is diathesis-stress?	What are neuro-leptics?	Who is Seymour Kety?	What is a high-risk study?

SHORT ANSWER

1.

4 A's	Current diagnostic term or concept
Association	Incoherence
Affect	Disturbance of affect
Ambivalence	Disturbance of motivation
Autism	Disturbed interpersonal relating ability

2. 5, 6, 2, 4, 3, 1

3.

Symptom	Potential impact
Disturbance of thought content: Delusions	Misinterpret behavior of others; form erroneous conclusions from daily experiences.
Disturbance in perceptions: Hallucinations	Images may be frightening and painful and are disruptive in daily life.
Disturbance of thinking, language, and communication: Disorganized speech	Difficulties in social interactions.
Disturbed behavior	Behavior looks odd to other people.
Negative symptoms	Loss of spontaneity and enjoyment in daily life, including the ability to experience pleasure from activities.
Social and occupational dysfunction	Lack of interaction with others causes loss of social skills which leads to further isolation; inability to keep a job influences standard of living.

4.

Basis of classification	Rationale in support of this classification	Arguments against this classification
Paranoid/catatonic/ disorganized/residual/un differentiated	Captures qualitative differences based on symptoms	Categories do not capture underlying dimensions of schizophrenia
Positive-negative dimension	Reliable system for predicting long-term outcome	Difficult to form clear-cut diagnosis and many clients have "mixed" symptoms
Process-reactive dimension	Intended to provide a useful system for diagnosis and estimation of prognosis	People with symptoms on reactive pole of dimension no longer regarded as having a diagnosis of schizophrenia

5.

Disorder	Current explanations	Treatment
Schizophreniform disorder	Biological links to schizophrenia as indicated by large brain ventricles, similar PET scans, and higher incidence in biological relatives	Antipsychotic medications, antianxiety medications, lithium, ECT, and psychotherapy
Schizoaffective disorder	Debate over whether disorder is a variant of schizophrenia or affective disorder	Lithium, antidepressant medications, antipsychotic medications, and psychotherapy
Shared psychotic disorder	Relationship issues in which dominant person feels isolated and seeks ally in weaker person who has come to rely on the other	Separation of the two individuals; therapy with submissive partner regarding vulnerability to domination

6.

Explanation	Dopamine hypothesis	Chromosomal abnormality
Mechanism of action	Increased dopamine activity.	Defect on a given chromosome underlies dopamine abnormality.
Supportive evidence	Antipsychotic drugs block dopamine receptors. Drugs related to dopamine increase frequency of psychotic symptoms.	Genetic mapping studies involving attempts to identify a susceptibility gene for schizophrenia have indicated several possible loci.
Criticisms	No difference exists between people with schizophrenia and normal individuals in dopamine metabolism.	Original findings have not been reliably replicated by other investigators.
Current understanding	Dopamine hypothesis may apply to Type 1 schizophrenia but not Type 2.	Researchers are still hoping to discover chromosomal abnormalities related to schizophrenia.

7.

Method	Purpose	Limitations
Family concordance	Relationship between proximity of biological relationship and concordance for schizophrenia.	Families share not only genetics factors but also the same environments.
Twin studies	Identical twins share same genetic endowment; concordance rate for schizophrenia reveals direct estimate of genetic contribution.	Identical twins share the same environment as well as identical genetic makeup.
Discordant twin-offspring study	Determination of whether offspring of discordant twins have higher concordance for schizophrenia provides further information on genetic determination of the disorder.	Still remaining unclear is why in the original discordant pairs one twin and not the other develops schizophrenia.
Adoption study	Rule out the influence of environmental factors in family concordance studies.	Adopting families may not be free of disorder and therefore not provide a "clean" environment.
Cross-fostering study	Evaluate the effect of environmental contributions to schizophrenia in the absence of genetic inheritance.	Very difficult to conduct due to small incidence of disordered adopting parents.

8. a. Labeling   Family systems explanations of schizophrenia.
    b. Cross-fostering   Brain changes.
    c. Neuroleptics   Behavioral treatments for schizophrenia.
    d. Schizophrenia spectrum   Biological markers for schizophrenia.
    e. Dopamine hypothesis   Concepts related to the vulnerability model of schizophrenia.

9.   a. All showed signs of disorder by the time they were in their 20s.

    b. As identical quadruplets, they shared the same genetic makeup; it is unusual to find such a family. In addition, they were studied over the course of their adult lives.

    c. Mrs. Genain was hypothesized to have given conflicting and confusing messages to her daughters, and to pressure the more competent ones to conform to the characteristics of the sisters who had more severe disturbance. It is necessary to interpret Mrs. Genain's role with caution because it would be a mistake to place too much importance on the effects of parenting style on the development of schizophrenia.

    d. The four sisters changed in order of degree of impairment with Hester and Iris originally showing more impairment than Nora and Myra; in the follow-up, Myra and Iris showed less impairment than the other two sisters.

    e. The fact that they all developed schizophrenia is convincing evidence for genetic contributions to the disorder; but the fact that their symptoms emerged in different ways over the years of adulthood and that their relative degree of impairment shifted suggests an interaction of genetics with environmental factors.

FOCUSING ON RESEARCH

1. Researchers believe that delusions are attributions or judgments that people make in an effort to make sense of particular experiences or perceptions. Individuals with schizophrenia may develop delusions to bring order and understanding to unusual, frightening, or hallucinatory experiences.

2. Cognitive therapists use verbal challenge and reality testing. In verbal challenge they examine the evidence supporting or contradicting the delusional beliefs and develop explanations that are more accurate and realistic. In reality testing, the therapist has client carry out activities aimed at invalidating the delusion.

FROM THE CASE FILES OF DR. SARAH TOBIN: THINKING ABOUT DAVID'S CASE

1. David was yelling about wanting to see Zoroaster. He said he had been appointed to protect the world from evil forces and that he was bearing a message of salvation.

2. David was experiencing hallucinations and delusions so Dr. Tobin could on conduct a 30-minute mental status examination. All of his answers focused on his beliefs about Zoroaster and aliens, including his name and the date. He had loose associations and bizarre behaviors. He was impaired in most areas of everyday functioning. He was socially isolated, and failed to take care of his personal hygiene. Dr Tobin diagnosed him as having the undifferentiated type schizophrenia.

3. David's aunt probably was a schizophrenic. He had been withdrawn most of his life, unlike his outgoing brother (to whom his parents gave most of their attention). The message David got from his parents was that they were not as concerned with him as with his brother.

4. Dr. Tobin recommended that David remain in the hospital for 3 months and be treated with antipsychotic medication. His hospital course went well after he was stabilized on medication. Upon discharge from the hospital, he attended a day treatment program for 12 months. He then got a job at the library and did well, gaining a promotion that involved a lot of contact with the public. However, the stress of exposure to many people caused him to relapse. Within 2 weeks of starting his new position, he had a full-blown psychotic episode and went back to the hospital. After a short stay, he went back to the day treatment program for 6 months, then agreed to move out of his parents' home into a group home for schizophrenics. He was able to go back to work. Dr. Tobin has seen him once a month for several years and David has remained stable. However, David does not seem to be getting much of out psychotherapy.

HOW **ARE** WE DIFFERENT?

1. According to the social causation hypothesis, membership in lower socioeconomic classes may cause schizophrenia because members of these classes experience highly stressful environmental factors that may be conducive to the development of schizophrenia. These include numerous economic hardships, do not have access to high-quality education, health care, and employment, and may experience discrimination. The downward social drift hypothesis downplays the effects of socioeconomic stresses in the development of the disorder, but says that once people develop the disorder their economic standing and social fortunes decline precipitously, in effect leading them into a lower socioeconomic class.

2. The social causation hypothesis is consistent with the "stress" component of the diathesis- stress model (that environmental stressors contribute to manifestation of a disorder). But the diathesis-stress model holds that there is a biological/genetic predisposition to schizophrenia and that stressors trigger the onset of the disease.

3. We need to know more about societal values and beliefs about mental illness that lead to differing criteria for diagnosis.

REVIEW AT A GLANCE

1. thought
2. perception
3. affect
4. sense of self
5. motivation
6. behavior
7. interpersonal functioning
8. six
9. delusions
10. hallucinations
11. disorganized speech
12. disturbed behavior
13. negative symptoms
14. prodromal
15. residual
16. social withdrawal
17. work productively
18. eccentricity
19. poor grooming
20. inappropriate

    emotionality
21. peculiar thought and speech
22. unusual beliefs
23. perceptual experiences
24. energy/initiative
25. residual
26. catatonic
27. speech
28. behavior
29. flat
30. inappropriate
31. delusions
32. auditory hallucinations
33. undifferentiated
34. residual
35. positive
36. hallucinations
37. negative
38. process-reactive

39. brief psychotic disorder
40. schizophreniform disorder
41. schizoaffective disorder
42. delusional disorders
43. shared psychotic disorders
44. biologically
45. predisposition
46. environmental
47. structure/function
48. genetic
49. markers
50. biological
51. biological
52. behavioral
53. milieu
54. family

MULTIPLE CHOICE

1. (a) is correct. (b) refers to lingering symptoms after a period of active schizophreina; (c) and (d) are not associated with graduate deterioration.
2. (c) is correct. (a) in incorrect, because anomie is not a feature; (b) because antagonism is not one; and (d) because affiliation is not a symptom.
3. (a) is correct. (b) is associated with increased dopamine levels, thus (d) is also incorrect; (c) is not associated with organic brain differences.
4. (a) is correct. (b) involves thoughts; (c) and (d) are not forms of delusions.
5. (b) is correct. (a), (c), and (d) are recognized symptoms
6. (d) is correct. (a), (b), and (c) are not types of research design.
7. (a) is correct. (b) and (c) are inaccurate statements; (d) concerns concordance rates.
8. (a) is correct. (b), (c), and (d) are incorrect because they are not temporary conditions.
9. (d) is correct. (a), (b), and (c) have not been associated with schizophrenia symptoms.

10. (a) is correct. There is no evidence that they are grandiose or jealous delusions (b) and (d); there is not such disorder as (c).
11. (b) is correct. (a), (b), and (c) are not related to Kraepelin's term or to his theory of schizophrenia.
12. (c) is correct. (a) involves more than one person; (b) has a range of symptoms; (d) is not a psychotic disorder.
13. (a) is correct. (b), (c), and (d) are inaccurate.
14. (c) is correct. (d) involves a research design not used in this case; (a) and (b) were not addressed in the research.
15. (d) is correct. (a), (b), and (c) have not been reported.
16. (c) is correct. (a) is not related to social factors; there is no evidence for (b); (d) may be true but it is not related to the downward drift hypothesis.
17. (d) is correct. (a), (b), and (c) are not characterized by these symptoms.
18. (a) is correct. (b) involves absence of speech, and affect; (c) refers to a loss of enjoyment of life, more a factor in depression; and (d) is not a term in current use.
19. (c) is correct. (a) refers to phases of the disorder; (b) and (d) to diagnostic types. (c) refers to type of symptoms.
20. (b) is correct. (a) is a measure of cognitive activity; (c) and (d) are not terms used in the context of schizophrenia.
21. (b) is correct. (a) coined the term; (c) and (d) made other contributions.
22. (d) is correct. (a) occurs after an active phase; (b) is the presence of full-blown symptoms; and there is no such phase as (c).
23. (a) is correct. (b) involves thought; (c) and (d) are not terms used to describe schizophrenia symptoms.
24. (b) is correct. (a), (c), and (d) do not match the described symptoms.
25. (b) is correct. (a), (c), and (d) do not match the described symptoms.
26. (c) is correct. (b) involves a more rapid onset; (c) and (d) are not terms used to describe the onset of schizophrenia.
27. (c) is correct. The course of the illness and response to treatment varies so that (a), (b), and (d) are not reasonable conclusions.
28. (c) is correct. (a) and (d) require longer expression of symptoms for a diagnosis; (b) is not a psychotic disorder.
29. (a) is correct. There is no serotonin hypothesis (d)l (b) and (c) would be unaffected by antipsychotic medication.
30. (a) is correct. (b) may be apparent in some clients, but it is a cognitive factor, not biological; (c) is a social factor stemming from family dynamics; and (d) is a measure of cognitive activity, not necessarily related to schizophrenia.

CHAPTER 11
DEVELOPMENT-RELATED DISORDERS

CHAPTER AT A GLANCE

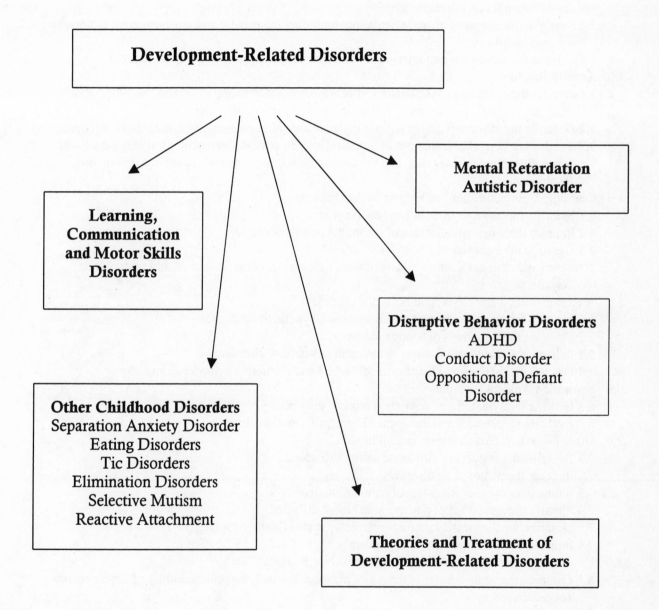

Development-Related Disorders

Learning, Communication and Motor Skills Disorders

Mental Retardation
Autistic Disorder

Disruptive Behavior Disorders
ADHD
Conduct Disorder
Oppositional Defiant Disorder

Other Childhood Disorders
Separation Anxiety Disorder
Eating Disorders
Tic Disorders
Elimination Disorders
Selective Mutism
Reactive Attachment

Theories and Treatment of Development-Related Disorders

Learning Objectives

1.0 Introductory Issues
  1.1 Discuss the controversies involved in the definition and diagnosis of development-related disorders.
2.0 Mental Retardation
  2.1 Identify the characteristics of mental retardation and the behavioral competencies associated with the different levels of retardation.
  2.2 Describe the causes of mental retardation, including the genetic and environmental factors, and prevention programs.
  2.3 Discuss the treatments and interventions best suited for people with mental retardation.
3.0 Autistic Disorder
  3.1 Identify the types and characteristics of pervasive developmental disorders, including Rett's disorder, childhood disintegrative disorder, and Asperger's disorder.
  3.2 Describe the characteristics of autistic disorder and those of its subtype, autistic savant syndrome.
  3.3 Summarize current explanations of autistic disorder, psychopharmacological and behavioral treatments of autistic disorder, and the controversies associated with aversive treatment techniques.
4.0 Learning, Communication, and Motor Skills Disorders
  4.1 Identify the characteristics of learning disorders.
  4.2 Indicate the diagnostic features of communication disorders.
  4.3 Describe the symptoms of motor skills disorders.
  4.4 Summarize current theories and treatments of learning, communication, and motor skills disorders.
5.0 Attention-Deficit and Disruptive Behavior Disorders
  5.1 Identify the characteristics of attention-deficit/hyperactivity disorder.
  5.2 Describe the symptoms of conduct disorder.
  5.3 Indicate the diagnostic features of oppositional-defiant disorder.
  5.4 Discuss the theories and treatments of ADHD and disruptive behavior disorders.
6.0 Separation Anxiety Disorder
  6.1 Indicate the symptoms of separation anxiety disorder.
  6.2 Evaluate the theories and treatment of separation anxiety disorder.
7.0 Other Disorders That Originate in Childhood
  7.1 Describe the features of childhood eating disorders.
  7.2 Indicate the nature of tic disorders.
  7.3 Summarize the characteristics of elimination disorders.
  7.4 Identify the symptoms of reactive attachment disorder.
  7.5 Describe the diagnostic criteria for stereotypic movement disorder.
  7.6 Indicate the features of selective mutism.
8.0 Development-Related Disorders: The Perspectives Revisited
  8.1 Compare the contributions of the major perspectives with the understanding of development-related disorders.
9.0 Chapter Boxes
  9.1 Evaluate the issues involved in the use of aversive treatment for autistic disorder.
  9.2 Examine the current research involving adults with attention-deficit/ hyperactivity disorder.

Identifying Symptoms

Write the name of the disorder in which the symptom described is a prominent feature.

1. _____ Delay or deficit in a particular academic skill.
2. _____ Refusal to talk when a social interaction is expected.
3. _____ Impulsive, restless, aggressive, and unable to focus on a task.
4. _____ Significantly below-average intellectual functioning and adaptive behavior.
5. _____ Involved in delinquent and criminal activities without remorse for one's actions.
6. _____ Massive impairment in ability to communicate and relate emotionally to others.
7. _____ Hostile, argumentative, and generally rebellious toward authority figures.
8. _____ Distress when parents are not present, even for short periods of time.
9. _____ Severely handicapped communication and emotional relatedness combined with extraordinary skill in an area such as memory or arithmetic.
10. _____ Repetitive, seemingly driven bodily behaviors that interfere with everyday functioning and can cause injuries.
11. _____ In females, impaired cognitive and neurological development between 5 months and 4 years of age.
12. _____ Difficulty understanding and expressing certain kinds of words or phrases.
13. _____ Normal development for first 2 years with loss of cognitive and adaptive skills before the age of 10.
14. _____ Obvious problems of verbal expression.
15. _____ Adequate cognitive and language development with severe impairment in social interaction and restricted, repetitive, and stereotyped patterns of behavior.

Matching

Put the letter from the right-hand column corresponding to the correct match in the blank next to each item in the left-hand column.

1. ___ Abnormalities in this neurotransmitter system are thought to be a source of attention-deficit/hyperactivity disorder.
2. ___ Level of mental retardation in which individual can be trained but is unlikely to progress beyond second-grade skills.
3. ___ Disorder in which child regurgitates food after it has been swallowed, possibly eating the vomit after it has been spit up.
4. ___ Speech and language disorder characterized by mispronunciations, substitutions, and omissions of speech sounds.
5. ___ Form of mental retardation caused by chromosomal abnormality present from conception.
6. ___ Disorder of childhood in which child lacks control of bowel movements.
7. ___ In developmental _____ disorder, an individual has difficulty performing simple physical tasks.
8. ___ Medication found to be helpful in reducing symptoms of attention-deficit/hyperactivity disorder.
9. ___ Childhood disorder involving recurrent eating of inedible substances such as hair, paper, and string.
10. ___ Approach that is mandated by U.S. federal law to integrate children with mental retardation into public schools.
11. ___ Level of retardation in which individual can respond to a very limited range of self-help training.
12. ___ Form of tic disorder that involves involuntary uttering of obscenities.
13. ___ Form of pervasive developmental disorder shown by the title character in Rainman, who could instantly make complex math calculations.
14. ___ Speech and language disorder characterized by limited vocabulary and use of grammatical structures.
15. ___ Disorder of childhood in which child lacks control over urination.

a. mainstreaming
b. pica
c. Tourette's syndrome
d. coordination
e. catecholamine
f. encopresis
g. moderate
h. expressive language disorder
i. autistic savant syndrome
j. enuresis
k. Down syndrome
l. rumination disorder
m. methylphenidate
n. phonological disorder
o. profound

Short Answer

1. In what ways are the following pairs of items the same?

a. Tay-Sachs disease and Fragile X syndrome: _____
b. Phonological disorder and receptive language disorder: _____
c. Echolalia and emotional unresponsiveness: _____
d. Pica and ruminative disorder: _____
e. Mathematics disorder and disorder of written expression: _____

f. White noise and cold showers: _____

g. Oppositional defiant disorder and conduct disorder: _____

h. Albert Einstein and Henry Ford: _____

i. Facial abnormalities and low birth weight: _____

2. Describe the possible role of biological factors as causes of each of the following development-related disorders:

Development-related disorder	Possible biological factors
Mental retardation	
Autistic disorder	
Language, communication, and motor skills disorders	
Attention-deficit/hyperactivity disorder	
Separation anxiety disorder	

3. Summarize long-term effects associated with each of the following disorders:

Disorder	Long-term effects
Autistic disorder	
Language, communication, and motor skills disorders	
Conduct disorder	
Attention-deficit/hyperactivity disorder	
Separation anxiety disorder	

187

4. Imagine that you are a parent of a child with attention-deficit/hyperactivity disorder. List three advantages and three disadvantages that you would consider if choosing medication such as Ritalin (methylphenidate) as a method of treatment?

Advantages	Disadvantages

5. Briefly describe the available behavioral treatments for each of the following development-related disorders:

Disorder	Behavioral treatment
Mental retardation	
Autistic disorder	
Learning, communication, and motor skills disorders	
Attention-deficit/hyperactivity disorder	
Conduct disorder	
Separation anxiety disorder	

ABC Puzzle

Fill in each of the following blanks that are in alphabetical order. The first letter of the answer is indicated at the beginning of the blank:

A_____ Disorder involving massive deficits in a person's ability to communicate and form emotional bonds with others.

B_____ Theoretical perspective on which aversive conditioning procedures are based.

C_____ Disorder in which a child becomes involved in criminal or delinquent activities and feels no sense of remorse.

D_____ Category of disorders that applies specifically to children.

E_____ Characteristic of autistic disorder in which the individual repetitively utters the sound of a verbalization.

F_____ Cause of mental retardation due to an abnormality on the "X" chromosome.

G_____ Category of causes of mental retardation due to deficits or abnormalities in a person's inherited potential.

H_____ Common term for a child who is incapable of sustaining attention on a task, becomes restless, and can irritate others by constant movement and aggressiveness.

I_____ Psychological variable on which categories of mental retardation are based.

J_____ Religious/ethnic background of people who are most vulnerable to inheriting Tay-Sachs disease.

K_____ Expert on autistic disorder who theorized that faulty mothering is the cause of the disorder.

L_____ Category of learning, communication, and motor skills disorders involving delays or deficits in academic areas.

M_____ Disorder in which individual suffers delays or deficits in acts involving coordination.

N_____ Historically renowned physicist who was a poor student in school and a failure in running the family farm.

O_____ Form of disruptive behavior disorder characterized by extreme stubbornness, rebelliousness, and resistance to authority.

P_____ Cause of mental retardation caused by failure (present at birth) to produce an enzyme needed for normal development.

Q_____ A child with selective mutism is very _____ because he or she refuses to speak.

R_____ Commonly known as "German measles," a disease that can cause mental retardation if the mother acquires it during the first trimester of pregnancy.

S_____ Disorder in which the individual shows a disturbance in the normal fluency and patterning of speech.

T_____ Rapid, recurring, involuntary movement or vocalization.

U_____ Environmental cause of mental retardation that is associated with high poverty levels.

V_____ Patterns of rising crime and _____ are seen as contributing to behavioral problems among inner-city youth.

W_____ Use of these on cigarette boxes and alcohol labels is regarded as aiding in prevention of mental retardation.

X_____ Computer-aided versions of this radiological test can provide important information about brain abnormalities in people with disorders such as autistic disorder.

Y_____ Synonym for childhood and adolescence.

Z_____ Snoring noise made by weary students.

Focusing on Research

Answer the following questions from "Research Focus: Adults with Attention-Deficit/ Hyperactivity Disorder."

1. Summarize the current research about adult ADHD.

_____

_____

2. Comment on a possible explanation for the difference in research findings.

_____

_____

From The Case Files of Dr. Sarah Tobin: Thinking About Jason's Case

Answer the following questions about the case of Jason Newman.

1. Describe Dr. Tobin's observations of Jason at their first meeting.

_____

_____

2. List Jason's symptoms as reported by his parents.

_____

_____

3. Identify the components of Dr. Tobin's assessment of Jason and her diagnosis.

_____

_____

4. Discuss the nature and course of Jason's treatment.

_____

_____

Review at a Glance

An IQ of (1)_____ or below indicates mental retardation. In addition to intellectual deficits, people with mental retardation have significant impairments in abilities such as (2)_____, (3)_____, (4)_____, and (5)_____ for self-care. Mental retardation can result from an (6)_____ condition or from an (7)_____ or _____ that takes place during development.

(8)_____ disorders are characterized by severe impairment in (9)_____ or (10)_____ skills or the presence of extremely odd (11)_____, (12)_____, and (13)_____. The most common of these disorders is (14)_____ disorder, characterized by massive impairment in an individual's ability to (15)_____ and relate (16)_____ to others. Support for the biological theory of autism includes patterns of (17)_____, as well as studies of brain (18)_____ and (19)_____. Psychological interventions aim at modifying the (20)_____ of autistic individuals.

A (21)_____ is a delay or deficit in (22)_____ that is evident when an individual's achievement on standardized tests is (23)_____ what would be expected for others of comparable (24)_____, (25)_____, and level of (26)_____. (27)_____ are characterized by impairment in the (28)_____ or (29)_____ of language. The primary form of (30)_____ disorder is (31)_____, a condition characterized by marked impairment in the development of (32)_____. Most developmental disorders are viewed as (33)_____ based, with various causes, such as damage during (34)_____ or (35)_____ or as the result of (36)_____ or a (37)_____. Interventions for children with these disorders generally occur in a (38)_____ setting.

Attention-deficit/hyperactivity disorder (ADHD) involves (39)_____ and (40)_____. Inattentiveness is characterized by behaviors such as (41)_____, forgetfulness in (42)_____, and other (43)_____ problems. The hyperactive-impulsive component is further divided into subtypes of (44)_____ and (45)_____. Hyperactivity is characterized by (46)_____,

(47)_____, (48)_____ inappropriately, having difficulty in (49)_____ quietly, and (50)_____ excessively. Impulsivity is evident in individuals who (51)_____, (52)_____, and (53)_____ or _____ on others. Young people with (54)_____ persistently (55)_____, while those with oppositional defiant disorder show a pattern of (56)_____, (57)_____, and (58)_____ behaviors that result in (59)_____ or _____ problems.

Extensive research on the causes of ADHD focuses on (60)_____ abnormality that accounts for impaired (61)_____ and (62)_____. The most common biological intervention is the medication (63)_____. Psychological interventions are based on (64)_____ principles.

(65)_____ involves the experience of intense and inappropriate anxiety concerning separation from (66)_____ or _____. Childhood eating disorders include conditions such as (67)_____, (68)_____ of infancy or early childhood, and (69)_____ disorder. Tic disorders, such as (70)_____ disorder, involve bodily (71)_____ or (72)_____. Elimination disorders, such as (73)_____ and (74)_____, are characterized by failure to maintain continence at an age-appropriate stage. (75)_____ is a severe disturbance in an individual's ability to relate to others. Individuals with (76)_____ disorders engage in repetitive, seemingly driven bodily movements. Those with (77)_____ refuse to talk in certain circumstances.

Multiple Choice

1. Researchers studying adults with ADHD have found that many experience
   a. other serious psychological disorders.
   b. higher than average intelligence.
   c. improved psychological adjustment.
   d. lower cognitive distractibility.

2. A form of mental retardation with brain changes similar to those found in Alzheimer's disease is
   a. Fragile X syndrome.
   b. Tay-Sachs disease.
   c. phenylketonuria.
   d. Down syndrome.

3. The most appropriate intervention for an individual diagnosed with PKU is
   a. exposure to full-spectrum light.
   b. a special diet.
   c. low dose radiation.
   d. neuroleptic medication.

4. Which of the following is a procedure that is used to detect chromosomal abnormalities in a developing fetus?
   a. amniocentesis
   b. chromosonography
   c. genetic mapping
   d. FAS screening

5. Mainstreaming is
   a. the establishment of institutions that are devoted to educating people with disabilities.
   b. the placement of children with disabilities in foster homes where they can be appropriately nurtured.
   c. the integration into society of people with mental and physical disabilities.
   d. legislation that requires alcohol and tobacco products to carry warnings about potential toxic effects.

6. Which of the following is characteristic of Asperger's disorder?
   a. normal cognitive and language development
   b. occurrence only in females
   c. severe social and motor impairments
   d. loss of adaptive functions before the age of 10 years

7. Eleven-year-old Jonah's speech is characterized by poor use of grammar and vocabulary relative to others of his age, although he is able to understand the speech of others. These are signs that he has which communication disorder?
   a. stuttering
   b. expressive language disorder
   c. phonological disorder
   d. mixed receptive-expressive language disorder

8. Michael is a third-grader who is often causing problems at home and school. He is disorganized, messy, impulsive, inattentive, and accident-prone. In all likelihood, Michael would be regarded as having
   a. attention-deficit/hyperactivity disorder.
   b. conduct disorder.
   c. oppositional defiant disorder.
   d. separation anxiety disorder.

9. Which disorder is diagnosed in children who have great difficulty relating to others and express this either in avoidance of social interactions or in inappropriate familiarity with strangers?
   a. selective mutism
   b. separation anxiety disorder
   c. atypical autistic disorder
   d. reactive attachment disorder

10. In what context is a restrained time-out station used?
    a. aversive treatment for individuals with autistic disorder
    b. positive reinforcement for individuals with learning disorders
    c. behavioral treatment of hyperactive children
    d. rehabilitation of mentally retarded individuals

11. In explaining the hypothesized causes of ADHD, experts currently believe that it
    a. develops as a result of inadequate intellectual stimulation.
    b. is a genetically acquired trait.
    c. develops primarily as a result of a disturbed family system.
    d. is biologically based, triggered by certain stressful environmental conditions.

12. The term used to describe behavior in which an individual has bowel movements in clothes or inappropriate places is
    a. encopresis.
    b. enuresis.
    c. dyslexia.
    d. coprolalia.

13. The metabolic disorder that causes neural degeneration and early death, usually before the child reaches the age of 4 is called
    a. Down syndrome.
    b. Fragile X syndrome.
    c. phenylketonuria.
    d. Tay-Sachs syndrome.

14. A syndrome involving mental retardation that develops in the child of a woman who regularly consumes excess amounts of liquor while she is pregnant is referred to as
    a. Fragile X syndrome.
    b. alcohol dependence syndrome.
    c. Tay-Sachs syndrome.
    d. fetal alcohol syndrome.

15. Autistic children usually form attachments to
    a. inanimate objects.
    b. pets.
    c. older siblings.
    d. their mothers.

16. CAT scans of the brains of individuals with autistic disorder reveal
    a. temporal lobe malformations.
    b. low levels of cortical arousal.
    c. enlarged ventricles.
    d. lesions in the hypothalamus.

17. Norm has just started 1st grade but does not understand what his teacher means when she asks him to count to 10. He is also baffled by her requests to add or subtract numbers. Norm might be diagnosed as having
    a. math phobia.
    b. mathematics disorder.
    c. expressive numeric disorder.
    d. dyscalcula.

18. Which of the following is the development-related disorder that is the precursor in childhood of antisocial personality disorder?
    a. overanxious disorder
    b. conduct disorder
    c. oppositional defiant disorder
    d. attention-deficit/hyperactivity disorder

19. In many ways, Sally seems like a typical teenager. However, she repeatedly argues with her parents, refuses to do what she is told, and at times does things to annoy people deliberately. If this behavior pattern is relatively long-term, Sally might have
    a. conduct disorder.
    b. attention-deficit/hyperactivity disorder.
    c. rumination disorder.
    d. oppositional defiant disorder.

20. Seth is constantly moving his head and twitching his shoulders. He utters loud, abrupt noises that others regard as strange. These movement and vocal patterns are uncontrollable. The term used to describe Seth's condition is
    a. Rett syndrome.
    b. Sack's disorder.
    c. Asperger's syndrome.
    d. Tourette's disorder.

21. In order to be considered mentally retarded, an individual's IQ must be
    a. between 100-120.
    b. between 80-100.
    c. between 75-80.
    d. less than 70.

22. The metabolic disorder that causes neural degeneration and early death, usually before the child reaches the age of four, is called
    a. Down syndrome.
    b. Fragile X syndrome.
    c. phenylketonuria.
    d. Tay-Sachs disease.

23. A condition caused by poverty and neglect in which the child does not grow at a normal rate either physically or mentally is known as
    a. failure to thrive.
    b. anoxia.
    c. retardation.
    d. Tay-Sachs disease.

24. A symptom of autistic disorder in which the child mimics other people's words or phrases is referred to as
    a. clanging.
    b. perseveration.
    c. reverberating.
    d. echolalia.

25. CT scans of the brains of individuals with autistic disorder reveal
    a. temporal lobe malformations.
    b. low levels of cortical arousal.
    c. enlarged ventricles.
    d. lesions in the hypothalamus.

26. Joshua has a specific developmental disorder that is characterized by the fact that words and letters get reversed when he is reading; for example the letter "b" looks like "d" and the word "frog" may look like "gorf." This problem makes him read aloud in a slow and broken way. Joshua may have
    a. disorder of written expression.
    b. cluttering.
    c. expressive language disorder.
    d. dyslexia.

27. Which disorders may be the result of difficulty integrating information from the brain areas involved in vision, speech, and language comprehension?
    a. disruptive behavior disorders
    b. learning, communication and motor skills disorders
    c. anxiety disorders of childhood
    d. pervasive developmental disorders

28. Victor generally has no difficulty sitting still, but cannot focus his attention on what the teacher is saying for long periods of time. Victor might be diagnosed as having
    a. attention-deficit/hyperactivity disorder, inattentive type.
    b. attention-deficit/hyperactivity disorder, hyperactive-impulsive type.
    c. attention-deficit/hyperactivity disorder, combined type.
    d. attention-deficit/hyperactivity disorder, overactive type.

29. While eating, Lindsay often spits her food back up and rechews it. Assuming that this is a persistent problem, Lindsay might be diagnosed with
    a. pica
    b. feeding disorder of early childhood
    c. rumination disorder
    d. bulimia nervosa

30. The disorder originating in childhood in which the individual voluntarily repeats nonproductive behaviors such as rocking or head banging is called
    a. elective mutism.
    b. childhood schizophrenia.
    c. stereotypic movement disorder.
    d. pica.

Answers

IDENTIFYING SYMPTOMS

1. learning disorder
2. selective mutism
3. attention-deficit/hyperactivity disorder
4. mental retardation
5. conduct disorder
6. autistic disorder
7. oppositional defiant disorder
8. separation anxiety disorder
9. autistic savant syndrome
10. stereotypic movement disorder
11. Rett's disorder
12. mixed receptive-expressive language disorder
13. childhood disintegrative disorder
14. expressive language disorder
15. Asperger's disorder

MATCHING

1.	e	4.	n	7.	d	10.	a	13.	i
2.	g	5.	k	8.	m	11.	o	14.	h
3.	l	6.	f	9.	b	12.	c	15.	j

SHORT ANSWER

1. a. Causes of mental retardation
   b. Communication disorders
   c. Symptoms of autistic disorder
   d. Eating disorders of childhood
   e. Learning disorders
   f. Aversive treatments for autistic disorder
   g. Disruptive behavior disorders
   h. Successful adults who had learning problems in school
   i. Characteristics of children born with fetal alcohol syndrome

2. a. There are several inherited causes of mental retardation, including phenylketonuria, Tay-Sachs disease, Fragile X syndrome, and Down syndrome.
   b. People with autistic disorder show abnormal EEGs, CAT scans, and MRIs, as well as serotonin abnormalities.
   c. Damage to various brain sites during fetal development, birth, or early childhood
   d. Some evidence exists for decreased activity in the frontal cortex, involved in controlling attention and motor activity.
   e. Separation anxiety in children related to increased panic disorder in parents, suggesting possible genetic link.

3.

Disorder	Long-term effects
Autistic disorder	Two-thirds of people with autistic disorder are unable to live an independent life as an adult.
Language, communication, and motor skills disorders	Increased risk of anxiety disorder, mood disorder, ADHD, conduct disorder, and adjustment disorder
Conduct disorder	Marital difficulties, decreased occupational and educational opportunities, poor social relationships, alcohol use, poorer physical health, and antisocial personality disorder

Disorder	Long-term effects
Attention-deficit hyperactivity disorder	Substance abuse, academic underachievement, decreased self-esteem, higher number of arrests (in men), and greater risk of depression (in women)
Separation anxiety disorder	Increased likelihood of developing anxiety disorder as an adult

4.

Advantages	Disadvantages
Increased attentional control	Decreased sleep
Decreased hyperactive behavior	Decreased appetite
Increased positive social interactions with peers, teachers, and parents	Development of twitches

5.

Disorder	Behavioral treatment
Mental retardation	Reinforcement for appropriate use of speech and language, and the development of social skills; parents can be taught to reward a child for appropriate behaviors and to respond negatively to inappropriate behaviors
Autistic disorder	Self-control procedures, relaxation training, covert conditioning, and in extreme cases, aversive therapy
Learning, communication, and motor skills disorders	In the school context, more structure, fewer distractions, presentation of new material that uses more than one sensory modality at a time
Attention-deficit/hyperactivity disorder	Teaching of self-control and changing of the contingencies in the environment; involvement of family in reducing child's destructive behaviors
Conduct disorder	Teach appropriate behaviors such as cooperation and self-control while unlearning problem behaviors such as aggression, stealing, and lying; use reinforcement, behavioral contracting, modeling, and relaxation training
Separation anxiety disorder	Systematic desensitization, prolonged exposure, and modeling; contingency management and self-management can also teach the child to react more competently to a fear-provoking situation

ABC PUZZLE

Autistic disorder
Behavioral
Conduct disorder
Development-related disorders
Echolalia
Fragile X

Genetic
Hyperactive
Intelligence
Jewish
Kanner
Learning disorders

Motor skills disorder
Newton (Sir Isaac)
Oppositional defiant disorder
Phenylketonuria
Quiet
Rubella

Stuttering	Violence	Youth
Tic	Warning labels	Z-Z-Z-Z (Sorry, we couldn't find
Undernutrition	X-rays	any "z" words in this chapter!)

FOCUSING ON RESEARCH

1. Research results are inconclusive and somewhat contradictory. Studies following ADHD children into adulthood (known as longitudinal studies) find that as many as 30 to 50 percent of ADHD children continue to meet the diagnostic criteria for ADHD in adulthood. However, data extrapolated from epidemiological studies suggest only a 3.3 percent prevalence for childhood and adult ADHD.

2. Adults may not meet the full diagnostic criteria yet may exhibit some symptoms of the disorder.

FROM THE CASE FILES OF DR. SARAH TOBIN: THINKING ABOUT JASON'S CASE

1. Jason had just knocked over a water cooler, causing water to go all over the floor. While Jason's mother scolded him Jason played a game on his handheld Nintendo. He made popping noises with his mouth and cheered his game results. When Dr. Tobin met with Jason alone, he ignored some of her questions, changed topics, interrupted her, and was constantly distracted.

2. He was unable to control his behavior, was antagonizing people at home and other children at school, out of control at home and school, recently set a fire at school, disrupting his classes at school, throwing things at other students, playing tricks on his teachers, refusing to wait his turn, unable to sit still at church, at a movie, or at dinner at home, and was not paying attention in school, or doing his homework.

3. He had recently had an IQ test at school, which placed him in the above-average range of intelligence on verbal and performance scales. She had parents and teachers complete the Connors Checklist of Child Behaviors. The results indicated learning problems, impulsivity, and hyperactivity. She diagnosed Jason with ADHD, combined type.

4. Jason started taking Ritalin and participated in individual therapy with a child psychiatrist, weekly for 6 months, then monthly thereafter. His parents were trained in a behavioral management program. He did not improve overnight, but he improved steadily. His parents were successful in following the home behavioral management plan.

REVIEW AT A GLANCE

1. 70
2. social skills
3. judgment
4. communication
5. capacity
6. inherited
7. event; illness
8. Pervasive developmental
9. social interaction
10. communication
11. behaviors
12. interests
13. activities
14. autistic
15. communicate
16. emotionally
17. familial inheritance
18. size
19. structure
20. maladaptive behaviors
21. learning disorder
22. academic skill
23. substantially below
24. age
25. education
26. intelligence
27. Communication disorders
28. expression
29. understanding
30. motor skills
31. developmental coordination disorder
32. motor coordination
33. neurologically
34. fetal development
35. birth
36. physical trauma
37. medical disorder
38. school
39. inattentiveness
40. hyperactivity-impulsivity
41. carelessness
42. daily activities
43. attentional
44. hyperactivity
45. impulsivity
46. fidgeting
47. being restless
48. running about
49. playing
50. talking
51. blurt out answers
52. cannot wait their turn
53. interrupt; intrude
54. conduct disorder
55. violate the rights of others
56. negativistic
57. hostile
58. defiant
59. family; school
60. neurological
61. behavioral inhibition
62. self-control
63. methylphenidate (Ritalin)
64. behavioral
65. Separation anxiety disorder
66. home; caregivers
67. pica
68. feeding disorder
69. rumination disorder
70. Tourette's
71. movement

72. vocalizations   74. enuresis   76. stereotypic movement

73. encopresis   75. Reactive attachment disorder   77. selective mutism

MULTIPLE CHOICE

1. (a) is correct. ADHD has not been found to be related to (b), (c), or (d).

2. (d) is correct. (a), (b), and (c) are dissimilar to Alzheimer's disease.

3. (b) is correct. (a), (c), and (d) are not used to treat PKU.

4. (a) is correct. There is no such procedure as (b); (c) is not a diagnostic procedure; (d) screens for fetal alcohol syndrome.

5. (c) is correct. (a) and (b) are antithetical to (c); (d) has nothing to do with integration of the disabled into society.

6. (c) is correct. (a), (b), and (d) are not associated with Asperger's disorder.

7. (b) is correct. (a) is an expressive disorder; (c) a receptive disorder; and (d) is a combination of both types of learning disorders.

8. (a) is correct. The described behaviors are not associated with (b), (c), or (d).

9. (d) is correct. (a) is a refusal to speak; (b) involves anxiety when separated from caregivers; and (d) is a pervasive developmental disorder.

10. (a) is correct. (b) rewards behavior; time-out may be used in the context of (c), but not with restraints; (d) is not a treatment.

11. (d) is correct. (a), (b), and (c) are not known to be related to ADHD.

12. (a) is correct. (b) involves urination; (c) is a reading disorder; (d) is a speech disorder.

13. (d) is correct. (a) and (b) do not result in early death; (c) will not result in death if a standard treatment regimen is followed.

14. (d) is correct. (a) may be related to mental retardation, but not as the result of a mother's alcohol consumption; (c) is not related to alcohol; and (b) is not related to mental retardation.

15. (a) is correct. They are not interested in (b), (c), or (d).

16. (c) is correct. There is not research evidence for (a), (b), or (d).

17. (b) is correct. (a) and (c) are not disorders; (d) is related to numbers, but does not fit the described example.

18. (b) is correct. (a) is not a disorder; (c) involves defiance of authority; (c) is an attentional disorder.

19. (d) is correct. (a) involves behaviors violating of the rights of others; (b) is an attentional disorder; and (c) is an eating disorder.

20. (d) is correct. (c) is a pervasive developmental disorder; (a) and (b) are not disorders.

21. (d) is correct. (a) and (b) are high and low average, respectively; and (c) would be considered low borderline.

22. (d) is correct. (a), (b), and (c) do not cause death before the age of 4.

23. (a) is correct. (b) is loss of oxygen to the brain; (c) a cognitive developmental disorder; and (c) a metabolic disorder that causes neural degeneration and early death.

24. (d) is correct. (a) involves repeating and making up words that sound similar; (b) is the repetition of words; (c) is not a disorder or symptom.

25. (c) is correct. CT scans have not revealed (a); (b) and (d) could not be detected by CT scans.

26. (d) is correct. (a) involves writing deficits; (c) is related to problems in speech; and (b) is not a disorder.

27. (b) is correct. (a), (c) and (d) are not related to integration of neural and sensory information.

28 .(a) is correct. (b) involves inability to sit still as well as focus attention; (c) ?; there is no such disorder as (d).

29. (c) is correct. (a) is eating nonfood items; (b) involves problems in regulation of feeding; and (d) is an eating disorder associated with bingeing and either purging or exercising excessively.

30. (c) is correct. (a) is when a child refuses to talk; (b) is a psychotic disorder; and (d) involves eating nonfood items.

CHAPTER 12
COGNITIVE DISORDERS

CHAPTER AT A GLANCE

Cognitive Disorders

Delirium

Dementia
Memory Loss
Aphasia, Apraxia, and Agnosia
Disturbance in Executive
Functioning

Amnestic Disorders
Substance-Induced
Pick's Disease
Parkinson's Disease
Lewy Body Dementia
Frontal Lobe Dementia
Huntington's Disease
Creutzfeldt-Jakob Disease

Alzheimer's Disease
Diagnosis
Theories and Treatment
Biological Perspective
Environmental Perspectives
Medical Treatment
Behavioral Management of Symptoms

Learning Objectives

1.0 The Nature of Cognitive Disorders
    1.1 Explain the characteristics of disorders involving cognitive impairment.
2.0 Delirium
    2.1 Describe the symptomatic features and possible causes of delirium.
3.0 Amnestic Disorders
    3.1 Outline the types and causes of amnesia.
4.0 Dementia
    4.1 Indicate the symptoms of dementia, including memory loss, aphasia, apraxia, agnosia, and disturbance in executive functioning.
5.0 Alzheimer's Disease (Dementia of the Alzheimer's Type)
    5.1 Describe the prevalence and course of Alzheimer's disease.
    5.2 Indicate the characteristic brain changes associated with Alzheimer's disease.
    5.3 Explain the stages of Alzheimer's disease.
    5.4 Indicate other physical diseases and psychological disorders that can lead to dementia resembling Alzheimer's disease.
    5.5 Contrast the biological and psychological perspectives regarding the causes and treatment of Alzheimer's disease.
6.0 Cognitive Disorder: The Perspectives Revisited
    6.1 Discuss the prospects for improved understanding and treatment of Alzheimer's disease in the coming decades.
7.0 Chapter Boxes
    7.1 Evaluate the research regarding caregivers of people with Alzheimer's disease.
    7.2 Discuss the nature of the discrimination faced by people with cognitive disorders caused by HIV and AIDS.

Identifying the Disorders

Write the name of the cognitive disorder in the blank next to the symptoms listed.

1. _____ Loss of memory for previously learned information or inability to learn new information.
2. _____ Progressive disease of the cortex involving memory loss, aphasia, apraxia, and agnosia.
3. _____ Patchy, stepwise deterioration of intellectual functioning.
4. _____ Cognitive and personality disturbances accompanied by involuntary spasmodic movements that eventually progress to the point of causing total disability.
5. _____ Symptoms mimicking Alzheimer's disease including depressed mood, disturbances in cognitive functioning, sleep and appetite, anxiety, suicidality, low self-esteem, guilt, and lack of motivation.
6. _____ Temporary disturbance in thoughts, level of consciousness, speech, memory, orientation, perceptions, and motor behavior.
7. _____ Deterioration of parts of the nervous system involved in control of motor movement.
8. _____ Degenerative disease that affects the frontal and temporal lobes of the cortex involving memory loss, social disinhibition, loss of motivation.

9. _____ Recurrent bodily seizures with associated changes in EEG patterns.
10. _____ Rare neurological disease transmitted from animals to humans, leading to dementia.

Matching

Put the letter from the right-hand column corresponding to the correct match in the blank next to each item in the left-hand column.

1. ____ Protein that forms the core of plaques found in Alzheimer's.
2. ____ Loss of the ability to carry out coordinated bodily movements.
3. ____ Discoverer of a form of language impairment in which the ability to produce language is lost.
4. ____ Physician who first identified senile dementia.
5. ____ Extreme muscle rigidity involving difficulty in initiating movement.
6. ____ Loss of memories for events prior to brain injury or damage.
7. ____ Neurological condition involving seizures and EEG abnormalities.
8. ____ Substance in the nervous system essential for the formation of acetylcholine.
9. ____ Loss of the ability to use language.
10. ____ Experimental drug used to treat Alzheimer's disease by altering levels of acetylcholine.
11. ____ Inability to recognize familiar objects or events.
12. ____ Discoverer of a form of language impairment in which comprehension abilities are lost.
13. ____ Loss of memories for events taking place after brain damage has occurred.
14. ____ Condition seen in neurons affected by Alzheimer's disease in which tiny strands form in the cell body.
15. ____ Loss or depletion of oxygen to the brain.

a. retrograde amnesia
b. Wernicke
c. epilepsy
d. aphasia
e. neurofibrillary tangles
f. agnosia
g. □-amyloid
h. anoxia
i. anterograde amnesia
j. tacrine(tetrahydro-aminoacrdine)
k. Alzheimer
l. akinesia
m. apraxia
n. Broca
o. choline acetyltransferase

Not-So-Trivial Pursuits Game

This "puzzle" follows the lines of the popular board game in which players must answer questions within a set of six categories. Answer the following questions within these categories.

SL = Sports & Leisure   H = History
AL = Arts & Literature   G = Geography
E = Entertainment   S = Science and Nature

CARD 1:

SL	What disease makes it impossible for people to engage in finely tuned motor activities such as those required for athletics and many hobbies?
AL	What is the name of a book written by Oliver Sacks describing people with various forms of brain damage or other neuropsychological disorders?
E	Who is the former actor who became president and was later diagnosed with Alzheimer's Disease?
H	Which neurologist discovered a form of aphasia in which the individual can produce but not comprehend language?
G	What is the country in which Alzheimer's disease was first discovered?
S	Which neurotransmitter system is thought to be most affected by Alzheimer's disease?

CARD 2:

SL	What is the metal in cooking utensils regarded by some as the basis for Alzheimer's disease?
AL	Who is the author of *The Shattered Mind,* which presented lengthy interviews of people with various forms of aphasia?
E	What communication systems are useful for providing support to family members of Alzheimer's patients?
H	What is the year in which Alzheimer's disease was first identified?
G	In which European river valley was there a clustering of families with Alzheimer's disease?
S	What part of the brain is thought to be most affected by the degenerative processes associated with Alzheimer's disease?

Short Answer

1. Describe three approaches to diagnosing Alzheimer's disease, including their intended purpose and problems associated with each:

Diagnostic approach	Intended purpose	Problems

2. List the seven major physical diseases or disorders that can mimic Alzheimer's disease, the nature of the disease or disorder involved in each, and how its symptoms differ from Alzheimer's:

Physical disease or disorder	Nature of disease or disorder	How symptoms differ from Alzheimer's disease

3. Summarize the genetic theories for each subtype of Alzheimer's disease, indicating the gene involved and the biochemical effect of the proposed genetic abnormality:

Type of Alzheimer's Disease	Proposed gene	Biochemical effect
Early-onset familial dementia (ages 30 to 60)		
Early-onset dementia as observed in descendants of families from the Volga River valley in Germany		

Type of Alzheimer's Disease	Proposed gene	Biochemical effect
Early-onset familial dementia (ages 40 to 65)		
Late-onset dementia (age 65 plus)		

4. For each of the following forms of treatment or interventions for Alzheimer's disease, describe its goals and methods of implementation:

Treatment or intervention	Goals	Methods of implementation
Community services		
Medications		
Caregiver support		
Behavioral treatment		
Cognitive-behavioral interventions		
Telephone information and referral services; computer networks		

5. How might each of the following indicators be used to differentiate depression (pseudodementia) from dementia due to Alzheimer's disease?

Indicator	Use in differentiating pseudodementia from dementia
Memory complaints	
Order of symptom development	

Nature of symptoms	
Exploration of recent life events	

6. Answer the following questions about the general category of cognitive disorders:

a. How was the term *organic* previously used in the context of psychological disorders?

_____

_____

b. Why did the DSM-IV move to the term "delirium, dementia, amnestic and other cognitive disorders" rather than "organic disorders" to describe disorders caused by brain damage or disease?

_____

_____

c. Provide four examples of psychological symptoms that can be caused by physical abnormalities:

_____ _____

_____ _____

d. What is the primary difficulty involved in diagnosing a cognitive disorder?

_____

_____

e. Why has epilepsy been inaccurately viewed for centuries as a psychological disorder?

_____

_____

7. Contrast delirium with dementia in terms of the following:

	Delirium	Dementia
Cause		
Course		
Primary symptoms		
Outcome		

8. Write in the blank next to the symptom the stage of dementia in which it first becomes evident, using the following symbols:

F	=	Forgetfulness		**MD**	=	Middle dementia
EC	=	Early confusional		**LD**	=	Late dementia
ED	=	Early dementia				

Stage   Symptom

____   Difficulty choosing clothes

____   Mild forgetfulness and appropriate concern

____   Getting lost in familiar places

____   Forgets name of spouse

____   Forgets telephone number

____   Denial of memory problems but with anxiety

____   Losing ability to handle finances

____   Occasional but not serious memory lapses

____   Withdrawal from challenging situation____   Becoming totally dependent on caregiver

____   Complete deterioration of social skills

____   Some date and time disorientation

____   Incapable of self-toileting

____   Obvious denial of memory problems

____   Loss of all verbal abilities

____   Poor reading comprehension

____   Loss of ability to walk

____   Family notices forgetfulness

Focusing on Research

Answer the following questions from "Research Focus: Caring for a Person with Alzheimer's Disease."

1. Describe the positive and negative experiences of people who care for family members with Alzheimer's disease.

_____

_____

2. Indicate what interventions and programs are most beneficial to these caregivers.

_____

_____

From The Case Files of Dr. Sarah Tobin: Thinking About Irene's Case

Answer the following questions about the case of Irene Heller.

1. List Irene's symptoms as observed by Dr. Tobin during her first meeting and as reported by Jonathan Heller.

_____

_____

2. Describe the results of Irene's neuropsychological assessment.

_____

_____

3. Discuss the nature and course of the interventions undertaken to help deal with Irene's Alzheimer's disease.

_____

_____

How Are We Different?

Answer the following questions from the text box "How People Differ: Discrimination Against People with AIDS."

1. How are people who experience AIDS-related dementia treated differently from those whose dementia is caused by other factors?

_____

_____

2. Describe the efforts to end discrimination against people with AIDS.

_____

_____

Review at a Glance

Cognitive disorders are characterized by (1)_____ that is caused by (2)_____ trauma, (3)_____, or (4)_____.

People with (5)_____ are (6)_____, have (7)_____ memories, and may have various other symptoms such as (8)_____ speech, (9)_____, (10)_____, and (11)_____ disturbances. Delirium is caused by a change in the (12)_____ of the brain and can result from various factors, including (13)_____ or _____, (14)_____ injury, high (15)_____, and (16)_____ deficiency. The onset is (17)_____ and the duration (18)_____.

People with (19)_____ disorders are unable to recall (20)_____ information or register (21)_____. (22)_____ use or medical conditions such as (23)_____ trauma, loss of (24)_____, or (25)_____ cause these disorders.

Dementia involves progressive deficits in a person's (26)_____ and learning of (27)_____, ability to (28)_____, (29)_____, and motor (30)_____. People with dementia also undergo changes in their (31)_____ and (32)_____ state, in addition to cognitive changes. Dementia is the result of profuse and progressive (33)_____ damage, associated with physical conditions such as (34)_____ diseases, (35)_____, (36)_____ trauma, (37)_____ substances, and various (38)_____ disorders. The most well known form of dementia is (39)_____, a condition associated with severe (40)_____ and (41)_____ changes in the brain. The four subtypes of Alzheimer's are: with (42)_____, with (43)_____, with (44)_____ and (45)_____. Theories about the cause of Alzheimer's focus on (46)_____ abnormalities involving the (47)_____ system, specifically changes in the neurons. These are the formation of (48)_____ and the development of (49)_____. Although there is no cure for Alzheimer's disease, medications such as (50)_____ alleviate its symptoms. Psychological interventions involve (51)_____ techniques for managing symptoms and strategies for alleviating (52)_____ burden.

Multiple Choice

1. Which of the following statements is true about people with AIDS who develop dementia?
   a. Education can reduce fear and prejudice against these individuals.
   b. They are likely to encounter accurate knowledge and understanding from society.
   c. Attitudes toward their condition are not related to attitudes toward gays and lesbians.
   d. They receive preferential treatment in housing, employment, and health care.

2. The term *organic* in regard to psychological disorders was traditionally used to refer to
   a. birth defects.
   b. physical illness.
   c. brain damage or dysfunction.
   d. refusal to eat pesticide-treated food.

3. Delirium is caused by
   a. changes in the metabolism of the brain.
   b. intense levels of emotional stress.
   c. too much sleep.
   d. dietary imbalance.

4. Individuals with anterograde amnesia suffer memory loss
   a. due to a traumatic emotional experience.
   b. as a result of epilepsy.
   c. for events prior to their amnesia.
   d. for new events that take place after the amnesia.

5. Controversy regarding chemical restraints for dementia patient centers on
   a. the ethics and wisdom of using medication for restraint.
   b. whether such methods are as effective as physical restraints.
   c. the high cost of these medications when used on a daily basis.
   d. the fact that they are more humane than behavioral treatments.

6. Which symptom is not commonly noted in people with dementia?
   a. aphasia
   b. apraxia
   c. agnosia
   d. anoxia

7. Which of the following statements about Alzheimer's disease is accurate?
   a. The number of cases has decreased.
   b. Women have higher rates of this disorder.
   c. It affects 25 percent of the U.S. population.
   d. The rate is lowest in those over 85.

8. Clusters of dead neurons mixed together with fragments of protein molecules in the brains of people with Alzheimer's disease are called
   a. amyloid plaques.
   b. neurofibrillary tangles.
   c. granulovacuoles.
   d. senillaries.

9. What is the name of the disorder which is a hereditary condition involving a widespread deterioration of the subcortical brain structures and parts of the frontal cortex that control motor movements?
   a. Parkinson's disease
   b. Huntington's disease
   c. Creutzfeldt's syndrome
   d. Brady's kinesia

10. Vascular dementia shows this characteristic pattern?
    a. pseudodementia
    b. patchy deterioration
    c. hydrocephalus
    d. sclerosis

11. Clinicians who provide services to families in which one member has Alzheimer's disease have focused increasingly on
    a. shared environmental toxins.
    b. genetic predispositions.
    c. the problem of pseudodementia.
    d. caregiver burden.

12. Dependence on caregiver, delusional symptoms, and loss of awareness of all recent events first occur in which stage of dementia?
    a. middle
    b. early
    c. forgetfulness
    d. late confusional

13. Jeremy, a person with epilepsy, has seizures during which he loses consciousness, stops breathing for a short period of time, and experiences body jerking. Jeremy has what type of seizures?
    a. petit mal
    b. generalized convulsive
    c. partial
    d. focal

14. Annie is a 78-year-old woman seen in the Emergency Room who is delusional, is unable to remember her last name, and slurs her speech. Her heart rate is rapid and she is sweating, but she is not intoxicated. From what might she be suffering?
    a. amnesia
    b. Alzheimer's disease
    c. Huntington's disease
    d. delirium

15. Which of the following is the most common cause of amnestic disorder?
    a. chronic alcohol use
    b. chronic marijuana use
    c. head injury
    d. viral infection

16. Aphasia is defined as the loss of ability to
    a. use language.
    b. recognize familiar objects.
    c. carry out verbal instructions.
    d. learn or remember events.

17. On autopsy, it is determined that a woman's cerebral cortex had degenerated and there were numerous amyloid plaques in the brain tissue. It is likely that this woman suffered from
    a. Alzheimer's disease.
    b. epilepsy.
    c. pseudodementia.
    d. Tay-Sachs disease.

18. Chronic exposure to the fumes of house paints and petroleum fuels can lead to symptoms that mirror which disease?
    a. Alzheimer's disease
    b. AIDS
    c. Tourette's disease
    d. amnesia

19. While at rest, Ray's hands shake uncontrollably and his head jerks sideways. These are early symptoms of
    a. Parkinson's disease.
    b. Pick's disease.
    c. Alzheimer's disease.
    d. Creutzfeldt-Jakob disease.

20. A link exists between Alzheimer's disease and which inherited disorder?
    a. Down syndrome
    b. autistic disorder
    c. attention-deficit/hyperactivity disorder
    d. pica

21. Why is it often difficult to diagnose organic disorders?
    a. because the individuals who suffer from these disorders often suffer from somatoform disorders as well
    b. because it is difficult to differentiate these disorders from psychophysiological disorders
    c. because often the symptoms are not recognized by individuals without training in psychiatry
    d. because many of the symptoms of these disorders are similar to those associated with psychological disorders

22. Tony has seizures during which he loses consciousness and experiences occasional twitching of his eyelids. With which type of seizures does Tony suffer?
    a. generalized convulsive
    b. partial
    c. focal
    d. petit mal

23. A condition in which a person's thoughts, level of consciousness, speech, memory, orientation, perceptions, and motor patterns are very confused, unstable, or otherwise grossly disturbed is called
    a. delirium.
    b. dementia.
    c. amnesia.
    d. tachycardia.

24. Disorders involving a biological loss of memory are called
    a. dissociative disorders.
    b. amnestic disorders.
    c. delirium-related disorders.
    d. neuroses.

25. The form of language impairment in which the individual is able to produce language, but has lost the ability to comprehend, so that these verbal productions have no meaning, is referred to as
    a. apraxia.
    b. agnosia.
    c. tachycardia.
    d. Wernicke's aphasia.

26. Which of the following statements about the incidence of Alzheimer's disease in the elderly population is true?
    a. Most elderly people will eventually develop Alzheimer's.
    b. A majority of the elderly develop Alzheimer's disease.
    c. Only a small percentage of the elderly develop Alzheimer's disease.
    d. Alzheimer's disease is much more common in middle-aged individuals.

27. The degenerative course of Alzheimer's disease typically can last up to
    a. 10 months.
    b. 10 years.
    c. 20 years.
    d. 30 years.

28. While he is resting, Ray's hands shake uncontrollably. At times his head appears to jerk from side to side. Ray may be showing the early symptoms of
    a. Parkinson's disease.
    b. Pick's disease.
    c. Alzheimer's disease.
    d. Creutzfeldt-Jakob disease.

29. One biological theory proposes that Alzheimer's disease is the result of disruptions in which neurotransmitter system?
    a. the GABA system
    b. the norepinephrine system
    c. the acetylcholine system
    d. the dopaminergic system

30. Supportive therapy may be useful in helping clients with Alzheimer's disease overcome their
    a. debilitating symptoms.
    b. hallucinations and delusions.
    c. neurological deficits.
    d. concerns over personal loss and mortality.

ANSWERS

IDENTIFYING DISORDERS

1.	amnestic disorder	5.	pseudodementia	9.	epilepsy
2.	dementia	6.	Delirium	10.	Creutzfeld-Jacob disease
3.	vascular dementia	7.	Parkinson's disease		
4.	Huntington's disease	8.	Pick's disease		

1.	g	5.	l	9.	d	13.	i
2.	m	6.	a	10.	j	14.	e
3.	n	7.	c	11.	f	15.	h
4.	k	8.	o	12.	b		

NOT-SO-TRIVIAL PURSUITS

CARD 1:

SL	Parkinson's Disease
A L	The Man Who Mistook His Wife for a Hat
E	Ronald Reagan
H	Wernicke
G	Germany
S	Acetylcholine

CARD 2:

SL	Aluminum
A L	Howard Gardner
E	Computer networks
H	1907
G	Volga
S	Hippocampus

SHORT ANSWER

1.

Diagnostic approach	Intended purpose	Problems
CAT and PET scans, MRI	Detect structural brain abnormalities (CAT and MRI) and metabolic defects (PET scans)	Measures not sensitive to brain changes specific to Alzheimer's disease
Neurological and neuropsychological evaluations involving cognitive tests	Identify patterns of abnormalities indicative of brain damage or cognitive processes of memory and learning	Can be used to help distinguish between pseudodementia and Alzheimer's disease but are not sensitive enough to Alzheimer's to make reliable diagnosis
Mental status examination	Assess functional deficits associated with Alzheimer's	Evidence of deficits in areas assessed by the examination is not sufficient basis for diagnosis.

2.

Physical disease or disorder	Nature of disease or disorder	How symptoms differ from Alzheimer's disease
Substance-induced persisting dementia	Brain damage resulting from exposure to toxins in the environment	Symptoms are progressive but occur in response to specific enviromental agents rather than disease.
Dementia due to head trauma	Brain injury	Similar to Alzheimer's but occur in a more sudden fashion.
Dementia due to HIV disease	Subtle deterioration in cognitive functioning due to AIDS	In addition to memory problems, symptoms include movement disturbances, delusions, hallucinations, extreme depression, apathy, and social withdrawal.
Pick's disease	Degenerative disease that affects frontal and temporal lobes of cortex.	Personality alterations precede memory problems.
Parkinson's disease	Neuronal degeneration of basal ganglia; deterioration of diffuse areas of cortex may also occur	Main features are motor disturbances, including akinesia, brady kinesia, shuffling gait, and loss of fine coordination.
Huntington's disease	Deterioration of subcortical brain structures and parts of frontal cortex that control motor movements; degeneration of corpus callosum.	Main symptoms are involuntary spasmodic and often tortuous movements.

Physical disease or disorder	Nature of disease or disorder	How symptoms differ from Alzheimer's disease
Creutzfeldt-Jakob disease	Neurological disease transmitted from animals to humans that leads to dementia and death	Initial symptoms are fatigue, anxiety, appetite disturbance, sleep problems and concentration difficulties; disease progression results in loss of motor coordination, vision problems, and further neural disturbance.
Vascular dementia	Death of selected groups of neurons in cerebral cortex when clusters of capillaries in the brain are cut off by infarctions	Patchy, stepwise cognitive deterioration

3.

Type of Alzheimer's disease	Proposed gene	Biochemical effect
Early-onset familial dementia (ages 30 to 60)	S182 gene on chromosome 14	Codes a protein embedded in a membrane of the neuron that might be involved in protein transport between neurons and possibly connected with amyloid plaques
Early-onset dementia as observed in descendants of families from the Volga River valley in Germany	STM2 on chromosome 1	Seems linked to S182 gene
Early-onset familial dementia (ages 40 to 65)	APP gene on chromosome 21	Interference with disposal mechanism for APP might lead to accumulation of -amyloid protein and eventual formation of amyloid plaques
Late-onset dementia (age 65 plus)	APOE on chromosome 14	The APo E 4 allele codes for the E4 form of Apo E, which may damage the microtubules within the neuron that play an essential role in transport throughout the cell; this damage may occur through the destruction of the tau protein, which stabilizes the microtubules

4.

Treatment or intervention	Goals	Methods of implementation
Community services	Maintain the individual for as long as possible at current level of functioning	Diagnostic and medical assessment, counseling, support groups, financial planning assistance, and home care services; day care and respite programs to aid caregivers
Medications	Offset the effects of the disease on the brain	Vasodilators or metabolic enhancers to increase blood flow to the brain, choline-based substances to increase activity of acetylcholine; tacrine, which decreases the activity of cholinesterase
Caregiver support	Help caregivers work through feelings of guilt and anger and other intense emotional reactions	Insight-oriented psychotherapy
Behavioral treatment	Maximize individual's ability to adapt to the environment and maintain independence	Teach daily living skills (dressing, bathing, cooking, and social skills) and reduce disruptive behaviors (wandering and incontinence)
Cognitive-behavioral interventions	Alleviate depression in afflicted individual and caregivers	Focus on compensation for memory problems and help caregivers with feelings of depression caused by dysfunctional attitudes about their role in treating the individual
Telephone information and referral services; computer networks	Provide caregivers with information as well as emotional support	Informal sharing of help and information in a readily accessible format

5.

Indicator	Use in differentiating pseudodementia from dementia
Memory complaints	Depressed individuals complain about their faulty memory, even though there is no physical basis for their complaints; the individual with Alzheimer's tries to conceal or minimize the extent of impairment or explain it away. As the disease progresses, the Alzheimer's patient may even falsely sense an improvement of memory functioning.
Order of symptom development	In depressed elderly people, mood changes precede memory loss; the reverse is true for Alzheimer's patients.
Nature of symptoms	People with pseudodementia show classic symptoms of depression, including anxiety, sleep and appetite disturbance, suicidal thoughts, low self-esteem, guilt, and lack of motivation. Their memory problems come on suddenly, and they may have a history of depression. People with dementia experience unsociability, uncooperativeness, hostility, emotional instability, confusion, disorientation, and reduced alertness. The course of memory impairment is gradual and progressive.
Exploration of recent life events	Depressed elderly persons are more likely to have suffered a recent stressful life event; life events are not thought to be a factor in the development of dementia.

6.
a. The term organic was traditionally used in psychology to refer to physical damage or dysfunction that affects the integrity of the brain.
b. Movement away from the term *organic* was suggested in recognition of the fact that many psychological disorders have their origins in brain dysfunction. The current term more accurately describes the nature of the dysfunction in this group of disorders.
c. hallucinations
   delusions
   mood disturbances
   extreme personality changes
d. It is difficult to differentiate symptoms associated with a psychological disorder from those arising in response to a physical disorder, even with the aid of sophisticated diagnostic technology.
e. Epilepsy has been misunderstood as a psychological disorder because people with this disorder may act in ways that appear odd or psychotic.

7.

	Delirium	Dementia
Cause	Change in metabolism of the brain	Progressive degeneration of the cortex
Course	Rapid onset and brief duration	Slow onset and long duration
Primary symptoms	Any or all of the following psychological changes: confusion, disturbance of consciousness, delusions, illusions, hallucinations, and emotional disturbances, as well as autonomic nervous system disturbance	Loss of memory, language abilities, orientation, motor abilities, judgment, and social skills as well as emotional instability
Outcome	Positive outcomes are possible such as natural recovery or positive response to treatment unless the delirium reflects a neurological disease or life-threatening condition	Death invariably occurs due to the development of secondary physical illness

8.

ED	MD	LC	LD	LC	LD
F	ED	F	ED	LD	EC
EC	EC	LC	LD	EC	

FOCUSING ON RESEARCH

1. The most common negative result is caregiver depression. Positive responses include a feeling of well being that they are coping with the difficult challenge of caregiving, gratification in the support from other family members and friends, and spiritual rewards from regarding their role as consistent with religious teachings.

2. Caregivers benefit most from brief psychodynamic and cognitive-behavioral therapies for depression and help with coping strategies. Community services that are beneficial include diagnostic and medical assessment programs, counseling, support groups, financial planning assistance, home care services, and electronic information services and bulletin boards on the World Wide Web. Daycare and respite care for the sufferers of the disease give the caregivers much needed breaks and vacations from caregiving.

FROM THE CASE FILES OF DR. SARAH TOBIN: THINKING ABOUT IRENE'S CASE

1. Memory problems, anger, confusion, paranoia, and denial that she had any problem other than being a little "forgetful"

2. Moderate cognitive deficits, problems with abstract reasoning and verbal fluency, disorientation as to time and place, memory impairment, and depression

3. The diagnosis was Dementia of the Alzheimer type. The treatment plan involved moving into an assisted-living apartment complex; multidisciplinary assistance from a psychologist, social worker, and counselor from the local Counsel of Aging; and assistance with self-care and independent living. She deteriorated rapidly and progressively. After 6 months in the assisted-living residence, she was moved to a nursing home because she was a danger to herself and others. She deteriorated to the point that she rarely recognized her son.

HOW ARE WE DIFFERENT?

1. Many AIDS patients are discriminated against for two main reasons:
   (1) Some believe that the diseases can be passed on through casual contact, so they suffer discrimination in availability of health care, housing and employment, and are shunned by friends and family members; and (2) Some people believe that AIDS is a punishment for sinful and wrong actions.

2. Efforts to end discrimination against people with AIDS fall into two broad categories: legal proceedings relying on the benefits of the Americans with Disabilities Act (ADA) and educational efforts targeted at specific prejudicial beliefs.

REVIEW AT A GLANCE

1. cognitive impairment
2. brain 3. disease
4. exposure to toxic substances
5. delirium
6. disoriented
7. foggy
8. rambling
9. delusions
10. hallusinations
11. emotional
12. metabolism
13. intoxication/withdrawal
14. head
15. fever
16. vitamin
17. rapid
18. brief amnestic
19. previously learned
20. new memories
21. Substance
22. head
23. oxygen
24. herpes simplex
25. memory
26. new information
27. communicate
28. judgment
29. coordination
30. personality
31. emotional
32. brain
33. vascular
34. AIDS
35. head
36. psychoactive
37. neurological
38. Alzheimer's disease
39. Cerebral atrophy
40. microscopic
41. delirium
42. delusions
43. depressed mood
44. uncomplicated
45. biological
46. nervous
47. neurofibrillary tangles
48. amyloid plaques
49. anticholinesterase
50. behavioral
52. caregiver

MULTIPLE CHOICE

1. (a) is correct. (b, (c), and (d) are more likely than not to occur.
2. (c) is correct. (a), (b), and (d) are unrelated to the term.
3. (a) is correct. (b), (c), and (d) are not known causes of delirium.
4. (d) is correct. (a), (b), and (c) refer to other types of amnesia.
5. (a) is correct. There is no controversy concerning (b); (c) and (d) are not accurate statements.
6. (d) is correct. (a), (b), and (c) may be associated with dementia, but (d) is loss of oxygen to the brain.
7. (b) is correct. (a), (b), and (d) are not accurate statements.
8. (a) is correct. (b) and (c) refer to other neurological states; there is no such thing as (d).
9. (b) is correct. (a), (c),and (d) are not associated with the described symptoms.
10. (b) is correct. (a) refers to false dementia; (c) to water on the brain; and (d) to a degenerative motor condition.
11. (d) is correct. (a), (b), and (c) are etiological and diagnostic issues, but only (d) is related to services to families.
12. (a) is correct. (c) and (d) are not stages; there is little dependence in (b).
13. (b) is correct. (a), (c), and (d) may have some, but not all, of the described occurrences.
14. (d) is correct. (a), (b), and (c) would not be indicated by these symptoms.
15. (a) is correct. (b), (c), and (d) may cause memory loss, but not to the degree that (a) does.
16. (a) is correct. (b) refers to agnosia; (c) to apraxia; and (d) to amnesia.
17. (a) is correct. (b), (c), and (d) would not be associated with this neurological symptom
18. (a) is correct. (b), (c), and (d) are not related to this environmental condition.
19. (a) is correct. (b), (c), and (d) are not associated with the described symptom.
20. (a) is correct. (b), (c), and (d) are not related to Alzheimer's disease.

21. (d) is correct. There is no support for (a), (b), and (c).
22. (d) is correct. (b) and (c) involve loss of consciousness; there is no disorder called (a).
23. (a) is correct. (b) and (c) both involve memory impairment; (d) involves a heart-related disorder.
24. (b) is correct. (a), (c), and (d) are not related to memory loss.
25. (d) is correct. (a) involves inability to form purposeful bodily actions; (b) is the failure to recognize things; and (c) is a heart-related condition.
26. (c) is correct. There is no support for (a), (b),and (d).
27. (b) is correct. (a) is an underestimate; (c) and (d) overestimates.
28. (a) is correct. (b), (c), and (d) are not related to the described physical symptoms.
29. (c) is correct. Alzheimer's has not been related to (a), (b), or (d).
30. (d) is correct. Supportive therapy cannot benefit (a), (b), and (c).

CHAPTER 13
SUBSTANCE-RELATED DISORDERS

CHAPTER AT A GLANCE

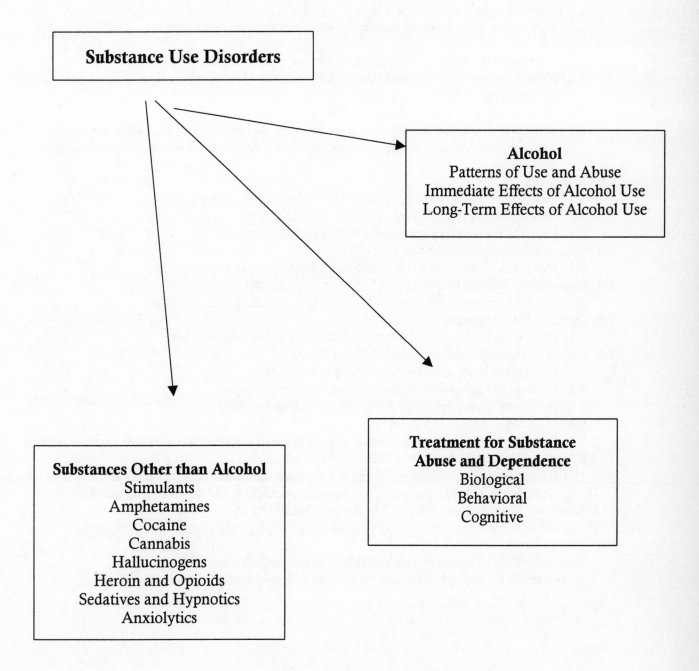

Substance Use Disorders

Alcohol
Patterns of Use and Abuse
Immediate Effects of Alcohol Use
Long-Term Effects of Alcohol Use

Substances Other than Alcohol
Stimulants
Amphetamines
Cocaine
Cannabis
Hallucinogens
Heroin and Opioids
Sedatives and Hypnotics
Anxiolytics

Treatment for Substance
Abuse and Dependence
Biological
Behavioral
Cognitive

Learning Objectives

1.0   The Nature of Substance Abuse and Dependence
    1.1   Describe the nature of a psychoactive substance.
    1.2   Indicate the prevalence of substance abuse disorders in the U.S. population.
2.0   Behaviors Associated with Substance-Related Disorders
    2.1   Explain the nature of substance-induced disorders, including intoxication, withdrawal, and tolerance.
    2.2   Discuss the issues involved in defining substance abuse and dependence.
3.0   Alcohol
    3.1   Summarize the demographic patterns of alcohol use and impact on the family.
    3.2. Identify the physical and psychological factors that produce the immediate and long-term effects of alcohol on the body.
    3.3   Discuss biological and psychological theories of alcohol dependence.
    3.4   Summarize biological and psychological treatment approaches to alcohol dependence.
    3.5   Describe how Alcoholic Anonymous approaches the development and treatment of alcohol dependence.
4.0   Stimulants
    4.1   Describe the effects of and physiological changes caused by amphetamines.
    4.2   Indicate the features involved in cocaine use and abuse.
    4.3   Explain the characteristics of caffeine-related disorders.
5.0   Cannabis-Related Disorders
    5.1   Indicate the behavioral and physiological effects of marijuana use.
6.0   Hallucinogen-Related Disorders
    6.1   Describe the types and effects of hallucinogens, including LSD and PCP.
7.0   Opioid-Related Disorders
    7.1   Outline the behavioral and lifestyle effects of opioid-related disorders.
8.0   Sedative-, Hypnotic-, and Anxiolytic-Related Disorders
    8.1   Indicate the short- and long-term effects of barbiturates.
    8.2   Describe the nature and effects of barbiturate-like substances.
    8.3   Outline the characteristics and effects of anxiolytic substances.
9.0   Other Substance-Related Disorders
    9.1   Describe the symptoms and disorders related to use of nicotine, inhalants, and anabolic steroids.
10.0 Substance Abuse and Dependence: General Treatment Issues
    10.1 Explain general principles pertaining to the causes and treatment of substance abuse and dependence including the role of biochemical mechanisms and psychological factors.
11.0 Substance Abuse and Dependence: The Perspectives Revisited
    11.1 Describe the integration of physiological and psychological factors in substance abuse.
12.0 Chapter Boxes
    12.1 Outline the variations by race and culture in patterns of alcohol use.
    12.2 Describe the research indicating the harmful effects of crack on prenatal development.

Identifying the Substance

Write the name of the substance that is described in the right-hand column.

1. _____ A stimulant drug that was an ingredient of a popular soft drink during the late 1800s.

2. _____ The most widely used illegal drug in the United States.

3. _____ An opioid whose use had declined steadily from a peak in the 1970s but which appears to be on the rise again.

4. _____ Used appropriately as anesthetics, anticonvulsants, and sleeping pills, drugs in this category have high addictive potential.

5. _____ 10% of adults in the United States abuse or are dependent on this substance.

6. _____ A stimulant ingested daily by at least 85% of the U.S. adult population.

7. _____ Hallucinogen that was a central component of the nationwide drug culture of the 1960s.

8. _____ An inexpensive form of a stimulant drug whose use skyrocketed in the 1980s due to its availability on the streets and inaccurate perception of its risk.

9. _____ The yearly cost of abuse of this substance in the U.S. averages at least $100 billion.

10. _____ A category of stimulant drugs whose legitimate medical use is appetite suppression, control of hyperactivity in children, and narcolepsy.

Matching

Put the letter from the right-hand column corresponding to the correct match in the blank next to each item in the left-hand column.

1. ___ Physiological and psychological reactions that can occur when a psychoactive substance is discontinued.

2. ___ Proposed subcategory of alcohol dependence theorized to be caused almost exclusively by genetic factors.

3. ___ The extent to which an individual requires larger doses of a substance to achieve its desired effects.

4. ___ A program that provides support and understanding for relatives and friends of people with alcohol dependence.

5. ___ Physiological factor that influences the extent to which a given amount of alcohol will have psychoactive effects.

6. ___ A psychological and physical need for a psychoactive substance.

7. ___ Alteration in behavior due to the accumulation of a psychoactive substance in the body.

8. ___ A pattern of drug use that creates significant problems for a person in everyday life.

9. ___ Physical condition involving autonomic system dysfunction, confusion, and seizures, caused by withdrawal from long-term heavy use of alcohol.

10. ___ Proposed subcategory of alcohol dependence caused by a hereditary predisposition interacting with environmental causes.

11. ___ Explanation of the biological mechanisms of alcohol that focuses on the changes in the body's cells caused by intake of alcohol.

12. ___ Psychological explanation of alcohol use proposing that a combination of beliefs about the effects of alcohol and reinforcement for these beliefs leads to alcohol dependence.

13. ___ Social movement that raised awareness of the impact of alcoholism on family members (abbreviation).

14. ___ The interpretation of a lapse by an alcohol dependent individual as a lack of ability to control drinking.

15. ___ Non-barbiturate substance with high abuse potential originally designed to replace barbiturates.

a. methaqualone
b. dependence
c. membrane hypothesis
d. Type 1 alcoholism
e. ACOA
f. intoxication
g. expectancy model
h. delirium tremens
i. tolerance
j. Al-Anon
k. substance abuse
l. metabolism rate
m. Type 2 alcoholism
n. withdrawal
o. abstinence violation effect

Diamond Puzzle

The clues below are all for the "across" direction this puzzle. Clue #1 is for the first row, #2 for the second row, and so on.

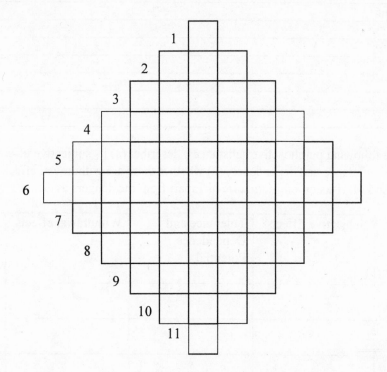

1. First letter of the abbreviation for a treatment approach for alcohol dependence which emphasizes commitment to group meetings, support networks, and spirituality.
2. Abbreviation for one of two enzymes that is responsible for metabolizing alcohol.
3. Use of a psychoactive substance in a way that places the individual at significant risk or harm in daily life.
4. Residential treatment program founded in the late 1950s based on the principle that substance dependent individuals benefit from a therapeutic community approach.
5. A drug that has THC as its active ingredient.
6. A drug used in treating alcohol dependence that is intended to reduce the desire for alcohol by acting on the GABA system.
7. Extent to which the individual can ingest larger amounts of a psychoactive substance without feeling its effects.
8. Stimulant drug thought to cause a "high" by blocking the reuptake in the nervous system of excitatory neurotransmitters, leading to stimulation of pleasure reward centers in the brain.
9. When the effects of cocaine wear off, a person is likely to experience a _____.
10. Hallucinogenic drug accidentally discovered by a scientist that became a central part of the 1960s drug culture.
11. Second letter of the abbreviation for the treatment approach for alcohol dependence in item 1.

Short Answer

1. List six types of medications used in the treatment of alcohol dependence and the intended effect of each medication.

Medication	Intent

2. For each of the following psychoactive substances, describe: (a) its subjective effects, (b) whether it has potential for tolerance and dependence, (c) whether there are withdrawal effects when it is discontinued, and (d) risks or long-term effects (apart from the dangers associated with withdrawal):

Psychoactive Substance	Subjective Effects	Tolerance and Dependence Potential	Withdrawal effects	Risks or long-term effects
Alcohol				
Amphetamines				
Cocaine				
Cannabis (Marijuana)				
Hallucinogens				
Opioids				
Barbiturates				
Barbiturate-like				
Anxiolylitics				

3. Link the terms in the left-hand column with the terms on the right by drawing a line from the term on the left to the matching term on the right. Explain how they are related to each other on the line that matches the term on the left:

How Terms Are Related

Wernicke	Caffeine
Cue Exposure	Enkephalins
Cocaine	Withdrawal
Endorphins	Korsakoff

4. Discuss the kinds of risks or accidents that result from the abuse of alcohol (be as specific as you can).

_____
_____
_____

5. Summarize the evidence for a biological theory of alcohol dependence in terms of each of the following areas of investigation:

Area of Investigation	Available evidence
Patterns of Inheritance	
Biological Matters	
Neurotransmitter Functioning	
Search for an "alcohol" gene	

6. What are four obstacles that stand in the way of recovery for substance abusers?

_____
_____

7. a. What is the central assumption of the relapse prevention model?

_____
_____

b. Four areas of focus involved in the relapse prevention model for treating alcohol dependence are:

_____

_____

c. What are the two central assumptions of Alcoholics Anonymous?

_____

_____

d. What four areas of treatment are similar in both the relapse prevention model and Alcoholics Anonymous?

_____

_____

e. In what two approaches to treatment does relapse prevention differ from Alcoholics Anonymous?

Alcholics Anonymous	Relapse Prevention

Focusing on Research

Answer the following questions from "Research Focus: Studying Crack Babies."

1. List the confounding variables that hamper the search to understand the effects on the infant of other prenatal crack-cocaine use.

_____

_____

2. Discuss the results of animal research testing the effects of prenatal crack-cocaine use by animal mothers.

_____

_____

3. Why is it important to intervene early in the lives of crack babies and their addicted mothers?

_____

_____

From the Case Files of Dr. Sarah Tobin: Thinking about Carl's Case

Answer the following questions about the case of Carl Wadsworth.

1. How was cocaine use negatively impacting Carl's life?

_____

_____

2. What was Dr. Tobin's formulation of Carl's case?

_____

_____

3. Discuss the course and outcome of Carl's treatment.

_____

_____

How <u>Are</u> We Different: The Influence of Race and Culture on Alcoholism

Answer the following questions from the text box, "How People Differ: The Influence of Race and Culture on Alcoholism."

1. Identify the general different patterns of drinking in European and American societies._____
   _____

2. What might help explain the comparative differences in alcohol-related problems of African-American and Caucasian men?
   _____
   _____

3. What are two reasons that help account for lower rates of alcoholism in some Asian countries relative to Western nations?
   _____
   _____

4. How do patterns of alcohol use differ for men and women, generally speaking?
   _____
   _____

Review at a Glance

A substance is a chemical that alters a person's (1) _____ or (2) _____ when (3)_____, (4)_____, (5) _____, (6) _____, or (7)_____. Substance (8) _____ is a temporary experience of (9) _____ or (10)_____ changes due to the accumulation of the substance in the body. When some substances are discontinued, some people may experience symptoms of substance (11)_____ that involve (12) _____

_____ and symptoms may develop a (14)_____ for the substance. Substance (15)_____ is the maladaptive pattern of use that leads to significant (16) _____ or (17) _____.

The short-term affect of alcohol is appealing because of its (18) _____ qualities. Long term use can cause serious harm to many (19)_____ or the body and can lead to (20) _____ problems and (21)_____. Researchers in the field of alcohol dependence first proposed the (22)_____ model of psychological disorder. The biological factor is most likely (23) _____. Psychological theories about alcohol dependence focus concepts derived from (24) _____, (25)_____, (26)_____ perspectives. According to the (27)_____ model, people develop problematic beliefs about alcohol early in life through (28)_____ and (29)_____ learning. The sociocultural perspective emphasizes the stressors within the (30)_____, (31)_____, and (32)_____ as factors that lead to alcohol dependence.

Biological treatments for alcohol problems include mediations to control (33)_____ symptoms and (34)_____ agents that provoke nausea after alcohol ingestion. Psychological interventions focus on (35)_____ and (36)_____ techniques. (37)_____ is a (38)_____ program built on the premise that alcoholism is a (39) _____.

(40) _____ have an (41)_____ effect on the nervous system. (42) _____ in moderate amounts cause feelings of (43) _____, increased (44) _____, (45) _____ and (46) _____. In moderate doses, (47) _____ leads to feelings of (48) _____, (49) _____ excitement, (50) _____, (51)_____, and

(52)_____. (53)_____ symptoms can develop with higher use of stimulants and cocaine. (54)_____ or marijuana, causes altered (55)_____, and (56) _____ sensations, as well as maladaptive (57) _____ and (58) _____ reactions. (59)_____ cause abnormal (60)_____ experiences in the form of (61)_____ and (62)_____. (63)_____ users experience intense (64)_____ sensations. (65)_____, (66)_____, and (67)_____ induce relaxation, sleep, tranquility, and reduced awareness.

Biological treatment for substance-related disorders involve (68)_____ that block or reduce (69)_____. Behavioral treatments involve techniques such as (70)_____, while cognitive-behavioral techniques are used to help clients modify their (71)_____, (72)_____, and (73)_____, associated with drug use.

Multiple Choice

1. Jared has found that he needs to drink 4 or 5 beers to achieve the level of relaxation that he was able to achieve with only two beers a year ago. This phenomenon is called
   a. withdrawal.
   b. intoxication.
   c. potentiation.
   d. tolerance.

2. Which of the following is not associated with the rate at which alcohol is absorbed into the bloodstream?
   a. concentration of alcohol in a beverage
   b. time of day when alcohol is consumed
   c. metabolic rate of the individual
   d. mixing a carbonated beverage with alcohol

3. Which of the following has contributed to the hypothesis of a genetic link in the development of alcoholism?
   a. Sons of alcoholics are four times more likely to become alcoholic than sons of nonalcoholics.
   b. Daughters of alcoholics are three times more likely to become alcoholic than daughters of nonalcoholics.
   c. Fraternal twins have a higher concordance rate for alcoholism than identical twins.
   d. Children of alcoholics have a stronger reaction to alcohol than children of nonalcoholics.

4. Marianne takes a medication that gives her a headache, nausea, and other unpleasant symptoms each time she has alcohol. This medication is:
   a. disulfiram.
   b. nalxetrone.
   c. acamprosate.
   d. aldehyde.

5. Compared to amphetamines, the stimulating effects of cocaine are:
   a. longer but less intense.
   b. shorter but more intense.
   c. longer but more intense.
   d. similar in duration and intensity.

6. This term describes the experience in which a cocaine user develops convulsions because the brain's threshold for seizures has been lowered by repeated exposure
   a. tolerance
   b. intoxication
   c. kindling
   d. potentiation

7. Cross-cultural research on patterns of alcohol use and abuse has shown that
   a. rates of alcohol abuse are remarkably stable across cultures.
   b. Asian societies discourage alcohol use among men.
   c. prevalence rates are highest among the Amish in America.
   d. cultural and social deprivations can contribute to high rates of abuse.

8. Opioids are also known as
   a. narcotics.
   b. hallucinogens.
   c. sedatives
   d. hypnotics.

9. The most frequently used drug in the category of barbiturate-like subances is
   a. clonazepam.
   b. secobarbital.
   c. diazepam.
   d. methaqualone.

10. Which of the following statements is true regarding research on babies whose mothers used crack cocaine when pregnant?
    a. It is difficult to separate the effects of crack from those of other substances.
    b. These infants have higher birth weight and larger head size.
    c. Early intervention cannot alter the developmental course of a crack baby's life.
    d. Withdrawal effects are shown in the infants for at least the first year of life.

11. What is the term used for programs that are intended to minimize the physiological changes associated with withdrawal from substances?
    a. milieu
    b. therapeutic community
    c. Alcoholics Anonymous
    d. detoxification

12. Psychologists who have tried to validate the existence of an "addictive personality" have found that
    a. this construct cannot be clearly identified.
    b. such individuals are unlikely to be depressed.
    c. they are addicted to substances but not food.
    d. their personality is linked to physiological factors.

13. The physical and psychological changes that accompany discontinuation of a psychoactive substance are referred to as
    a. tolerance
    b. intoxication.
    c. withdrawal.
    d. potentiation

14. When two or more psychoactive substances are combined, the intoxicant effect can be greater than the effect due to each substance acting alone, a situation referred to as
    a. sedation.
    b. inebriation.
    c. metabolism.
    d. potentiation.

15. Paul is a chronic alcoholic with dementia. He also has difficulties remembering past events and forming new memories. He suffers from
    a. Type 1 Alcoholism.
    b. Alzheimer's disease.
    c. Wernicke's disease.
    d. Korsakoff's syndrome.

16. Joyce is alcohol dependent and trying to abstain from drinking. However, she went to a party, broke down, and had a drink. According to the expectancy model, how should she view this behavior?
    a. She should view it as a sign of a character flaw.
    b. She should view it as a sign of personal weakness.
    c. She should not view it as a result of social pressure.
    d. She should not view it as a loss of self-control.

17. Which treatment program is heavily grounded in spirituality?
    a. Alcoholics Anonymous
    b. cue exposure method
    c. relapse prevention therapy
    d. detoxification

18. Amphetamines have their effect by enhancing the action of which neurotransmitter?
    a. serotonin
    b. norepinephrine
    c. GABA
    d. dopamine

19. Spontaneous hallucinations, delusions, or disturbances in mood that are not the result of ingestion of a hallucinogen are called
    a. psychotic breaks.
    b. delirium tremens.
    c. flashbacks.
    d. illusory spasms.

20. Enkephalins and endorphins are
    a. natural pain-killing substances produced by the brain.
    b. narcotics.
    c. hallucinogens.
    d. produced only in heavy narcotic users.

21. The experience of altered behaviors due to the accumulation of a substance in the body is referred to as
    a. tolerance
    b. intoxication
    c. withdrawal.
    d. dependence.

22. Which of the following is the main feature of substance abuse?
    a. use of a substance in order to prevent withdrawal
    b. continued use of a drug despite risks or problems in living
    c. usage of increased amounts of a drug to achieve the same high
    d. subjective feeling of a need for the substance

23. Dwayne went out drinking despite the fact that he has been taking sleeping pills. As a consequence he has lapsed into a coma. Dwayne has experienced the effects of drug
    a. abuse.
    b. dependence.
    c. tolerance.
    d. potentiation.

24. The permanent form of dementia in which the individual develops retrograde and anterograde amnesia, leading to an inability to remember recent events or learn new information is called
    a. Wernicke's disease.
    b. Broca's disease.
    c. Korsakoff's syndrome.
    d. Tourette's syndrome.

25. Which neurotransmitter system may be involved in the effects of alcohol?
    a. the norepinephrine system
    b. the GABA system
    c. the enkephalin system
    d. the cholinergic system

26. According to Woititz, which one of the following is one of the characteristic behavior patterns apparent in adult children of alcoholics?
    a. They fail to establish intimate relationships.
    b. They act in extremely antisocial ways.
    c. They are often overly shy and reticent.
    d. They tend to be abusive to their own children.

27. Aldehyde dehydrogenase (ALDH) is
    a. a medication prescribed to threat alcoholism.
    b. the same thing as disulfiram.
    c. an enzyme responsible for the metabolism of alcohol.
    d. a medication used to treat heroin addicts.

28. The condition that develops from chronic abuse of amphetamine, or from one very large does of amphetamine, is referred to as
    a. schizophrenia.
    b. delirium tremens.
    c. Korsakoff's syndrome.
    d. stimulant psychosis.

29. The most widely abused illegal drug in the United States is
    a. cocaine.
    b. marijuana.
    c. alcohol.
    d. caffeine.

30. The synthetic opioid that produces a safer and more controlled reaction than heroin is referred to as
    a. endorphin.
    b. enkaphalin.
    c. morphine.
    d. methadone.

ANSWERS

IDENTIFYING THE SUBSTANCE

1. cocaine
2. marijuana
3. heroin

4. barbiturates
5. alcohol
6. caffeine

7. LSD
8. crack cocaine
9. alcohol

10. amphetamine

MATCHING

1. n
2. m
3. i.
4. j
5. l

6. b
7. f
8. k
9. h
10. d

11. c
12. g
13. e
14. o
15. a

DIAMOND PUZZLE

```
        A
       A D H
      A B U S E
     S Y N A N O N
    M A R I J U A N A
   A C A M P R O S A T E
    T O L E R A N C E
      C O C A I N E
       C R A S H
        L S D
         A
```

SHORT ANSWER

1.

Medication	Intent
Benzodiazepines	Manage symptoms of withdrawal and delirium tremens.
Acamprosate	Reduce desire for alcohol by acting on the GABA neurotransmitter system.
Citalopram	Reduce desire for alcohol by inhibiting the uptake of serotonin.
Buspirone	Reduce desire for alcohol by inhibiting the uptake of serotonin.
Naltrexone	Reduces pleasurable feelings associated with alcohol use by altering opioid receptors.
Disulfiram	Produces aversive reaction to alcohol by causing a violently unpleasant reaction when mixed with alcohol.

2.

Psychoactive Substance	Subjective effects	Tolerance and Dependence	Withdrawal	Risks or long-term effects
Alcohol	**Small amounts**: sedative effects **Larger amounts**: disinhibition **Very large amounts**: sleepiness, uncoordination, dysphoria, irritability	Yes	Yes	Brain damage, liver disease, damage to the gastrointestinal system, osteoporosis, cancer, reduced functioning of immune system.
Amphetamines	**Moderate amounts**: euphoria, confidence, talkativeness, energy. **Large amounts**: surge or "rush" of extremely pleasurable sensations.	Yes	Yes	Amphetamine-induced psychosis, also called stimulant psychosis.
Cocaine	**Moderate doses**: Euphoria, sexual excitement, potency, energy, and talkativeness; **Higher doses**: delusions, hallucinations, confusion, suspicion, agitation, and violence.	Yes	Yes	Heart failure and convulsions.
Cannabis (Marijuana)	**Moderate doses**: relaxation and feeling that time is slowed down, heightened sensual enjoyment, hunger, greater awareness of surroundings, possible impairment of short-term memory; **Higher doses**: visual hallucinations and paranoid delusions.	Not clear from available evidence	No	Nasal and respiratory problems, higher risk of cancer and cardiovascular disease, negative effects on reproductive functioning particularly in men; possible loss of motivation; increased risk of accidents.
Hallucinogens	**LSD**: Dizziness, weakness, euphoria, hallucinations; **Psilocybin**: relaxation and euphoria; **PCP**: low doses like depressant; larger doses cause distorted perceptions that can lead to violence.	Information not in text.		**LSD**: Flashbacks and hallucinogen persisting perception disorder. **PCP**: coma, convulsions, brain damage, disorientation so severe that it can lead to accidental death.
Opioids	Intensely pleasurable physical sensations and subjective feelings of euphoria.	Yes	Yes	Highly addictive. Long-term effects: decrease in respiratory efficiency, high blood pressure, and difficulty withdrawing.
Barbiturates	**Low doses**: feeling of calm and sedation, sociability, talkativeness, euphoria. **Higher doses**: sleep.	Yes	Yes	Accidental suicide due to respiratory failure. Alcohol potentiates the effect of these drugs, so risk is greater when they are combined with alcohol.
Barbiturate-like substances	Dissociation, loss of inhibitions, greater euphoria during sexual encounters.	Yes	Not discussed in text	Not discussed in text
Anxiolytics	Calm and relaxation.	Yes	Yes	Text discussion includes only withdrawal symptoms, which can be severe.

232

3. Wernicke and Korsakoff: names of dementias associated with long-term heavy alcohol consumption.
   Cue exposure and relapse prevention: two psychological treatments for alcohol dependence.
   Cocaine and caffeine: stimulants.
   Endorphins and enkephalins: two natural pain-reducing substances in the nervous system.
   Tolerance and withdrawal: two patterns associated with substance dependence.
4. Alcohol is responsible for more than half of the fatal automobile accidents in the U.S.
   Intoxicated pedestrians are four times more likely than nonintoxicated pedestrians to be hit by a car.
   Alcohol increases the risks of accidental drownings, falls, fires, and burns.
   Greater likelihood of serious trauma when an intoxicated person is involved in an accident.
   Increased risk of domestic violence as indicated by the finding that almost two-thirds of husbands who abused their wives were under the influence of alcohol when violent.
5.

Area of investigation	Available evidence
Patterns of inheritance	Higher concordance rate among identical than fraternal twins. Sons of alcoholics are four times more likely to become alcohol dependent than are sons of nonalcoholic parents, and the risk is higher for children of alcoholics regardless of whether they are raised by their biological parents or not.
Biological markers	Subjective reaction to alcohol: Nonalcoholic children of alcoholics show less of a subjective reaction than do children of nonalcoholics. P300 wave: Similar to alcoholics, children of alcoholic fathers show a lowering of the P300 wave after presentation of a stimulus.
Neurotransmitter functioning	Abnormalities have been examined in the GABA, serotonin, and dopamine neurotransmitter systems.
Search for an "alcohol" gene	Attempts have been made to find an "alcohol" gene that influences dopamine receptors but so far have been unsuccessful.

6. In the case of alcohol dependence, alcohol is so much a part of Western society that people may not even realize that excessive consumption is a problem.
   Alcohol dependent individuals tend to deny that they have a problem.
   The individual may be unwilling to reveal the problem to others.
   There is an inherently reinforcing property of psychoactive substance use.
   The painful nature of withdrawal symptoms makes it difficult for the user to achieve abstinence.
7.
a. Alcohol-dependent individuals are faced with the temptation to have a drink and at some point fail to abstain; according to the abstinence violation effect, if the individual's self-efficacy is lowered, a relapse is likely.
b. Decision-making for analyzing situations presenting a high risk of alcohol use.
   Skills training to express and receive feelings, initiate contact with others, and reply to criticism.
   Alternate coping methods for handling high-risk situations.
   Self-efficacy for maintaining abstinence.
c. Alcoholism is an illness or disease.
   A person never completely recovers from alcoholism, no matter how long abstinence has been maintained.
d. Avoid self-blame for lapses from abstinence.
   Develop alternate coping skills for handling situations involving potential alcohol use.
   Receive help through support and contact with others.
   Be motivated to participate in treatment.

e.

Alcoholics Anonymous	Relapse prevention
Control over drinking is seen as due to an outside force.	Control over drinking is seen as due to internal factors.
The client is encouraged to seek help from outside.	The client learns to draw on personal coping resources.

FOCUSING ON RESEARCH ABOUT CRACK BABIES

1. It is difficult to isolate the effect of cocaine on the developing fetus because many pregnant women who are addicted to cocaine also use alcohol, marijuana, and tobacco, making it difficult to determine which substance, or combination of substances, might be causing congenital disabilities such as lower birth weight, stunted body length, and smaller head size. Studies also suggest that how much and for how long crack was consumed in pregnancy may be a factor. Further, many addicted women fail to obtain adequate prenatal care in general, placing the health of the fetus at even greater risk.

2. Researchers have studied the effects of cocaine on pregnant rats and their pups. Rats injected with cocaine gave birth to pups with brains that were 20 percent smaller and bodies that were 25 percent lighter than those in the control group. However, we cannot conclude that there would be comparable negative effects on developing human fetuses.

3. Early intervention with mother and child in efforts to improve the home environment will give a crack baby the chance to overcome the effects of prenatal crack, as well as the limited ability its mother may have to provide a nurturing and healthy home for the growing child.

FROM THE CASE FILES OF DR. SARAH TOBIN: THINKING ABOUT CARL'S CASE

1. Financial problems caused by his expensive cocaine habit, spending more time away from home, becoming sloppy in his work as a resident, being abrupt and insensitive to patients and nursing staff, losing control of his interactions with his wife and daughter, being irritable and impatient.

2. Carl grew up with intense pressure to become a doctor, as if to be anything else would result in his father's rejection of him. Carl depended on others heavily to succeed, and probably married his wife because he needed a caretaker. She could not help him in his search for greater self-esteem. Carl turned to cocaine, a substance that deluded him into believing that he was happy, competent, and successful.

3. After a four-week in-patient program, he began intensive psychotherapy that was confrontational and cognitive in approach. He was involved in a support group of local physicians with similar problems. He gained insight into his problems, changed his priorities, and made a dramatic improvement.

HOW ARE WE DIFFERENT: THE INFLUENCE OF RACE AND CULTURE ON ALCOHOLISM

1. In some American societies alcohol use is discouraged or prohibited, such as in certain conservative religions and among the Amish. In many European societies, alcohol is integrated into the daily diet and often a standard accompaniment to meals.

2. One study found that African-American men and Caucasian men develop alcoholism at similar rates, yet African-American men have more alcohol-related problems, including health and interpersonal problems. Disadvantages in health care, employment, and education may contribute to higher alcohol-related problems in African-American men.

3. Although some Asian men drink heavily in certain work settings, drinking outside of social situations is often discouraged and women are discouraged from drinking. Further, some members of Asian cultures are vulnerable to the buildup of potentially toxic by-products of alcohol, making intoxication an unpleasant physical experience.

4. While men may drink to suppress painful emotions, women seem more likely to drink to escape painful interpersonal situations. In traditional male-dominated societies, such as Hispanic and Asian cultures, there are strong prohibitions against women becoming intoxicated.

REVIEW AT A GLANCE

1. mood
2. behavior
3. smoked
4. injected
5. drunk
6. inhaled
7. swallowed
8. intoxication
9. behavioral
10. psychological
11. withdrawal
12. physical
13. psychological
14. tolerance
15. abuse
16. impairment
17. distress
18. sedating
19. organs
20. medical
21. dementia
22. biopsychosocial
23. genetic
24. behavioral
25. cognitive-behavioral
26. social learning
27. expectancy
28. reinforcement
29. observational
30. family
31. community
32. culture
33. withdrawal
34. aversive
35. behavioral
36. cognitive-behavioral
37. Alcoholics Anonymous
38. 12-step
39. disease
40. stimulants
41. activating
42. amphetamines
43. euphoria
44. confidence
45. talkativeness
46. energy
47. cocaine
48. euphoria
49. sexual
50. potency
51. energy
52. talkativeness
53. Psychotic
54. Cannabis
55. perception
56. bodily
57. behavioral
58. psychological
59. Hallucinogens
60. perceptual
61. illusions
62. hallucinations
63. Opioid
64. bodily
65. Sedatives
66. hypnotics
67. anxiolytics
68. medications
69. craving
70. contingency management
71. thoughts
72. expectancies
73. behaviors

MULTIPLE CHOICE

1. (d) is correct. (a) is the physiological response to discontinued use of alcohol; (b) the is temporary state occasioned by alcohol use; and (c) is the combined effect of two or more psychoactive substances.
2. (b) is correct. All of the other choices are associated with the rate of alcohol absorption.
3. (a) is correct. There is no support for (b), (c), or (d).
5. (d) is correct. (b), (c), and (d) do not have the described effects.
6. (b) is correct. There is no support for (a), (c), or (d).
7. (d) is correct. There is no support for (a), (b), or (c).
8. (a) is correct. Other drugs belong to the classes named in (b), (c), and (d).
9. (d) is correct. There is no support for (a), (b), or (c).
10. (a) is correct. There is no support for (b), (c), or (d).
11. (d) is correct. (a) is an in-patient setting where patient and health-care providers work closely together, (b) is a residential setting combining community living arrangements, work, and therapy; and (c) is a 12-step support group.
12. (a) is correct. There is no support for (b), (c), or (d).
13. (c) is correct. (a) is the need for more of a substance to achieve the desired effect; (b) is a temporary state occasioned by substance use; and (d) is the combined effect of two or more psychoactive substances.
14. (d) is correct. (a) is one effect of a certain type of psychoactive substance; (b) is sometimes used to mean the same thing as intoxication; (c) is the body's breakdown and processing of any ingested substance.
15. (d) is correct. (a) is not necessarily associated with dementia; (b) and (c) are forms of dementia not related to alcohol use.
16. (d) is correct. (a), (b), and (c) would undermine her abstinence efforts.
17. (a) is correct. There is no support for (b), (c), or (d).
18. (b) is correct. Other psychoactive substances effect (a), (c), and (d).
19. (c) is correct. (a), (b), and (d) may be associated with the use of a hallucinogen.
20. (a) is correct. (b) and (c) are synthetic psychoactive substances; and there is no evidence for (d).

21. (b) is correct. (a) involves a decreased sensitivity to the substance; (c) to the physiological reaction of not ingesting the substance; and (d) to using a substance in spite of ill effects.
22. (b) is correct. (a) is associated with dependence; (c) with tolerance; and (d) with craving.
23. (d) is correct. (a) involves continued use of drugs despite risks or problems in living; (b) is using drugs to achieve a mood or physical state; and (c) usage of increased amounts to achieve the same result.
24. (c) is correct. (a) is another form of dementia; (b) is not a disorder; and (d) is a tic and motor disorder.
25. (b) is correct. There is no evidence for (a), (c) and (d).
26. (a) is correct. (b), (c), and (d) are not necessarily associated with alcohol.
27. (c) is correct. (d) is methadone; there is no medication to treat alcoholism, as such (a), though medications are used to treat some symptoms; and (b) is a substance used to cause an aversive biological response to drinking alcohol.
28. (d) is correct. (a) is not related to drug use; (b) is a symptom involved in withdrawal from alcohol; and (c) is a form of dementia associated with prolonged alcohol use.
29. (b) is correct. (c) is the most widely abused legal substance; (d) is a legal substance; (a) is popular but not as widely used as marijuana.
30. (d) is correct. (a) and (b) natural pain-killing substances produced by the brain; and (c) is an opioid similar to heroin.

CHAPTER 14
EATING DISORDERS AND IMPULSE-CONTROL DISORDERS

CHAPTER AT A GLANCE

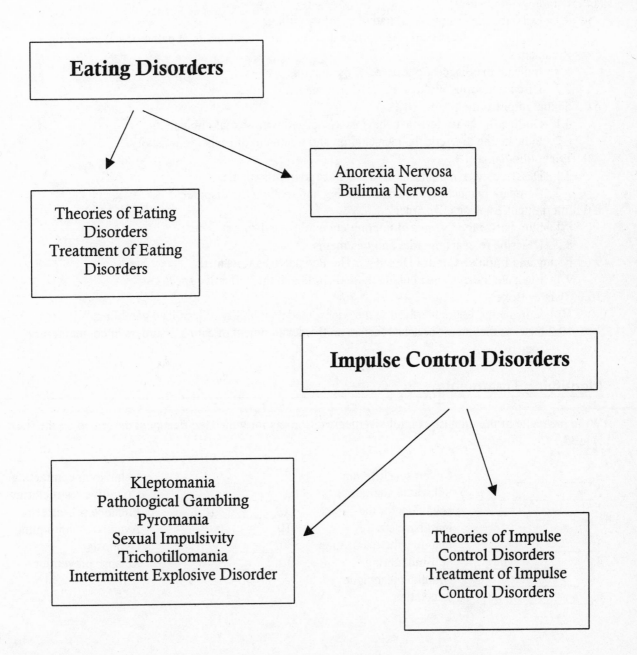

Eating Disorders

Theories of Eating
Disorders
Treatment of Eating
Disorders

Anorexia Nervosa
Bulimia Nervosa

Impulse Control Disorders

Kleptomania
Pathological Gambling
Pyromania
Sexual Impulsivity
Trichotillomania
Intermittent Explosive Disorder

Theories of Impulse
Control Disorders
Treatment of Impulse
Control Disorders

Learning Objectives

1.0 Eating Disorders
    1.1 Indicate the characteristics of anorexia nervosa.
    1.2 Identify the features of bulimia nervosa.
    1.3 Compare and contrast the theories and treatments of eating disorders.
2.0 Nature of Impulse-Control Disorders
    2.1 Identify the essential features common to the impulse-control disorders.
3.0 Kleptomania
    3.1 Summarize the characteristics of kleptomania.
    3.2 Indicate the relevant theories and treatments of kleptomania.
4.0 Pathological Gambling
    4.1 Describe the symptoms of pathological gambling.
    4.2 Contrast the theoretical perspectives used to understand and treat pathological gambling.
5.0 Pyromania
    5.1 Indicate the diagnostic features of pyromania.
    5.2 Discuss theories and treatments of pyromania.
6.0 Sexual Impulsivity
    6.1 Outline the characteristic behaviors associated with sexual impulsivity.
    6.2 Indicate the theoretical understanding and treatment of sexual impulsivity.
7.0 Trichotillomania
    7.1 Describe the symptoms used to diagnose trichotillomania.
    7.2 Compare perspectives to understanding and treating the disorder.
8.0 Intermittent Explosive Disorder
    8.1 Summarize the features of intermittent explosive disorder.
    8.2 Describe relevant theories and treatments.
9.0 Eating and Impulse-Control Disorders: The Perspectives Revisited
    9.1 Evaluate the evidence linking these disorders to the "affective spectrum."
10.0. Chapter Boxes
    10.1 Indicate the issues involved in the widespread availability of legalized gambling.
    10.2 Discuss the impact of social factors on the development of eating disorders in contemporary society.

Identifying Treatments

Write the name of the impulse-control disorder or disorders for which the treatment described on the right is used.

1._____ Covert sensitization

2._____ Substitute alternative behaviors for the impulsive act

3._____ Imaginal desensitization

4._____ Self-monitoring

5._____ Graphing technique

6._____ Relaxation

7. _____ Behavioral contracting

8. _____ Cognitive restructuring

9. _____ Enhance self-esteem

10._____ Aversive conditioning

11._____ Hypnosis

12._____ Relapse prevention.

Matching

Put the letter from the right-hand column corresponding to the correct match in the blank next to each item in the left-hand column.

1. ___ Neurotransmitter system thought to play a role in the development of kleptomania, pyromania, intermittent explosive disorder, and eating disorders.
2. ___ Behavioral technique used in the treatment of pyromania.
3. ___ Physical disorder thought to be linked to intermittent explosive disorder.
4. ___ Type of bulimia nervosa in which the individual tries to force out of the body excess food taken in during a binge by vomiting or using laxatives.
5. ___ Term used to identify personality type seen in childhood firestarters characterized by hyperactivity and proneness to destruction and thievery.
6. ___ Hormone that may be present in unusually high levels in individuals with sexual impulsivity.
7. ___ Psychiatrist who established the first U.S. clinic for treatment of pathological gambling.
8. ___ Axis II disorder thought to be linked to eating disorder.
9. ___ Well-known sports figure who was publicly exposed as a pathological gambler.
10. ___ Medication found to be effective in reducing kleptomanic behavior.
11. ___ Type of bulimia nervosa in which the individual tries to compensate for binges by engaging in fasting or excessive exercise.
12. ___ Bet that results in a large amount of money and is influential in propelling an individual to become a pathological gambler.
13. ___ Serial murderer, also known as "Son of Sam," who set more than 2000 fires in New York City during the 1970s.
14. ___ Term used to identify a personality type, seen in childhood firestarters, characterized by mood swings, intense anger, phobias, and a tendency toward violence.
15. ___ Psychological disorder thought to be linked to trichotillomania.

a. testosterone
b. borderline psychotic
c. Robert Custer
d. obsessive-compulsive disorder
e. big win
f. Pete Rose
g. serotonin
h. nonpurging type
i. impulsive neurotic
j. fluoxetine
k. David Berkowitz
l. graphing technique
m. borderline personality disorder
n. purging type
o. epilepsy

Word Scramble Puzzle

This puzzle is like the popular word game in which players form words from tiles that each has a certain value. The following letters are the ones in your "pile" with their assigned values. These letters can be combined in different ways to form the words described in the clues at the left. When you arrange the letters correctly, you will have the point value listed in parentheses. You can use each letter more than once to solve the clues.

Letter	Value	Letter	Value	Letter	Value	Letter	Value
A	1	H	4	N	1	T	1
B	3	I	1	O	1	U	1
C	3	K	5	P	3	V	4
E	1	L	1	R	1	X	8
G	2	M	3	S	1	Y	4

1. An impulse-control disorder characterized by a persistent and compelling urge to start fires.
   _____ (16 points)
2. An impulse-control disorder involving the persistent urge to steal _____. (19 points)
3. In intermittent _____ disorder, the individual experiences uncontrollable violent bursts of anger. (21 points)
4. In the eating disorder _____ nervosa, the individual has a view of herself as overweight even though she may be near starvation _____. (15 points)
5. The behavior engaged in by individuals with eating disorders when they attempt to rid themselves of food they have already eaten _____. (11 points)
6. In _____ nervosa, the individual may maintain a normal weight, though she yields to uncontrollable urges to overeat and then rid herself of what she has eaten. (11 points)
7. An uncontrollable urge to act is called an _____. (11 points)
8. An impulse-control disorder involving the uncontrollable and compulsive urge to pull out one's hair _____. (23 points)

240

Short Answer

1. What are three essential features of the behavior of people with an impulse-control disorder?

_____

_____

2. For each of the following disorders, describe a somatic treatment found to be helpful in reducing symptoms and the proposed mechanism of action of this treatment:

Disorder	Somatic treatment	Mechanism of action
Kleptomania		
Sexual impulsivity		
Trichotillomania		
Intermittent explosive disorder		
Eating disorders		

3. What are the two key differences between anorexia nervosa and bulimia nervosa?

_____

_____

4. Describe the role of faulty cognitions in the development of pathological gambling and eating disorders:

Disorder	Role of faulty cognitions
Pathological gambling	
Eating disorders	

5. What three lines of evidence regarding the relationship between mood disorders and impulse control disorders support the contention that these disorders are on the same "affective spectrum"?

_____

_____

_____

6. Summarize the main features of each of the following stages involved in the development of pathological gambling:

Stage	Main features
Recreational gambling	
Early winning stage	

Stage	Main features
The big win	
Chasing	
Establishment of pathological gambling cycle	

7. Describe the hypothesized role of family relationships in the development or maintenance of the following disorders:

Disorder	Role of family relationships
Pathological gambling	
Sexual impulsivity	
Trichotillomania	
Eating disorders	

From The Case Files of Dr. Sarah Tobin: Thinking About Rosa' Case

Answer the following questions about the case of Rosa Nomirez.

1. Describe how Rosa's symptoms met the diagnostic criteria for anorexia nervosa.

_____

_____

2. What was Dr. Tobin's case formulation for Rosa's diagnosis of anorexia nervosa?

_____

_____

3. Discuss the nature and course of Rosa's treatment.

_____

_____

4. How did Dr. Tobin respond to Rosa's refusal to participate in group therapy?

_____

_____

How Are We Different?

Answer the following questions from the text box "How People Differ: Does Modern Society Cause Eating Disorders?"

1. Comment on the pattern of eating disorders in African American and Caucasian women in the United States.

_____

_____

_____

2. What possible explanations are there to explain the relative infrequency of eating disorders in non-Western cultures?

_____

_____

_____

3. What individual characteristics may contribute to eating disorders?

_____

_____

_____

Review at a Glance

People with anorexia nervosa show four kinds of symptoms. They refuse or are unable to (1)_____; have an intense fear of (2)_____ or (3)_____; have a (4)_____ perception of their (5)_____ or _____; and experience (6)_____, if they are post-puberty. People with bulimia nervosa alternate between (7)_____ and (8)_____. Biological explanations for eating disorders focus on abnormalities in the (9)_____ and (10)_____ neurotransmitter systems. The psychological perspective sees people who have eating disorders as suffering from a great deal of (11)_____ and as turning to food for (12)_____ and (13)_____. Cognitive theories focus on the client's (14)_____ and resistance to (15)_____. Sociocultural explanations emphasize both the (16)_____ system and society's attitudes toward (17)_____ and (18)_____. Interventions include (19)_____, individual (20)_____, (21)_____ and (22)_____ techniques, and (23)_____ therapy.

People with (24)_____ disorders repeatedly engage in behaviors that are potentially harmful, and they feel unable to (25)_____ and a sense of (26)_____ if they are thwarted in their desires. People with (27)_____ are driven by a persistent urge to steal because they experience a (28)_____ while engaging in stealing. Treatments include medication, usually (29)_____, and (30)_____ treatments, such as (31)_____.

(32)_____ have an intense urge to gamble. Biological factors can be seen as a

243

drive for (33)_____ and (34)_____ feelings. Certain personality characteristics, such as (35)_____ and (36)_____, also predispose people to develop this condition. Sociocultural factors, such as the spread of (37)_____, may aggravate some people's tendencies to become immersed in such behavior. Treatments include medications, such as (38)_____, which are helpful, as are (39)_____ and (40)_____ techniques. Many pathological gamblers also benefit from participation in peer groups, such as (41)_____.

People with (42)_____ have an intense desire to prepare, set, and watch (43)_____. This disorder seems rooted in (44)_____ problems and (45)_____ behavior. Adults with pyromania typically have problems with (46)_____ and (47)_____. Interventions aimed at adults are designed to address the client's (48)_____, (49)_____, (50)_____ problems, and inability to control (51)_____.

People with (52)_____ are unable to control their sexual behavior. Individuals with this condition commonly suffer coexisting conditions, such as (53)_____, (54)_____ disorder, (55)_____, or some (56)_____ symptoms. Treatment usually combines (57)_____ -oriented, (58)_____, and (59)_____ systems approaches.

People with (60)_____ have an irresistible urge to pull out their hair. This condition is associated with (61)_____ disorders, (62)_____ abnormalities, disturbed (63)_____ relationships, and the fact that the behavior relieves (64)_____. The most common intervention is a form of (65)_____ therapy, aimed at (66)_____.

People with (67)_____ disorder feel an inability to resist assaultive or destructive acts of (68)_____, caused by an interaction of (69)_____ and (70)_____ factors. Treatment may involve both (71)_____ and (72)_____.

Multiple Choice

1. During the course of committing an impulsive act, people with impulse-control disorders
   a. usually feel tension and anxiety immediately after engaging in the impulsive act.
   b. may experience arousal before engaging in the impulsive act that they liken to sexual excitement.
   c. feel intensely conflicted at the moment of choosing to engage in the impulsive act.
   d. often experience feelings of regret and remorse immediately before engaging in the impulsive act.

2. Which of the following statements is true regarding people with kleptomania?
   a. They are driven by a desire to accumulate expensive possessions.
   b. They limit their stealing to situations in which they are taking items from people whom they know personally.
   c. They are driven by the desire to steal, not the desire to have.
   d. They rarely suffer from psychological disorders other than the problem of kleptomania.

3. Researchers investigating the role of biological factors in pathological gambling have found that these individuals
   a. show more norepinephrine activity than nongamblers.
   b. have thyroid abnormalities.
   c. have lower levels of dopamine than nongamblers.
   d. show evidence of specific biological markers.

4. A treatment of pathological gambling involving clients imagining scenes in which they feel tempted to gamble and relaxing as they imagine each successive behavior involved in the scene is called
   a. covert sensitization.
   b. flooding.
   c. *in vivo* desensitization.
   d. imaginal desensitization.

5. The type of bulimia nervosa in which one rids the body of food with vomiting, laxatives, or diuretics is
   a. anorexic.
   b. purging.
   c. depressive.
   d. nonpurging.

6. According to government estimates, the highest rates for legalized gambling occur in states in which
   a. casinos are built in expensive resort areas.
   b. gambling has been legalized for many years.
   c. there are lotteries but not casinos.
   d. new casinos and lotteries have been developed.

7. Prior to engaging in a seemingly uncontrollable act, people with intermittent explosive disorder experience a phenomenon similar to that experienced by people with
   a. epilepsy.
   b. high blood pressure.
   c. cardiovascular disease.
   d. migraine headache disorder.

8. Research on the relationship between dieting and eating disorders indicates that
   a. dieters are at lower risk for developing eating disorders.
   b. there is no relationship between dieting and eating disorders.
   c. dieters are at greater risk for developing eating disorders.
   d. exercisers but not dieters are likely to develop eating disorders.

9. Proponents of which theoretical model propose that people with bulimia translate society's attitudes toward thinness into extreme restraints and rigid rules about food?
   a. societal
   b. psychodynamic
   c. family systems
   d. cognitive-behavioral

10. Extreme cases of sexual impulsivity are sometimes treated biologically with
    a. antiandrogenic medication.
    b. testosterone.
    c. ECT.
    d. neuroleptics.

11. According to Custer's views regarding the development of pathological gambling, the transition to becoming a pathological gambler becomes evident when the gambler:
    a. starts to gain an identity as a winner.
    b. starts to develop fears of becoming a loser.
    c. begins to experience family problems.
    d. seeks professional help for the gambling problem.

12. The Goldfarb Fear of Fat Scale would be used in the diagnosis of
    a. bulimia nervosa.
    b. anorexia nervosa.
    c. eating disorders involving possible medical complications.
    d. any eating disorder.

13. Which behavioral technique involves having the individual with kleptomania imagine disgusting images, such as vomit, when the compulsion to steal is beginning?
    a. free association
    b. flooding
    c. covert sensitization
    d. in vivo desensitization

14. Which of the following techniques involves having the client with pyromania construct a chart that corresponds to the individual's behaviors, feelings, and experiences associated with firesetting?
    a. the graphing technique
    b. the thought stopping technique
    c. aversive conditioning
    d. in vivo desensitization

15. According to the family systems perspective, adults with sexual impulsivity are more likely to grow up in families with
    a. restrictive attitudes regarding sex.
    b. permissive attitudes regarding sex.
    c. liberal opinions regarding sex.
    d. open attitudes about sex.

16. Trichotillomania is an impulse-control disorder involving the persistent urge to
    a. pull one's hair.
    b. bite one's nails.
    c. binge, then purge.
    d. engage in sexual intercourse.

17. While stopped in his car at a stoplight, Tim occasionally experiences an aura, followed by an intense urge to get out of the car and pummel the person in the car ahead of him for no apparent reason. He has been arrested several times for acting on this urge. What impulse-control disorder might Tim suffer from?
    a. antisocial personality disorder
    b. oppositional defiant disorder
    c. intermittent explosive disorder
    d. passive aggressive personality disorder

18. Which of the following is considered to be the core feature of anorexia nervosa?
    a. frequent binging
    b. normal body weight
    c. consumption of nonnutritive substances
    d. body image disturbance

19. The highest rates for anorexia nervosa are found in
    a. China.
    b. France.
    c. India.
    d. the United States

20. Which of the following facts might support a conclusion that an individual's gambling behavior was beyond the boundaries of social gambling?
    a. He was seeking a big win.
    b. He started drinking while he was gambling.
    c. His wife approved of his gambling.
    d. He promised his wife that he would stop, but did not.

21. Which of the following is considered to be the core feature of anorexia nervosa?
    a. frequent binging
    b. normal body weight
    c. consumption of nonnutritive substances
    d. body image disturbance

22. Which of the following is one of the main differences between anorexics and bulimics?
    a. Anorexics are comfortable with their body image; bulimics are not.
    b. Anorexics are typically overweight; bulimics are typically underweight.
    c. Anorexics have a normal body weight; bulimics are typically overweight.
    d. Anorexics have a distorted body image; bulimics generally do not.

23. Family systems theorists view the anorexic behavior of the teenage girl as being an effort to
    a. assert her independence.
    b. express her concerns.
    c. modify her position in the family structure.
    d. reduce anxiety.

24. Which medication reduces the symptoms of bulimia by increasing serotonin levels?
    a. Prozac
    b. Halcion
    c. Mellaril
    d. Ritalin

25. Anne has a persistent urge to shoplift. However, her motivation for stealing is not based in need. She steals for the sake of fulfilling her impulse to do so. Which impulse-control disorder might she be diagnosed as having?
    a. antisocial personality disorder
    b. pyromania
    c. trichotillomania
    d. kleptomania

26. Which behavioral technique involves having the individual with kleptomania imagine disgusting images such as vomit when the compulsion to steal is beginning?
    a. free association
    b. flooding
    c. covert sensitization
    d. *in vivo* desensitization

27. The gain of a large amount of money in one bet through which a compulsive gambler becomes propelled into a pattern of gambling is referred to as the
    a. jackpot.
    b. big stakes.
    c. big win.
    d. obsession.

28. The impulse-control disorder characterized by a persistent urge to start fires is called
    a. kleptomania.
    b. rumination disorder.
    c. trichotillomania.
    d. pyromania.

29. According to family theorists, childhood neglect and abuse may result in which impulse control disorder?
    a. anorexia nervosa
    b. kleptomania
    c. sexual impulsivity
    d. bulimia nervosa

30. Andrea is an 8-year-old girl who compulsively pulls her hair out and occasionally eats it. She continues this behavior despite the fact that she has very noticeable bald spots. Which impulse-control disorder might she have?
    a. intermittent explosive disorder
    b. stereotypy/habit disorder
    c. pica
    d. trichotillomania

Answers

IDENTIFYING TREATMENTS

1. Kleptomania
   Sexual impulsivity
2. Trichotillomania
   Sexual impulsivity
3. Pathological gambling
4. Eating disorders
5. Pyromania
6. Trichotillomania
7. Sexual impulsivity
8. Eating disorders
9. Sexual impulsivity,
   Eating disorders
10. Pathological gambling
11. Trichotillomani
12. Eating disorders

MATCHING

1. g	4. n	7. c	10. j	13. k
2. l	5. i	8. m	11. h	14. b
3. o	6. a	9. f	12. e	15. d

WORD SCRAMBLE PUZZLE

1. PYROMANIA
2. KLEPTOMANIA
3. EXPLOSIVE
4. ANOREXIA
5. PURGING
6. BULIMIA
7. IMPULSE
8. TRICHOTILLOMANIA

SHORT ANSWER

1. They are unable to stop from acting on impulses that are harmful to self or others.
Before they act on their impulse, they feel pressured to act.
Upon acting on their impulse, they feel a sense of pleasure or gratification similar to sexual release.

2.

Disorder	Somatic treatment	Mechanism of action
Kleptomania	Fluoxetine (Prozac)	Increases availability of serotonin
Sexual impulsivity	Antiandrogenic medication	Reduces level of testosterone
Trichotillomania	Lithium Clomipramine	Not described in text Antidepressant that reduces obsessional symptoms
Intermittent explosive disorder	Benzodiazepines Lithium Beta blockers	Used to reduce explosive behavior in people with certain personality disorders Both reduce emotional reactivity by lowering norepinephrine functioning

Disorder	Somatic treatment	Mechanism of action
Eating disorders	Fluoxetine	Increases availability of serotonin
	Antidepressants	Reduce depressive symptoms and reduce eating disorder behaviors specifically
	MAO inhibitors	No longer used because of undesirable side effects.

3. **Body image**: People with anorexia nervosa see themselves as overweight, no matter how emaciated they may be; people with bulimia nervosa have normal body image.
   Amount of weight loss: People with anorexia nervosa are significantly below the norm for weight; people with bulimia are of normal or above average weight.

4.

Disorder	Role of faulty cognitions
Pathological gambling	Pathological gamblers hold the faulty beliefs that they are in control of the probabilities that affect the outcome of their bets; this leads them to develop grandiose ideas that lead them to become convinced of their ultimate success.
Eating disorders	The individual's incorporation of society's beliefs about thinness leads the individual to adopt a set of rules and restrictions regarding food; in the case of bulimia nervosa, these rules break down when the individual becomes hungry, and a binge pattern is set in motion.

5.
a. Several impulse-control disorders have been found to co-occur with mood disorders, including kleptomania, pathological gambling, and eating disorders. Trichotillomania is thought to be linked to obsessive-compulsive disorder, another disorder that would fall on a proposed affective spectrum.
b. Altered functioning of serotonin and norepinephrine neurotransmitters, systems that are thought to play a role in mood disorders, has been observed in people with impulse-control disorders, including kleptomania, pathological gambling, pyromania, and eating disorders.
c. Treatments used for mood disorders have been successfully applied to the impulse-control disorders kleptomania, trichotillomania, intermittent explosive disorder, and eating disorders.

6.

Stage	Main features
Recreational gambling	The person's behavior is indistinguishable from that of a gambler who enjoys gambling as a social activity.
Early winning stage	The individual begins to win and starts to gain gambling skills. Development of identity as a "winner" occurs, and, through continued wins, that identity becomes reinforced.
The big win	A gain of a large amount of money in one bet is so highly reinforcing that the individual becomes possessed with the need to re-experience it. The gambler is convinced of the possession of unique luck and skill and starts to make riskier bets.

Stage	Main features
Chasing	After losses inevitably start to occur, the individual begins to bet more and more to recoup earlier losses. As desperation mounts, the individual is launched into an intensive and all-consuming enterprise. Poor judgment combined with desperation lead to larger and larger losses.
Establishment of pathological gambling cycle	In a continued search for another big win, the individual has periodic wins that maintain his or her unreasonable optimism. In time, however, the individual's resources become depleted, and the person may consider drastic action, such as suicide, running away, or a life of crime to support the behavior.

7.

Disorder	Role of family relationships
Pathological gambling	Spouses and children of pathological gamblers are affected by the disorder. Spouses report detrimental changes in emotional functioning; dysfunctional coping behaviors; emotional, verbal, or physical abuse; and feelings of suicidality. Children experience significant behavioral and adjustment problems in school and at home and involvement in drug or alcohol abuse, crime, or gambling-related activities. Families also suffer financially due to the heavy betting expenses.
Sexual impulsivity	The disorder is thought to result from either unduly restrictive attitudes toward sex in a child's family or childhood neglect and abuse. The disorder may result in or be maintained in adulthood by dysfunctional communication patterns in the sexual domain between sexual partners.
Trichotillomania	Described in terms of psychodynamic theory, disturbed parent-child relationships are thought to create feelings of neglect, abandonment, or emotional burdening in a child who attempts to gain attention or gratification through hair-pulling.
Eating disorders	Family systems theorists propose that a girl may develop anorexia nervosa in an effort to assert her independence from the family, perhaps in situations where the girl feels that her parents are standing in the way of her becoming autonomous. Other contributing factors may be a family that is chaotic, incapable of resolving conflict, unaffectionate, and lacking in empathy.

FROM THE CASE FILES OF DR. SARAH TOBIN: THINKING ABOUT ROSA'S CASE

1. Her MMPI-2 profile showed her to be defensive, hypersensitive, depressive, and a perfectionist, features commonly associated with eating disorders. She had lost nearly 20 percent of her body weight in the past several months, had stopped menstruating, and had showed signs of anemia, dehydration, and electrolyte disturbance. She had an intense fear of gaining weight, even though she was drastically underweight, and she had a disturbed perception of her body weight and figure.

2. Her problems went back to childhood, when her parents became overprotective of her after the death of her brother at the age of 5. Her parents expected a lot of her, and she did not want to disappoint them. She strove for perfection in every area of her life, but when she began college she feared that she would not meet the expectations of her parents and others. As her self-doubts increased she developed distorted concepts of her intelligence, personality, and attractiveness. She stopped eating in an effort to become more attractive. At 117 pounds, she thought she was fat.

3. Rosa developed a nutritional and meal plan with a nutritionist and had individual therapy with Dr. Tobin for 6 months. Dr. Tobin used mainly cognitive techniques to help Rosa develop more accurate views of herself, the world, and her potential. She complied with the medical treatment and improved in all areas of her life. She was able to talk to her parents about her need to feel less pressure from them, and she survived the tennis team's loss of the championship.

4. Dr. Tobin was sensitive to the fact that, in the Puerto Rican culture, seeking help for psychological problems carried a great stigma. She understood Rosa's insistence that she could not talk about her problem with peers.

HOW <u>ARE</u> WE DIFFERENT?

1. Within the United States, eating disorders are far less prevalent among African American women, compared with Caucasian women, and a similar pattern holds true for specific symptoms, such as restrictive dieting and body image distortion.

2. The ideal body image for a woman, according to the American cultural ideal, is tied to thinness. Over the past several decades, the ideal woman has gotten thinner and thinner. At the same time, the average body mass and height of women has increased (perhaps due to improvements in health and nutrition), making the cultural ideal increasingly difficult to obtain. There is evidence that, as women from other cultures adopt Western standards of beauty, restrictive dieting eating disorders becomes more prevalent.

3 .Men and women with personality characteristics of perfectionism, obsessiveness, or a sense of personal ineffectiveness and people with biological predispositions and problems in psychosocial development may be more prone to eating disorders.

REVIEW AT A GLANCE

1. maintain normal weight
2. gaining weight
3. becoming fat
4. distorted
5. weight; shape
6. amenorrhea
7. binging
8. purging
9. norepinephrine
10. serotonin
11. inner turmoil
12. comfort
13. nurturance
14. rigidity
15. change
16. family
17. eating
18. diet
19. medication
20. therapy
21. cognitive-behavioral
22. interpersonal
23. family
24. impulse control
25. stop themselves

26. desperation
27. kleptomania
28. thrill
29. fluoxetine
30. behavioral
31. covert sensitization
32. Pathological gamblers
33. stimulation
34. pleasurable
35. impulsivity
36. psychopathy
37. legalized gambling
38. selective serotonin reuptake inhibitors
39. behavioral
40. cognitive-behavioral
41. Gamblers Anonymous
42. pyromania
43. fires
44. childhood
45. firesetting
46. substance abuse
47. relationship difficulties
48. low self-esteem
49. depression

50. communication
51. anger
52. sexual impulsivity
53. depression
54. phobic
55. substance abuse
56. dissociative
57. insight
58. behavioral
59. family
60. trichotillomania
61. obsessive-compulsive
62. brain
63. parent-child
64. tension
65. behavior
66. habit reversal
67. intermittent explosive
68. aggression
69. biological
70. environmental
71. medication
72. psychotherapy

MULTIPLE CHOICE

1.   (b) is correct. They do not feel either (a), (b), or (c).
2.   (c) is correct. (a), (b), and (d) are not true.
3.   (a) is correct. There is no evidence for the existence of (b), (c), and (d).
4.   (d) is correct. Neither (a), (b), nor (c) involve imagining scenes.
5.   (b) is correct. (a) does not involve binging and purging; (c) and (d) are not forms of bulimia.
6.   (b) is correct. There is no evidence for (a), (c), or (d).
7.   (a) is correct. There is no evidence of (b), (c), or (d).
8.   (c) is correct. (a) and (b) are false, in fact the opposite is usually true; there is not evidence for (c).
9.   (c) is correct. (a) is not a theoretical model: (b) believes that childhood experience and intrapsychic conflict are contribute to the disorder; (c) that dysfunctional family dynamics play a role.
10.   (a) is correct. (b) may increase sexual desire; (c) and (d) would not be used as treatment.
11.   (a) is correct. (b), (c), and (d) have nothing to do with increasing gambling behavior.
12.   (b) is correct. The scale is not used with (a), (c), or (d).
13.   (c) is correct. (a) is a psychodynamic therapy technique; (b) and (d) involve real situations.
14.   (a) is correct. (b), (c), and (d) do not involve charting behavior.
15.   (a) is correct. (b), (c), and (d) may mitigate against sexual impulsivity,
16.   (a) is correct. (b) and (d) are not impulse-control disorders; (c) is bulimia nervosa.
17.   (c) is correct. (a) could account for violent acts, but not as described: (b) and (d) are not generally associated with violence and out-of-control behavior.
18.   (d) is correct. (a) is a factor of bulimia, not anorexia; (b) is definitely not a factor in anorexia; (c) is related to a disorder known as pica.
19.   (d) is correct. Rates are much lower in (a), (b), and (c) than in (d).
20.   (d) is correct. (a), (b) and (c) may contribute to the behaviors, but (d) indicates that it is becoming addictive.
21.   (d) is correct. (a) and (b) are associated with bulimia nervosa (c) with pica.
22.   (d) is correct. (a), (b), and (c) are all incorrect comparisons.
23.   (a) is correct. (b), (c) and (d) are not considered factors in the development of anorexia nervosa.
24.   (a) is correct. (b), (c), and (d) do not affect serotonin levels and are not used to treat bulimia.
25.   (d) is correct. (a) is a disorder associated with criminal behavior and violations of rights of others; (b) with fireseting; and (c) with pulling out one's hair.
26.   (c) is correct. (a) is a psychoanalytic technique; and (b) and (d) other forms of behavioral therapy.
27.   (c) is correct. (a) may be the source of a large payoff; (b) has to do with what one has wagered; and (d) is an intrusive thought.
28.   (d) is correct. (a) is compulsive stealing; (b) regurgitating food; and (c) pulling out one's hair.
29.   (c) is correct. Childhood abuse has not been linked to (a), (b), or (d).
30.   (d) is correct. (a) is uncontrolled violent outbursts; (b) a repetitive behavior; and (c) eating nonfood items.

CHAPTER 15
ETHICAL AND LEGAL ISSUES

CHAPTER AT A GLANCE

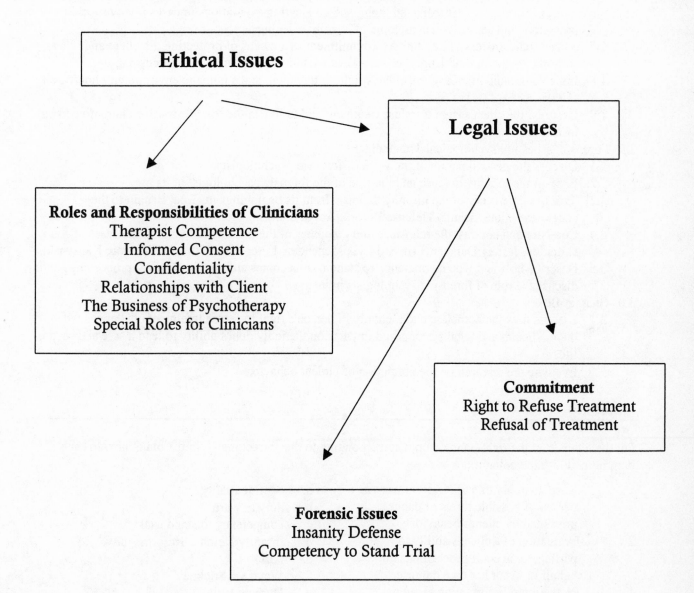

Ethical Issues

Legal Issues

Roles and Responsibilities of Clinicians
Therapist Competence
Informed Consent
Confidentiality
Relationships with Client
The Business of Psychotherapy
Special Roles for Clinicians

Commitment
Right to Refuse Treatment
Refusal of Treatment

Forensic Issues
Insanity Defense
Competency to Stand Trial

Learning Objectives

1.0 Ethical Issues
1.1 Identify the roles and responsibilities of mental health clinicians.
1.2 Describe the concept of informed consent and discuss its relevance to psychological treatment.
1.3 Explain the importance of confidentiality and the related concept of privileged communication, and discuss the exceptions to these principles, such as the duty to warn.
1.4 Discuss the nature of a clinician's relationships with clients.
1.5 Outline the major concerns of the business of psychotherapy.
1.6 Distinguish the special roles clinicians may play, including testifying in court as an expert witness, serving as a guardian ad litem, and conducting evaluations in cases involving child protection and adults with symptoms of cognitive decline.
1.7 Discuss the process of involuntary commitment as a means of protecting the client and others from the expression of dangerous behaviors, including the principle of parens patriae.
1.8 Indicate the importance of the client's right to treatment and a humane environment, liberty, and safety.
1.9 Describe the client's right to refuse treatment and to live in the least restrictive alternative to an institution.
2.0 Forensic Issues in Psychological Treatment
2.1 Discuss the general nature of the work of forensic psychologists.
2.2 Explain the insanity defense and the role of the forensic psychologist in its use.
2.3 Discuss the history of the insanity defense, from its beginnings in Great Britain to the enactment of the Insanity Defense Reform Act of 1984.
2.4 Compare and contrast the relevance and outcomes of the insanity defenses in the cases of John Hinckley, Jeffrey Dahmer, Erik and Lyle Menendez, Lorena Bobbitt, and Theodore Kaczynski.
2.5 Describe how and why competency to stand trial becomes an issue in criminal proceedings and discuss the role of forensic psychologists in its use.
3.0 Chapter Boxes
3.1 Discuss how the homeless and mentally ill person's right to refuse treatment challenges the mental health and legal systems and impacts on the individual's ability to lead a safe and secure life.
3.2 Evaluate the research on the prediction of violent behavior.

Matching

Put the letter from the right-hand column corresponding to the correct match in the blank next to each item in the left-hand column.

1. _____ Responsibility of a clinician to warn a person of possible threat or danger presented by client's behavior
2. _____ Evaluation of a client's ability to participate in court proceedings on behalf of his or her own defense.
3. _____ Protection of information about a client obtained in the process of providing treatment.
4. _____ Need to "appreciate" the wrongfulness of an act.

a. confidentiality
b. duty to warn
c. competency to stand trial
d. Insanity Defense Reform Act
e. ALI
f. Waytt vs. Stickney
g. Durham Rule
h. M'Naghten
i. informed consent
j. Least Restrictive environment
k. guardian ad litem

254

5. ____ Proof of "insanity" needed
6. ____ Legal procedure designed to protect individuals incapable of doing so such as a minor or incapacitated adult.
7. ____ Insanity defense
8. ____ Appointed by a court to make decisions privileged for a person
9. ____ Client's participation in setting, understanding, and agreeing to treatment goals
10. ____ Treatment setting that provides the fewest constraints on a client's freedom
11. ____ Legal requirement that professionals notify appropriate authorities about cases in which children and other vulnerable individuals are being abused
12. ____ Authority of the state to protect those who are unable to protect themselves
13. ____ Information provided by a client to a clinician that cannot be disclosed in court without the client's permission

l. mandated reporting
m. privileged communication
n. parens patriae
o. communication

Short Answer

1. Answer each of the following questions about forensic issues in psychological treatment.

   a. Why was there a difference between the outcome of the Jeffrey Dahmer case and that of the John Hinckley case?

   _____

   _____

   b. What have been the major issues identified in legislation and judicial rulings regarding the definition of insanity?

   _____

   _____

   c. What factors are assessed in determining a person's competency to stand trial?

   _____

   _____

   d. How do clinicians attempt to balance the need to commit a person involuntarily to treatment against the individual's right to the least restrictive alternative?

   _____

   _____

e. What issues are involved in a clinician's protecting a client's confidentiality versus the need to notify potential victims of harm?

_____

_____

f. What are the basic components of treatment to which hospitalized clients are entitled by law?

_____

_____

2. Answer the following pursuant to the Guidelines for Psychological Evaluations in Child Protection Matters.

a. The primary purpose of the evaluation is

_____

_____

b. Whose interests and well-being are paramount?

_____

_____

c. The evaluation addresses:

_____

_____

d. What do the guidelines mandate about reporting on the psychological functioning of any individual?

_____

_____

e. What must be the basis for any recommendations made by the psychologist?

_____

_____

3. Answer the following concerning the Guidelines for the Evaluation of Dementia and Age-Related Cognitive Decline.

a. What must the psychologist at least attempt to obtain before beginning the evaluation of a person with dementia or age-related cognitive decline?

_____

_____

b. What assessment procedures should be used if possible?

_____

_____

c. What should the examiner attempt to provide in addition to conducting an assessment?

_____

_____

_____

4. Answer the following from "Critical Issue: Homeless and Mentally Ill: The Right to Refuse Treatment."

    a. State the evidence that homeless people with schizophrenia experience more severe symptoms than those who are not homeless.

_____

_____

    b. What aspect of medication is cited as one reason for widespread homelessness among people with schizophrenia?

_____

_____

    c. What do we need to know about the relationship between homelessness and noncompliance with medication for schizophrenia?

_____

_____

Focusing on Research

Answer the following questions from "Research Focus: The Prediction of Violent Behavior."

1. What is the single best predictor of violence?

_____

_____

2. Discuss the problems inherent in psychologists' attempts to predict a person's behavior.

_____

_____

3. Summarize the guidelines for psychologists' prediction of violence suggested by forensic psychologist John Monahan.

_____

_____

From The Case Files of Dr. Sarah Tobin: Thinking About Mark's Case

Answer the following questions about the case of Mark Chen.

1. Why did Dr. Tobin have no choice but to ask Tanya to commit Mark involuntarily to the hospital?

_____

_____

2. Discuss Dr. Tobin's assessment and diagnosis of Mark.

_____

_____

3. What was Dr. Tobin's formulation of Mark's case?

_____

_____

4. Describe the nature and course of Mark's treatment.

_____

_____

Review at a Glance

Clinicians are expected to have the intellectual competence to (1)_____, (2)_____, and (3)_____ clients whom they accept into treatment. When beginning work with clients, they should obtain the client's (4)_____ to ensure that the client understands the (5)_____ of treatment, the process of (6)_____, the client's (7)_____, the therapist's (8)_____, treatment (9)_____, (10)_____ that will be used, (11)_____ issues, and the limits of (12)_____.

Confidentiality is the principle that (13)_____ in therapy must be safeguarded by the therapist as (14)_____. With only a few exceptions, the content of therapy is considered (15)_____ communication, that is, the clinician may not disclose any information about the client without the client's (16)_____. Exceptions to this include instances involving (17)_____ reporting and duty to (18)_____. Mental health professionals are mandated by law to report information involving the (19)_____ or _____ of a child or people who are unable to (20_____. The duty to warn involves the clinician's responsibility to take action to inform a (21)_____ of a client's (22)_____ to that person.

In their relationships with clients, clinicians must avoid (23)_____ relationships, such as (24)_____ with clients, and are expected to maintain (25)_____ and (26)_____ in their dealings with clients. Sometimes clinicians are called upon for special roles that present unique ethical challenges, such as being an (27)_____, preparing (28)_____ and evaluating people with (29)_____.

Clinicians are sometimes involved in the process of (30)_____, an emergency procedure for the involuntary hospitalization of a person deemed to be likely to create (31)_____ for self or (32)_____ as a result of (33)_____. Hospitalized clients have the right to a (34)_____ environment and to (35)_____ and (36)_____. Clients also have the right to refuse (37)_____ unless a court intervenes. clients also have the right to be placed in the (38)_____ to treatment in an institution.

The major forensic issues that pertain to the field of mental health involve the (39)_____ and the competency to (40)_____. A client may plead insanity if, due to the existence of a (41)_____, he or she should not be held (42)_____ for (43)_____ actions. The determination of competency to stand trial pertains to the question of whether a defendant is (44)_____ and able to (45)_____ criminal proceedings.

Multiple Choice

1. Which of the following is a guarantee that a clinician is capable of providing treatment to a client?
   a. A doctoral degree in clinical psychology
   b. A degree in medicine
   c. A state license to practice.
   d. None of the above.

2. Dr. Ward does not feel that she has the resources necessary to effectively treat Cindy's condition and so she give Cindy the name and phone number of another clinician. Dr. Ward provided Cindy with
   a. informed consent.
   b. a referral.
   c. the right to refuse treatment.
   d. a mandated report.

3. Informing the client about the potential risks and benefits of therapy, confidentiality and its limits, and the expected length of therapy is necessary so that the client can
   a. understand his or her duty to warn.
   b. choose the least restrictive alternative.
   c. provide informed consent.
   d. establish commitment to therapy.

4. Nathan has been brought to the emergency room. He is extremely disoriented and is out of touch with reality. He has just attempted to commit suicide and Dr. Gallina believes he is still at risk. Unfortunately, Nathan does not seem capable of providing informed consent for treatment. Dr. Gallina should
   a. respect Nathan's right to refuse treatment.
   b. get a court order to forcibly provide treatment.
   c. wait until Nathan becomes lucid.
   d. get consent from Nathan's family.

5. Why is confidentiality in therapy important?
   a. It is necessary in order for clients to feel comfortable disclosing intimate details about themselves during therapy.
   b. It is important for the clients to feel confident about improvement in their condition.
   c. It is a courtesy that has been brought about by the traditions of secrecy in the confessional.
   d. Most clients are collecting medical benefits and fear that if their bosses find out that they will lose the money.

6. Dr. Blanchard is being pressured by the local police department for information on one of his client's who is suspected of murder. Dr. Blanchard must be careful to remember the principle of
   a. mandated reporting.
   b. privileged communication.
   c. informed consent.
   d. duty to warn.

7. The clinician's responsibility to notify a potential victim of a client's harmful intent toward that individual is referred to as
   a. primary prevention.
   b. notification of intent.
   c. duty to warn.
   d. legal commitment.

8. When a clinician is called on to provide specialized information not commonly known by people outside the mental health profession during court cases he/she is considered to be a(n)
   a. *guardian ad litem*.
   b. expert witness.
   c. *parens patriae*.
   d. impartial party.

9. A person appointed by the court to represent or make decisions for a person who is legally incapable of doing so in a civil legal proceeding is referred to as a
   a. legal witness.
   b. *parens patriae*.
   c. parental authority.
   d. *guardian ad litem*.

10. If someone has not committed a crime but is viewed as being a potential threat to self or others, he or she may be
    a. involuntarily committed to a psychiatric hospital.
    b. judged incompetent to stand trial.
    c. judged as not guilty by reason of insanity.
    d. judged as guilty but insane.

11. The legal principle that the state has the authority to protect those who are unable to protect themselves is referred to as
    a. commitment.
    b. *guardian ad litem*.
    c. *ad hominen*.
    d. *parens patriae*.

12. Wendy has been involuntarily committed to a psychiatric hospital. When she tries to use the ward pay phone, the staff members stand nearby and listen to her conversation. Occasionally they have actually interrupted her calls and have hung the phone up on her. Which of Wendy's rights is being violated?
    a. the right to stand trial
    b. the right to treatment
    c. the right to a humane environment
    d. the right to refuse treatment

13. Which of the following is among the rights that apply to psychiatric patients?
    a. the right to refuse treatment
    b. the right to the most restrictive environment
    c. the right to legal counsel
    d. the right to die

14. Carol has been hospitalized after her most recent bout with depression, which nearly resulted in her suicide. Her doctor insists that she receive electroconvulsive therapy. Despite the fact that she does not want the treatment, her doctor performs it anyway. Which of Carol's rights are being violated?
    a. the right to the least restrictive environment
    b. the right to refuse treatment
    c. the right to a humane environment
    d. the right to treatment

15. The subjective analysis of what the client would decide if he or she were cognitively capable of making the decision is
    a. *parens patriae.*
    b. *in loco parentis.*
    c. substituted judgement.
    d. informed consent.

16. What is the name of the rapidly growing subfield of psychology that examines issues pertaining to the relationship between criminal behavior and psychological disturbance?
    a. psychopathology
    b. clinical psychology
    c. forensic psychology
    d. legal psychology

17. Which of the following legal "tests" of insanity is based on the idea that people should not be judged guilty if a mental disorder prevents them from knowing the difference between right and wrong?
    a. the M'Naghten Rule
    b. the irresistible impulse test
    c. the Durham Rule
    d. the ALI guidelines

18. A person is not guilty if the "unlawful act was the product of mental disease or defect." This is the key feature of
    a. the M'Naghten Rule.
    b. the Durham Rule.
    c. the irresistible impulse test.
    d. the ALI guidelines.

19. What alternative verdict have some states utilized to separate the questions of guilt and mental disorder?
    a. not competent to stand trial
    b. the irresistible impulse verdict
    c. the least restrictive environment verdict
    d. the guilty, but mentally ill verdict

20. Which of the following individuals was found guilty but insane, and sent to prison?
    a. Jeffrey Dahmer
    b. John Hinkley
    c. David Berkowitz
    d. Lorena Bobbitt

ANSWERS

MATCHING

1. b	4. e	7. f	10. k	13. l
2. c	5. d	8. h	11. i	14. n
3. a	6. o	9. g	12. j	15. m

SHORT ANSWERS

1.
a. The Insanity Defense Reform Act of 1984 had tightened the criteria for a person's psychological disorder to be regarded as grounds for insanity, partly in response to the criticisms of the outcome of the John Hinckley case. Further, Dahmer was diagnosed as having a sexual disorder, but not a psychotic disorder, unlike Hinckley.

b. Legislation and judicial rulings regarding the determination of "insanity" focus on whether a person has the capacity to judge the rightness or wrongness of an act, to control his or her impulses to act, and, appreciate the wrongfulness of an act.

c. Determination of competency to stand trial involves predicting whether the defendant will have the cognitive capacity, emotional strength, and freedom from symptoms to make it possible to participate in court proceedings.

d. Clinicians must determine whether the risk presented by a client to the self or others outweighs the client's right to live independently outside an institution.

e. Clients are protected by the confidentiality of the clinician-client relationship, except when the clinician is obligated to follow through on a "duty to warn" another person about whom the client has expressed harmful intent or in cases where the client might inflict self-harm.

f. Clients are entitled to provision of psychotherapeutic services; privacy; appropriate clothing; opportunities to interact with other people, to receive and send mail, to use the telephone, and to have visitation privileges; comfortable surroundings; exercise, and adequate diet.

2.
a. To provide relevant, professionally sound results or opinions in matters where a child's health may have been and/or may be harmed in the future

b. The child's interest and well-being are paramount.

c. The particular psychological and developmental needs of the child and/or parent(s) that are relevant to child protection issues, such as physical abuse, sexual abuse, neglect, and/or serious emotional harm

d. Psychologists should provide an opinion regarding the psychological functioning of an individual only after conducting an evaluation of the individual adequate to support their statements or conclusions.

e. Recommendations, if offered, are based on whether the child's health and welfare have been and/or may be seriously harmed.

3.
a. Informed consent

b. Clinical interview and standardized psychological and neuropsychological tests

c. Constructive feedback, support, education, and a therapeutic alliance

4.
a. Those who were homeless experienced more hallucinations, persecutory delusions, emotional problems, impulsive behavior, and problems with alcohol and drug use, and were more likely to be noncompliant with their medications.

b. Forty percent or more schizophrenic outpatients refuse medication or fail to take it as prescribed, which they have the legal right to do. Treatment can be mandated only if they are a danger to themselves or others.

c. We need to know why clients who are schizophrenic refuse medication despite the sometimes dire consequences. Is it because it does not eliminate their symptoms or causes unpleasant side effects, or do they not appreciate its importance?

FOCUSING ON RESEARCH

1. A history of previous violence

2. Many factors can contribute to violent behavior, including violent history, violent family background, history of drug abuse, being male, frequently moving, being unemployed, low intelligence, growing up in a violent subculture, and the availability of weapons and victims. However, many men with all of these factors don't commit violence. Thus, psychologists are reluctant to predict that men with these risk factors may be violent in the future. Further, not all men who are violent have these identifiable factors in their background, thus leaving open the possibility of false negatives (incorrectly predicting that someone won't be violent, when, in fact, they are) and false positives (incorrectly predicting that someone will be violent, when, in fact, they are not).

3. The clinician should (1) know what risk factors to look for in an assessment of a client's potential harm to others, such as previous history of violence and the base rate of specific types of violent crimes; (2) attempt to gather information about past treatment and arrests; (3) apply a prediction model that takes into account both demographic characteristics of the client and features of the client's particular disorder; and (4) ensure that this information is communicated to others and is documented in the client's records. Then preventive action can be taken, such as institutionalizing the client, warning the victim, and increasing contact with the client in the community.

FROM THE CASE FILES OF DR. SARAH TOBIN: THINKING ABOUT MARK'S CASE

1. When Dr. Tobin saw Mark in the Emergency Room, Mark was immobilized, in a catatonic state. He was unshaven, unkempt, and unresponsive to questions, but he suddenly grabbed a pen and gouged at his wrist. He did not appear to comprehend anything Dr. Tobin was saying. His wife reported that Mark had not eaten in days and was not sleeping much. He had recently urinated and defecated in his clothing, unaware that he was doing so. He was clearly a danger to himself.

2. Because of Mark's catatonic state, Dr. Tobin could not administer any assessment instruments. She had to rely on what she observed and what his wife reported about his recent history. She gave him the diagnosis of Major Depressive Disorder, Recurrent, with Catatonic Features.

3. Mark had a biological and psychological predisposition to a mood disorder. His mother suffered from recurrent depression, and some of Mark's experiences, such as the death of his father when he was only 5, and his inability to manage intense stress as he got older, were psychological factors contributing to his depression. He had struggled with depression for years and had had a major episode in college. This time, his anxiety about being a parent seemed to trigger the depressive episode.

4. During Mark's hospitalization, he received six ECT treatments. He improved dramatically. He was discharged on antidepressant medication and had individual therapy with Dr. Tobin for 8 months. The therapy sessions focused on helping Mark develop strategies to minimize a relapse. Mark did fine until his son was born. He then became sad and tearful. Dr. Tobin saw his twice weekly for the next few weeks and increased the dosage of his antidepressant. Weekly sessions with Dr. Tobin resumed for another year; after which he saw her once a month and, eventually, twice yearly. He continued to take a low dose of antidepressant medication. He has been fine for several years.

REVIEW AT A GLANCE

1. assess	16. consent	32. other people
2. conceptualize	17. mandated	33. mental illness
3. treat	18. warn	34. humane
4. informed consent	19. abuse; neglect	35. liberty
5. goals	20. protect themselves	36. safety
6. therapy	21. possible victim	37. unwanted treatment
7. rights	22. intention to do harm	38. least restrictive alternative
8. responsibilities	23. inappropriate	39. insanity defense
9. risks	24. sexual intimacy	40. stand trial
10. techniques	25. neutrality	41. mental disorder
11. financial	26. distance	42. legally responsible
12. confidentiality	27. expert witness	43. criminal
13. disclosures	28. child custody	44. aware of
14. private	29. dementia	45. participate in
15. privileged	30. commitment	
	31. harm	

MULTIPLE CHOICE

1. (d) is correct. Education (a and b) and licensing (c) are no guarantee of professional competence.
2. (b) is correct. (a) has to do with client consent to treatment; (c) the right of a hospitalized patient to refuse treatment; and (d) the requirements of mental health professionals to report certain types of abuse.

3. (c) is correct. (a) involves duty of a mental health professional to warn persons a client has threatened to harm; (b) involves the duty to provide the least intrusive treatment option; and (d) is determining if the client is committed to participating in treatment.

4. (d) is correct. (a) and (c) are incorrect because the professional must act if the client is a danger to himself; (b) is not necessary unless the family does not give consent.

5. (a) is correct. (c) is technically correct, but it is not why confidentiality is important; (c) and (d) have nothing to do with therapist-client confidentiality.

6. (b) is correct. Client confidentiality becomes a legal privilege if the client is involved in any legal proceeding; (a) involves duty to report certain types of abuse; (c) concerns the client's understanding of and agreement with treatment; and (d) involves therapist duty to warn people the client may have threatened to harm.

7. (c) is correct. (a) has nothing to do with responsibility to victims; (b) is not a term used in the context of treatment; and (d) are legal proceedings to protect a client who is a danger to himself or others.

8. (b) is correct. (a) involves being court-appointed to represent the interest of someone who cannot protect their legal interests; (c) is the doctrine that allows the government to intervene in a person's life in order to protect their well-being; and (d) has nothing to do with the described activity.

9 .(d) is correct. There is not such term as (a); (b) is the doctrine that allows the government to intervene in a persons' life in order to protect their well-being; and (c) is not relevant to the described activity.

10. (a) is correct. (b), (c), and (d) would only become issues if someone had been charged with a crime.

11. (d) is correct. (a) involves the legal proceeding to get treatment for a person who is a danger to self or others; (b) is a person who protects the legal interests of persons who cannot do so for themselves; and (c) is a Latin term that has nothing to do with mental health treatment.

12. (c) is correct. (a), (b),and (d) are unrelated to the described scenario.

13. (a) is correct. (b) is the opposite of what patients are supposed to have; patients do not have (c) and (d).

14. (b) is correct. Carol has (a), (c) and (d), but they are not being violated in this scenario.

15 .(c) is correct. (a) and (b) involve the government's rights to protect those who can't protect themselves; and (d) has to do with a client's knowledge of and consent to treatment.

16. (c) is correct. (d) is not a subfield; (a) is a term for mental illness; and (b) involves the treatment of mental illness.

17 .(a) is correct. (b), (c), and (d) are variations the insanity defense.

18. (b) is correct. (a), (c), and (d) are variations of the insanity defense.

19. (d) is correct. (a) is not concerned with guilty or innocence; (b) is a variation on the insanity defense; and there is no such thing as (c).

20. (a) is correct. (b) and (d) were found not guilty by reason of insanity; and (c) was found guilty in spite of an insanity plea.

CHAPTER 1
UNDERSTANDING ABNORMALITY:
A LOOK AT HISTORY AND RESEARCH METHODS

CHAPTER AT A GLANCE

Abnormal Behavior

What Causes It?
Biological Causes
Psychological Causes
Sociocultural Causes

What Is It?
Distress
Impairment
Risk to Self and Others
Socially Unacceptable
Behavior

What Are Its Effects?
Impact on the Individual
Impact on the Family
Impact on the Community
Impact on Society

Abnormal Psychology

What Are Its Research Methods?
The Scientific Method
The Experimental Method

What Is Its History
Prehistoric Times
Ancient Greece and Rome
Europe and the United States in the 1700s
The 1800s to the 1900s
The Late Twentieth Century

Adoption Study	Asylum	Baseline
Population	Biological Markers	Double-Blind Technique
Placebo Condition	Electroconvulsive Therapy	Genetic Mapping
Prevalence	Experimental Group	Biopsychosocial
Experimental Method	Probability	Case Study

The period in which a participant is observed prior to being given treatment, the purpose being to document the frequency of the target behavior. (p. 24)	Literally a place of refuge or safety, the term was originally used to describe a psychiatric facility and later came to have negative connotations. (p. 11)	A method of comparing genetic versus environmental contributions to a disorder by tracking the incidence of disorders in children whose biological parents have diagnosed psychological disorders but whose rearing parents do not. (p. 25)
An experimental procedure in which neither the person giving the treatment nor the person receiving the treatment has knowledge of whether the participant is in the experimental or control group. (p. 22)	Measurable characteristics or traits whose patterns parallel the inheritance of a disorder or other inherited characteristic. (p. 25)	The entire group of individuals sharing a particular characteristic. (p. 20)
The attempt by biological researchers to identify the structure of each gene and the characteristics each gene controls. (p. 25)	The application of electrical shock to the head for the purpose of inducing therapeutically effective seizures. (p. 24)	The condition used in experimental research in which people are given an inert substance or treatment that is similar in all other ways to the experimental treatment. (p. 21)
A model in which the interaction of biology, psychology, and sociocultural factors are seen as influencing the development of the individual. (p. 7)	The group of participants that receives the "treatment" thought to influence the behavior under study. (p. 21)	The number of people who have ever had a disorder at a given time or over a specified period. (p. 24)
An intensive study of a single person described in detail. (p. 24)	The odds or likelihood that an event will happen. (p. 19)	A research method that involves altering or changing the conditions to which participants are exposed (independent variable) and observing the effects of this manipulation in the behavior of the participants (dependent variable). (p. 21)

Psychoanalysis	Hypnotism	Concordance Rate
Psychoanalytic Model	Hypothesis Formation	Control Group
Psychosurgery	Hysteria	Correlation
Psychotherapy	Incidence	Cross fostering Study
Quasi-experimental Design	Diathesis-Stress Model	Independent Variable

Agreement ratio between people diagnosed as having the disorder and their relatives. (p. 25)	The process of inducing a trance state. (p. 16)	A theory and system of practice that relies heavily on the concepts of the unconscious mind, inhibited sexual impulses, early development, and the use of "free association" technique and dream analysis. (p. 16)
The group of participants that does not receive the treatment thought to influence the behavior under study. (p. 21)	The stage of research in which the researcher generates ideas about cause-effect relationships between the behaviors under study. (p. 19)	An approach that seeks explanations of abnormal behavior in the workings of unconscious psychological processes. (p. 15)
An association, or co-relation, between two variables, that can range in value from +1.00 to −1.00. (p. 22)	A disorder in which psychological problems become expressed in physical form. (p. 16)	A form of brain surgery, the purpose of which is to reduce psychological disturbance. (p. 20)
A method of comparing genetic versus environmental contributions to a disorder by tracking the incidence of disorders in children who are adopted by parents with psychological disorders but whose biological parents are psychologically healthy. (p. 25)	The frequency of new cases within a given time period. (p. 23)	The treatment of abnormal behavior through psychological techniques. (p. 16)
The variable whose level is adjusted or controlled by the experimenter. (p. 21)	A proposal that people are born with a predisposition (diathesis) that places them at risk for developing a psychological disorder. (p. 8)	A design like an experimental design but lacking the key ingredient of random assignment to groups. (p. 22)

Representativeness	Deinstitutionalization	Medical Model
Sample	Demand Characteristics	Mesmerism
Single-Subject Design	Dependent Variable	Monozygotic Twins
Survey Method	Dizygotic Twins	Moral Treatment
Multiple Baseline Approach	Trephining	Variable

The view that abnormal behaviors result from physical problems that should be medically treated. (p..15)

The release of psychiatric patients into community treatment sites as a result of dramatic changes in public policy. (p. 17)

The extent to which a sample adequately reflects the characteristics of the population from which it is drawn. (p. 21)

Derived from the name, Mesmer, used to refer to a process of bringing about a state of heightened suggestibility through the words and actions of a charismatic individual. (p. 16)

The expectations of participants in an experiment about what is going to happen to them or the proper way to respond. (p. 22)

A selection of individuals from a larger group. (p. 20)

Identical twins who share the same genetic inheritance. (p. 25)

The variable whose value is the outcome of the experimenter's manipulation of the independent variable. (p. 21)

An experimental procedure in which one person at a time is studied in both the experimental and the control conditions. (p. 24)

The philosophy that people, with proper care, develop self-control over their own disturbed behaviors. (p. 13)

Nonidentical or fraternal twins who are genetically alike only to the same degree as other siblings. (p. 25)

A research tool used to gather information from a sample of people considered representative of a particular population in which participants are asked to answer questions about a topic of concern. (p. 23)

A dimension along which people, things, or events differ. (p. 21)

The drilling of a hole in the skull presumably as a way of treating psychological disorders. (p. 9)

Observing different dependent variable in the same person over the course of treatment, or observing the behavior as it occurs under different conditions. (p. 25)

CHAPTER 2
CLASSIFICATION AND TREATMENT PLANS

CHAPTER AT A GLANCE

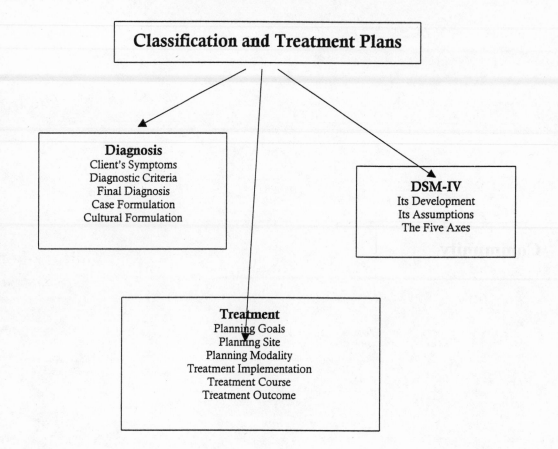

Classification and Treatment Plans

Diagnosis
Client's Symptoms
Diagnostic Criteria
Final Diagnosis
Case Formulation
Cultural Formulation

DSM-IV
Its Development
Its Assumptions
The Five Axes

Treatment
Planning Goals
Planning Site
Planning Modality
Treatment Implementation
Treatment Course
Treatment Outcome

272

Adjustment Disorder	Axis	Base Rate
Case Formulation	Client	Clinical Psychologist
Community Mental Health Centers	Comorbid	Culture-bound Syndromes
Day Treatment Programs	Decision Tree	*Diagnostic and Statistical Manual of Mental Disorders (DSM)*
Differential Diagnosis	Family Therapy	Global Assessment of Functioning (GAF)

The frequency with which a disorder occurs in the general population (p. 38)	A class of information regarding an aspect of the individual's function. (p. 42)	A reaction that is more extreme than would be expected under the circumstances (p. 43)
A mental health professional with training in the behavioral sciences who provides direct service to clients. (p. 37)	A person seeking psychological treatment. (p. 36)	A clinician's analysis of the factors that might have influenced the client's current psychological status. (p. 49)
Recurrent patterns of abnormal behavior or experience that are limited to specific societies or cultural areas. (p. 50)	Multiple diagnostic conditions that occur simultaneously within the same individual. (p. 37)	Outpatient clinics that provide psychological services on a sliding fee scale to serve individuals who live in certain geographical areas. (p. 55)
A book published by the American Psychiatric Association that contains standard terms and definitions of psychological disorders. (p. 38)	A strategy used for diagnosis, consisting of a series of yes/no questions that guide clinicians in ruling in or out psychological disorders. (p. 48)	A structured program in a community treatment facility that provides activities similar to those provided in a psychiatric hospital. (p. 55)
Axis V of the *DSM-IV*, a scale that rates the individual's overall level of psychological health. (p. 46)	Psychological treatment in which the therapist works with several or all members of the family. (p. 55)	The process of systematically ruling out alternative diagnoses. (p. 48)

Group Therapy	Halfway Houses	Individual Psychotherapy
Milieu Therapy	Modality	Multiaxial System
Neurosis	Patient	Principle Diagnosis
Prognosis	Psychiatrists	Psychological Testing
Psychosis	Reliability	Syndrome

Psychological treatment
in which the therapist works
on a one-to-one basis
with the client. (p. 55)

A community treatment
facility designed for
deinstitutionalizing clients
coming out of a hospital who
are not yet ready for
independent living. (p. 55)

Psychological treatment in
which the therapist facilitates
discussion among a group of
several clients who talk
together about problems.
(p. 55)

A multidimensional
classification and diagnostic
system that summarizes a variety
of relevant information about an
individual's physical and
psychological functioning.
(p. 42)

The form in which
psychotherapy is offered.
(p. 55)

A treatment approach used in
an inpatient psychiatric
facility in which all facets of the
milieu, or environment,
are components of the
treatment. (p. 55)

The disorder that is
considered to be the primary
reason the individual seeks
professional help. (p. 49)

Consistent with the medical
model, a term used to refer to
someone who receives
treatment. (p. 36)

A nontechnical term used to refer
to behavior that involves
symptoms that are distressing to
the individual and that the
person recognizes as unacceptable.
(p. 42)

A broad range of measurement
techniques, all of which involve
having people provide
scorable information about
their psychological
functioning. (p. 38)

Medical doctors with
advanced training in treating
people with psychological
disorders. (p. 37)

A client's
likelihood of recovering
from a disorder. (p. 46)

A collection of
symptoms that together
form a definable pattern.
(p. 41)

The consistency of
measurements or
diagnoses. (p. 38)

A nontechnical term
used to describe various forms
of behavior involving loss
of contact with reality.
(p. 42)

Validity

How well a test measures
what it is designed to measure.
The extent to which a
diagnosis or rating accurately
and distinctly characterizes
a person's psychological
status. (p. 38)

CHAPTER 3
ASSESSMENT

CHAPTER AT A GLANCE

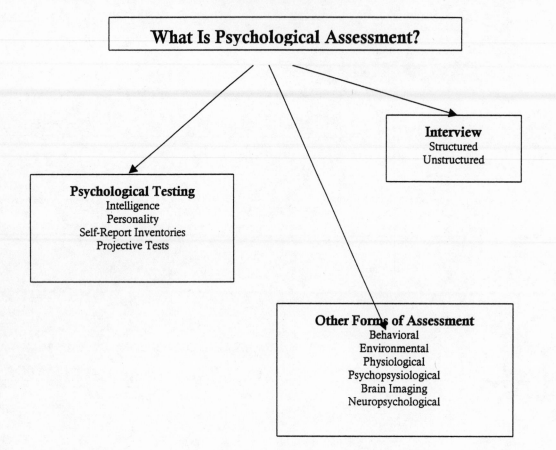

What Is Psychological Assessment?

Interview
Structured
Unstructured

Psychological Testing
Intelligence
Personality
Self-Report Inventories
Projective Tests

Other Forms of Assessment
Behavioral
Environmental
Physiological
Psychopsysiological
Brain Imaging
Neuropsychological

Assessment	Unstructured Interview	Personal History
Family History	Structured Interview	Mental Status
Mental Status Examination	Motor Behavior	Hyperactivity
Psychomotor Agitation	Psychomotor Retardation	Catatonia
Compulsion	Orientation	Content of Thought

Information gathered in a psychological assessment regarding important events and relationships in areas of the client's life such as school performance, peer relationships, employment, and health. (p. 65)	A series of open-ended questions aimed at determining the client's reasons for being in treatment, symptoms, health status, family background, and life history. (p. 64)	The evaluation of a person in Terms of the psychological, physical, and social factors that have the most influence on the individual's functioning. (p. 64)
A term used by clinicians to describe what the client thinks about and how the client thinks, talks, and acts. (p. 66)	A standardized series of assessment questions, with a predetermined wording and order. (p. 65)	Information gathered in a psychological assessment regarding the sequence of major events in the lives of the client's relatives, including those who are closest to the client as well as more distantly related family. (p. 65)
A motor pattern involving abnormally energized physical activity, often characterized by quick movements and fast talking. (p. 66)	How a person moves. May refer to fine movements such as handling small objects or large movements involved in walking. (p. 68)	A method of objectively assessing a client's behavior and functioning in a number of spheres with particular attention to the symptoms associated with psychological disturbance. (p. 67)
Extreme Motor disturbances in a psychotic disorder not attributable to physiological causes. (p. 68)	A motor pattern involving abnormally slow movements and lethargy. (p. 68)	A motor pattern involving an obvious level of discomfort in which the individual appears to be restless and stirred up. (p. 68)
Ideas that fill a client's mind. (p. 68)	A person's awareness of time, place, and identity. (p. 68)	A repetitive and seemingly purposeful behavior performed in response to uncontrollable urges or according to a ritualistic or stereotyped set of rules. (p. 68)

Obsession	Delusions	Overvalued Idea
Magical Thinking	Thinking Style and Language	Affect
Inappropriate Affect	Intensity of Affect	Mobility of Affect
Range of Affect	Mood	Normal Mood
Euthymic Mood	Dysphoric Mood	Euphoric Mood

A thought that has an odd and absurd quality but is not usually bizarre or deeply entrenched. (p. 69)	Deeply entrenched false beliefs not consistent with the client's intelligence or cultural background. (p. 69)	An unwanted thought, word, phrase, or image that persistently and repeatedly comes into a person's mind and causes distress. (p. 68)
An individual's outward expression of emotion. (p. 69)	To indicate how a person thinks. This includes information on the client's vocabulary use and sentence structure. (p. 69)	A peculiarity of thinking in which an individual makes a connection between two objects or events that other people would see as unrelated. (p. 69)
The ease and speed with which people move from one kind of feeling or level of emotional intensity to another. (p. 69)	Strength of emotional expression. (p. 69)	The extent to which a person's emotional expressiveness fails to correspond to the content of what is being discussed. (p. 69)
A feeling state that is neither unduly happy nor sad, but shows day-to-day variations within a relatively limited range considered to be appropriate. (p. 71)	A person's experience of emotion. (p. 70)	The extent and variety of an individual's emotional expression. (p. 70)
A feeling state that is more cheerful and elated than average, possible even ecstatic. (p. 71)	Unpleasant feelings such as sadness or irritability. (p. 71)	Normal mood (p. 71)

Hallucination	Auditory Hallucination	Command Hallucination
Visual Hallucination	Olfactory Hallucination	Somatic Hallucination
Gustatory Hallucination	Depersonalization	Identity Confusion
Insight	Judgment	Psychometrics
Reliability	Validity	Standardized

A hallucination in which an individual hears an instruction to take some action. (p. 72)

A hallucination that involves hearing sounds, often voices or even entire conversations. (p. 72)

A false perception not corresponding to the objective stimuli present in the environment. (p. 71)

A hallucination involving the false perception of bodily sensation. (p. 73)

A hallucination involving the perception of a smell. (p. 72)

A hallucination involving the false visual perception of objects or persons. (p. 72)

A lack of clear sense of who one is, ranging from confusion about one's role in the world to actual delusional thinking. (p. 73)

An altered experience of the self, ranging from feeling that one's body is not connected to one's mind to the feeling that one is not real. (p. 73)

A hallucination involving the false sensation of taste, usually unpleasant. (p. 72)

Literally means "measurement of the mind," reflecting the goal of finding the most suitable tests for psychological variables under study. (p. 74)

The intellectual process in which an individual considers and weighs options in order to make a decision. (p. 73)

A sense of understanding and awareness about oneself and one's world. (p. 73)

Uniform procedures used for both test administration and scoring. (p. 74)

The extent to which a test, diagnosis or rating accurately and distinctly characterizes a person's psychological status. (p. 74)

The consistency of measurements or diagnoses. (p. 74)

Percentile Score	Intelligence Quotient	Deviation IQ
Self-report Clinical Inventory	Projective Test	Behavioral Assessment
Behavioral Self-Report	Behavioral Interviewing	Antecedents
Consequences	Self-Monitoring	Target Behavior
Behavioral Checklists and Inventories	Behavioral Observation	*In vivo* Observation

An index of intelligence derived from comparing the individual's score on an intelligence test with the mean score for that individual's reference group. (p. 76)	A method of quantifying performance on an intelligence test, originally calculated according to the ratio of a person's tested age to that person's chronological age, and changed in the 1960 revision of the Stanford-Binet to the deviation IQ. (p. 76)	The percent of those who obtain scores below a certain number on a test. (p. 74)
A number of measurement techniques based on objective recording of the individual's behavior. (p. 86)	A technique in which the test-taker is presented with an ambiguous item or task and asked to respond by providing his or her own meaning or perception. (p. 83)	A psychological test with standardized questions having fixed response categories that the test-taker completes independently, "self"-reporting the extent to which the responses are accurate characterizations. (p. 77)
Events preceding a specified behavior. (p. 86)	A specialized form of interviewing in which the clinician asks for information on the behavior under consideration as well as what preceded and followed that behavior. (p. 86)	A method of behavioral assessment in which the individual provides information about the frequency of particular behaviors. (p. 86)
A behavior of interest or concern in assessment. (p. 87)	A self-report technique in which the client keeps a record of the frequency of the specified behaviors. (p. 87)	Events following a specified behavior. (p. 86)
A form of behavioral assessment in which the individual is observed in the natural context where the target behavior occurs. (p. 87)	A behavioral method of assessment in which the clinician observes the individual and records the frequency of specific behaviors along with any relevant situational factors. (p. 87)	Behavioral assessment devices in which the client checks off or rates whether certain events or experiences have transpired. (p. 87)

Reactivity	Analog Observation	Environmental Assessment Scales
Electrocardiogram (ECG)	Blood Pressure	Electromyography (EMG)
Electrodermal Response	Galvanic Skin Response (GSR)	Electroencephalogram (EEG)
Computerized Axial Tomography (CAT scan)	Magnetic Resonance Imaging (MRI)	Functional Magnetic Resonance Imaging
Positron Emission Tomography (PET scan)	Single Photon Emission Computerized Tomography (SPECT)	Neuropsychological Assessment

Measures of key environmental dimensions hypothesized to influence behaviors. (p. 88)	A form of behavioral assessment that takes place in a setting or context specifically designed for observing the target behavior. (p. 87)	Change in a person's behavior in response to knowledge that he or she is being observed. (p. 87)
A measurement of electrical activity of the muscles. (p. 88)	The resistance offered by the arteries to the flow of blood as it is pumped from the heart. (p. 88)	A measure of electrical impulses that pass through the heart. (p. 88)
A measure of changes in the electrical activity of the brain. (p. 88)	See Electrodermal response. (p. 88)	Minor electrical changes in the skin that result from sweating. Also called galvanic skin response (GSR). (p. 88)
A variant of the traditional MRI, which makes it possible to construct a picture of actual activity in the brain. (p. 89)	Uses radiowaves rather than X-rays to construct a picture of the living brain based on the water content of various tissues. (p. 89)	A series of X-rays taken from various angles around the body that are integrated by a computer to produce a composite picture. (p. 89)
A process of gathering information about a client's brain functioning on the basis of performance on psychological tests. (p. 90)	A variant of the PET scan that permits a longer and more detailed imaging analysis. (p. 89)	A measure of brain activity in which a small amount of radioactive sugar is injected into an individual's bloodstream, following which a computer measures the varying levels of radiation in different parts of the brain and yields a multicolored image. (p. 89)

CHAPTER 4
THEORETICAL PERSPECTIVES

Chapter At A Glance

Theoretical Perspectives and Treatment

Humanistic Perspective
Person-Centered
Self-Actualization
HumanisticTreatment

Psychodynamic Perspective
Freudian Psychoanalytic
Post-Freudian Theorists
Object Relations Theorists
Psychodynamic Treatment

Biological Perspective
Nervous System
Endocrine System
Genetic Influences
Biological Treatment
Medication
Psychosurgery
ECT
Biofeedback

Sociocultural Perspective
Family Perspective
Social Discrimination
Social Influences
Historical Events
Sociocultural Treatment
Family Therapy
Group Therapy
Milieu Therapy

Behavioral and Cognitive Perspectives
Classical Conditioning
Operant Conditioning
Social Learning
Social Cognition
Behavioral and Cognitive Therapies
Conditioning Techniques
Contingency Management Techniques
Modeling and Self-Efficacy Training
Cognitive Restructuring
REBT

Anal Stage	**Attachment Style**	**Automatic Thoughts**
Aversive Conditioning	**Behavioral Perspective**	**Biofeedback**
Biological Perspective	**Cell Body**	**Cerebral Cortex**
Cerebral Hemispheres	**Chromosomes**	**Classical Conditioning**
Complex Traits	**Cognitive Restructuring**	**Cognitive-Behavioral Perspective**

Ideas so deeply entrenched that the individual is not even aware that they lead to feelings of unhappiness and discouragement.
(p. 118)

The way a person relates to a caregiver.
(p. 107)

A period of psychosexual development in which the toddler's pleasure focuses on anal stimulation and holding onto and expelling feces.
(p. 103)

A procedure in which people learn to monitor and control their autonomic responses, such as blood pressure, heart rate, skin conductance, and muscular tension.
(p. 130)

A theoretical perspective in which it is assumed that abnormality is caused by faulty learning experiences.
(p. 115)

A form of conditioning in which a painful stimulus is paired with an initially neutral stimulus. (p. 116)

The thin covering of neural tissue surrounding the outer surface of the brain.
(p. 124)

The part of the neuron that houses the structures responsible for keeping the neuron alive.
(p. 123)

A theoretical perspective in which it is assumed that disturbances in emotions, behavior, and cognitive processes are caused by abnormalities in the functioning of the body.
(p. 122)

The learning connection between an originally neutral and a naturally evoking stimulus that produces an automatic reflexive reaction.
(p. 115)

Structures found in each cell that contain the genes and exist in a pair, with one chromosome contributed from each parent at conception. (p. 127)

The two parts (or lobes) of the cerebral cortex.
(p. 125)

A theoretical perspective in which it is assumed that abnormality is caused by maladaptive thought processes that result in dysfunctional behavior. (p. 115)

An acquired response to a stimulus that was previously neutral. (p. 116)

Characteristics that reflect an inheritance pattern that does not follow the simple rules of dominant and recessive genes. (p. 108)

Client-centered	Conditioned Response	Conditioned Stimulus
Conditions of Worth	Congruence	Contingency Management
Corpus Callosum	Counterconditioning	Defense Mechanisms
Deficit Needs	Dendrites	Deoxyribonucleic Acid (DNA)
Diathesis-Stress Model	Discrimination	Dominant

A previously neutral stimulus that, after repeated pairings with the unconditioned stimulus, elicits a conditioned response. (p. 115)

An acquired response to a stimulus that was previously neutral. (p. 116)

An approach based on the belief held by Rogers that people are innately good and that the potential for self-improvement lies within the individual. (p. 108)

A form of behavioral therapy that involves the principle of rewarding a client for desired behaviors and not providing rewards for undesired behaviors. (p. 120)

A central feature of Roger's theory which states that a well-adjusted person's self-image should match with the person's experiences. (p. 108)

Conditions in which the child receives love only when he or she fulfills certain demands. (p. 108)

Tactics that keep unacceptable thoughts, instincts, and feelings out of conscious awareness and thus protect the ego against anxiety. (p. 99)

The process of replacing an undesired response to a stimulus with an acceptable response. (p. 120)

The band or bundle of axons connecting the right and left hemispheres of the brain. (p. 125)

A molecule whose characteristics will be expressed in the phenotype no matter what gene is paired with it from the other parent. (p. 128)

The fibers on neurons that receive information from other neurons. (p. 123)

Needs that are lower on Maslow's hierarchy of needs because they describe a state in which the individual seeks to obtain something that is lacking. (p. 109)

A gene whose characteristics will be expressed in the phenotype no matter what gene is paired with it from the other parent. (p. 128)

The process through which learning becomes increasingly specific to a given situation. (p. 116)

The proposal that people are born with a predisposition (diathesis) that places them at risk for developing a psychological disorder if exposed to certain extremely stressful life experiences. (p. 129)

Dream Analysis	Dysfunctional Attitudes	Ego
Electroconvulsive Therapy (ECT)	Excitatory Response	Existential
Extinction	Family Dynamics	Family Perspective
Fixation	Free Association	Frontal Lobe
Fully Functioning	Gene	Generalization

The structure of personality that gives the individual the mental powers of judgment, memory, perception, and decision making, enabling the individual to adapt to the realities of the external world. (p. 99)	Personal rules or values people hold that interfere with adequate adjustment. (p. 118)	A method used in psychoanalysis in which the client relates the events of a dream to the clinician and free associates these events. (p. 105)
A theoretical position in psychology that emphasizes the importance of fully appreciating each moment as it occurs. (p. 108)	A synapse in which the message communicated to the receiving neuron makes it more likely to trigger a response. (p. 123)	The application of electrical shock to the head for the purpose of inducing therapeutically effective seizures (p. 129)
A theoretical perspective in which it is assumed that abnormality is caused by disturbances in the pattern of interactions and relationships within the family. (p. 112)	The pattern of interactions among members of a family. (p. 112)	The cessation of behavior in the absence of reinforcement. (p. 117)
The lobe of the cerebral cortex near the forehead which is involved in movement. (p. 125)	A method used in psychoanalysis in which the client speaks freely, saying whatever comes to mind. (p. 105)	Arrested development at a particular stage of psychosexual development attributable to excessive or inadequate gratification at that stage. (p. 103)
The expansion of learning from the original situation to one that is similar. (p. 116)	The basic unit of heredity. (p. 127)	A term used to describe an individual with an accurate view of self and experiences. (p. 108)

Genital Stage	Genitality	Genome
Genotype	Heritability	Hierarchy of Needs
Hippocampus	Humanistic	Hypothalamus
Id	Incongruence	Inhibitory Response
Irrational Beliefs	Latency	Libido

The complete set of instructions for "building" all the cells that make up an organism. (p. 127)	The ability to express sexual feelings in a mature way and in appropriate contexts, reached when the individual is able to "work" and "love." (p. 104)	A period of psychosexual development coinciding with the resurfacing of sexual energy just prior to puberty. (p. 103)
According to Maslow, the order in which human needs must be fulfilled. (p. 109)	The proportion of the offspring's phenotype that is due to genetic causes. (p. 129)	The genetic program that guides the growth and activity of the body's cells. (p. 127)
A small structure in the brain that coordinates the activities of the central nervous system with systems involved in the control of emotion, motivation, and bodily regulation. (p. 125)	An approach to personality and psychological disorder that regards people as motivated by the need to understand themselves and the world and to derive greater enrichment from their experiences by fulfilling their unique potential. (p. 107)	A limbic system structure responsible for the consolidation of short-term memory into long-term memory. (p. 125)
A synapse in which the message communicated to the receiving neuron decreases the activity of the receiving neuron. (p. 123)	A mismatch between a person's self-perception and reality. (p. 108)	The structure of personality that contains the sexual and aggressive instincts. (p. 98)
An instinctual pressure for gratification of sexual and aggressive desires. (p. 99)	A period of psychosexual development during which the child interacts with peers and imitates the behavior of parents and other adults of the same biological sex as the child. (p. 103)	Views about the self and the world that are unrealistic, extreme, and illogical. (p. 118)

Limbic System	**Milieu Therapy**	**Modeling**
Multi-factorial Polygenic Threshold Model	**Mutations**	**Negative Reinforcement**
Neuron	**Neurotransmitter**	**Neutrality**
Object Relations	**Occipital Lobe**	**Operant Conditioning**
Oral Stage	**Parasympathetic Nervous System**	**Parietal Lobe**

Acquiring new behavior by imitating that of another person. (p. 117)	A treatment approach used in an inpatient psychiatric facility in which all facets of the milieu, or environment, are components of the treatment. (p. 114)	A set of loosely connected structures that form a ring within the center portion of the brain and that provide the neurological basis for the interaction between "rational" and "irrational" human behaviors. (p. 125)
The removal of aversive conditions when certain behaviors are performed. (p. 117)	An alteration that develops in genes when DNA reproduces itself. (p. 127)	The position that several genes with varying influence are involved in the transmission of a disorder or characteristic. (p. 129)
An attitude displayed by clinicians in which the clinician does not reveal his or her preferences, personal background, or reactions to the client's revelations in therapy. (p. 105)	A chemical substance released from the transmitting neuron into the synaptic cleft, where it drifts across the synapse and is absorbed by the receiving neuron. (p. 124)	The nerve cell; the basic unit structure and function within the nervous system. (p. 123)
A learning process in which an individual acquires a set of behaviors through reinforcement. (p. 116)	The part of the cerebral cortex at the back of the head above the spinal column which is involved in vision. (p. 125)	One's unconscious representations of important people in one's life. (p. 105)
The part of the cerebral cortex which spans the top of the head and is involved in the perception of bodily sensations such as touch. (p. 125)	The part of the autonomic nervous system that carries out the maintenance functions of the body when it is at rest, directing most of the body's activities to producing and restoring energy so that it can be used when the body is in action. (p. 126)	A period of psychosexual development in which the infant's pleasure comes from stimulation of the mouth. (p. 103)

Participant Modeling	Peak Experiences	Penetrance
Peripheral Nervous System	Person-centered Theory	Phallic Stage
Phenotype	Pituitary Gland	Pleasure Principle
Polygenic	Positive Reinforcement	Prefrontal Area
Primary Process Thinking	Primary Reinforcers	Psychodynamic Perspective

The extent to which a genotype is expressed in the individual's phenotypes. (p. 121)

Feelings of tremendous inner happiness and being totally in harmony with oneself and the world. (p. 109)

A form of therapy in which the therapist first shows the client a desired behavior and then guides the client through the behavioral change. (p. 121)

A period of psychosexual development in which the genital area of the body is the focus of the child's sexual feelings. (p. 103)

The humanistic theory that focuses on the uniqueness of each individual, the importance of allowing each individual to achieve maximum fulfillment of potential, and the need for the individual to confront honestly the reality of his or her experiences in the world. (p. 108)

The branch of the nervous system with pathways that lie outside the brain and spinal cord. (p. 122)

A motivating force oriented toward the immediate and total gratification of sensual needs and desires. (p. 98)

A major gland in the endocrine system, located in the brain and under the control of the hypothalamus; sometimes called the "master" gland. (p. 126)

The expression of the genetic program in the individual's physical and psychological attributes. (p. 127)

The area at the very front of the cerebral cortex responsible for abstract planning and judgment. (p. 125)

Providing reward when certain behaviors are performed. (p. 117)

A model of inheritance in which more than one gene participates in the process of determining a given characteristic. (p. 128)

The theoretical orientation in psychology that emphasizes unconscious determinates of behavior. (p. 129)

Rewards that satisfy a biological need. making them intrinsically rewarding. (p. 117)

A loosely associated, idiosyncratic, and distorted cognitive representation of the world. (p. 99)

Psychdynamics	Psychosexual Stages	Psychosurgery
Punishment	Reality Principle	Recessive
Reinforcement	Resistance	Reticular Formation
Secondary Process Thinking	Secondary Reinforcers	Selective Serotonin Reuptake Inhibitors
Self-actualization	Self-efficacy	Shaping

A form of brain surgery, the purpose of which is to reduce psychological disturbance. (p. 129)	According to psychoanalytic theory, the normal sequence of development through which each individual passes between infancy and adulthood. (p. 99)	The processes of interaction among personality structures that lie beneath the surface of observable behavior. (p. 99)
A gene whose characteristic will be expressed only if paired with a recessive gene. (p. 128)	A motivational force that leads the individual to confront the constraints of the external world. (p. 99)	The application of an aversive stimulus. (p. 117)
A diffuse collection of ascending and descending pathways that controls the level and direction of arousal or brain activity through the excitation of certain pathways and the inhibition of others. (p. 124)	The unconscious blocking of anxiety-provoking thoughts and feelings. (p. 106)	The "strengthening" of a behavior. (p. 117)
Medications that block the reuptake of serotonin at the synapse, enabling more of this neurotransmitter to be available at the receptor sites. (p. 130)	Rewards that derive their value from association with primary reinforcers. (p. 117)	The kind of thinking involved in logical and rational problem solving. (p. 99)
A learning technique in which reinforcement is provided for behaviors that increasingly resemble a desired outcome. (p. 117)	The individual's perception of competence in various life situations. (p. 118)	The maximum realization of the individual's potential for psychological growth. (p. 109)

Social Cognition	Social-cognitive Theory	Social Learning
Sociocultural Perspective	Somatic Nervous System	Somatic Therapies
Stimulus Discrimination	Subcortical Structures	Superego
Sympathetic Nervous System	Synapse	Synaptic Cleft
Systematic Desensitization	Theoretical Perspective	Token Economy

A theoretical perspective that focuses on how people develop personality and psychological disorders through their personal relationships with others and through observation of other people. (p. 118)	A theoretical perspective that focuses on thought processes and how those processes influence overt behavior. (p. 118)	The factors that influence the way people perceive themselves and other people form judgments about the causes of behavior. (p. 118)
A term given to therapies that involve treatments that act on known or presumed causes of the disorder. (p. 129)	The branch of the nervous system involving pathways that carry sensory information to and from the brain and spinal cord. (p. 122)	The theoretical perspective that emphasizes the ways in which individuals are influenced by people, social situations, and social forces in the world around them. (p. 112)
The structure of personality that includes the conscious and the ego ideal; it incorporates societal prohibitions and exerts control over the seeking of instinctual gratification. (p. 99)	Part of the brain that operates much of the time as a relay station to prepare information for processing in the cerebral cortex and to carry out instructions for action that the cerebral cortex gives to the muscles and glands. (p. 124)	Differentiation between two stimuli that possess similar but essentially different characteristics. (p. 116)
The gap at the juncture between neurons. (p. 123)	Points of communication between neurons. (p. 123)	The part of the autonomic nervous system primarily responsible for mobilizing the body's stored resources when these resources are needed for activities that require energy. (p. 126)
A form of contingency management in which a client who performs desired activities earns chips or tokens that can later be exchanged for tangible benefits. (p. 121)	An orientation to understanding the causes of human behavior and the treatment of abnormality. (p. 98)	A variant of counterconditioning that involves presenting the client with progressively more anxiety provoking images in a relaxed state. (p. 120)

Transference	Unconditional Positive Regard	Unconditioned Response
Unconditioned Stimulus	Vicarious Reinforcement	Working Through

A reflexive response that occurs naturally in the presence of the unconditioned stimulus without having been learned. (p. 116)

A method used in client-centered therapy involving total acceptance of what the client says, does, and feels. (p. 110)

The carrying over toward the therapist of the feelings the client had toward parents or other significant people in the client's life. (p. 105)

A phase of psychoanalytic treatment in which the clinician helps the client achieve a healthier resolution of issues that had occurred in the client's early childhood environment. (p. 106)

A form of learning in which a new behavior is acquired through the process of watching someone else receive reinforcement for the same behavior. (p. 118)

The stimulus that naturally produces a response without having been learned. (p. 115)

CHAPTER 5
PERSONALITY DISORDERS

CHAPTER AT A GLANCE

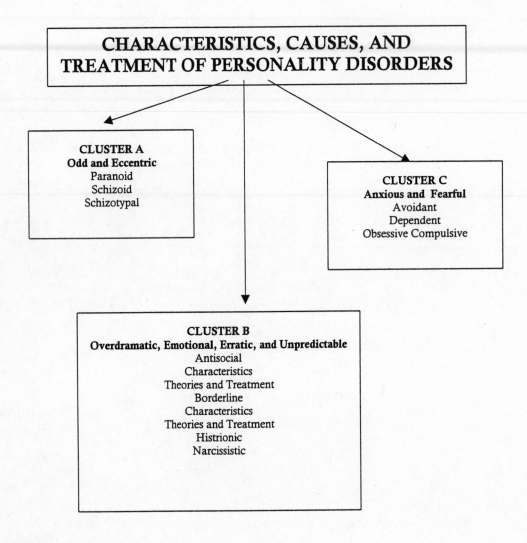

CHARACTERISTICS, CAUSES, AND TREATMENT OF PERSONALITY DISORDERS

CLUSTER A
Odd and Eccentric
Paranoid
Schizoid
Schizotypal

CLUSTER C
Anxious and Fearful
Avoidant
Dependent
Obsessive Compulsive

CLUSTER B
Overdramatic, Emotional, Erratic, and Unpredictable
Antisocial
Characteristics
Theories and Treatment
Borderline
Characteristics
Theories and Treatment
Histrionic
Narcissistic

Adult Antisocial Behavior	**Antisocial Personality Disorder**	**Avoidant Personality Disorder**
Borderline Personality Disorder	**Dependent Personality Disorder**	**Grandiosity**
Histrionic Personality Disorder	**Identity**	**Latent**
Narcissistic Personality Disorder	**Obsessive-compulsive Personality Disorder**	**Paranoid Personality Disorder**
Parasuicide	**Personality Disorder**	**Personality Trait**

A personality disorder whose prominent feature is that the individual desires, but is fearful of, any involvement with other people and is terrified at the prospect of being publicly embarrassed. (p. 142)	A personality disorder characterized by a lack of regard for society's moral or legal standards. (p. 141)	Illegal or immoral behavior, such as stealing, lying, and cheating. (p. 142)
An exaggerated view of oneself as possessing special and extremely favorable personal qualities and abilities. (p. 152)	A personality disorder whose main characteristic is that the individual is extremely passive and tends to cling to other people, to the point of being unable to make any decisions or to take independent action. (p. 158)	A personality disorder characterized by a pervasive pattern of poor impulse control and instability in mood, interpersonal relationships, and self-image. (p. 145)
A state in which a disorder is present and capable of becoming evident but is not yet obvious or active. (p. 156)	One's self-concept or sense of who one is. (p. 147)	A personality disorder characterized by exaggerated emotional reactions, approaching theatricality, in everyday behavior. (p. 151)
A personality disorder whose outstanding feature is that the individual is extremely suspicious of others and is always on guard against potential danger or harm. (p. 154)	A personality disorder characterized by recurrent obsessions or compulsions that are inordinately time-consuming or that cause significant distress and impairment. (p. 160)	A personality disorder primarily characterized by an unrealistic, inflated sense of self-importance and a lack of sensitivity to the needs of other people. (p. 152)
An enduring pattern of perceiving, relating to, and thinking about the environment and others. (p. 140)	Ingrained patterns of relating to other people, situations, and events with a rigid and maladaptive quality. (p. 140)	A suicidal gesture to get attention from loved ones, family, or professionals. (p. 147)

Psychopathy	Schizoid Personality Disorder	Schizophrenia Spectrum Disorders
	Schizotypal Personality Disorder	Splitting

A term used by some researchers to characterize a continuum of disorders, including schizophrenia, schizoid personality disorder, and schizotypal personality disorder. (p. 155)	A personality disorder primarily characterized by an indifference to social relationships, as well as a very limited range of emotional experience and expression. (p. 155)	A personality type characterized by a cluster of traits that constitutes the core of what is now called antisocial personality disorder. (p. 141)
A defense common in people with borderline personality disorder, in which individuals perceive others, or themselves, as being all good or all bad, usually resulting in disturbed interpersonal relationships. (p. 147)	A personality disorder that primarily involves peculiarities and eccentricities of thought, behavior, appearance, and interpersonal style. People with this disorder may have peculiar ideas, such as magical thinking and beliefs in psychic phenomena. (p. 147)	

CHAPTER **6**
ANXIETY DISORDERS

CHAPTER AT A GLANCE

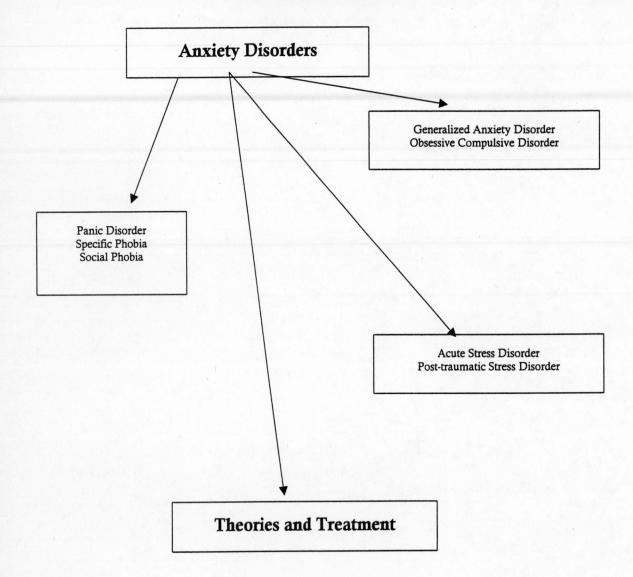

Anxiety Disorders

Panic Disorder
Specific Phobia
Social Phobia

Generalized Anxiety Disorder
Obsessive Compulsive Disorder

Acute Stress Disorder
Post-traumatic Stress Disorder

Theories and Treatment

Acute Stress Disorder	Agoraphobia	Anxiety
Anxiety Disorders	Aversions	Benzodiazepines
Compulsion	Conditioned Fear Reaction	Denial/Intrusion Phase
Fear	Flashback	Flooding
Generalized Anxiety Disorder	Graduated Exposure	Hypervigilent

A future-oriented and global response, involving both cognitive and emotional components in which the individual is inordinately apprehensive, tense, and uneasy about the prospect of something terrible happening. (p. 174)	Intense anxiety about being trapped or stranded in a situation without help if a panic attack occurs. (p. 175)	An anxiety disorder that develops after a traumatic event with symptoms such as depersonalization, numbing, dissociative amnesia, intense anxiety, hypervigilance, and impairment of everyday functioning. (p. 192)
Medications that slow down central nervous system reactions that are thought to contribute to anxiety. (p. 178)	Responses of discomfort or dislike to a particular object or situation. (p. 179)	A group of disorders characterized by intense, irrational, and incapacitating apprehension. (p. 174)
A period following a traumatic event during which the person alternates between denial, the experience of forgetting the event or pretending it did not occur, and intrusion. (p. 194)	Acquired associations between an internal or external cue and feelings of intense anxiety. (p. 177)	A repetitive and seemingly purposeful behavior performed in response to uncontrollable urges or according to a ritualistic or stereotyped set of rules. (p. 187)
A behavioral technique in which the client is immersed in the sensation of anxiety by being exposed to the feared situation in its entirety. (p. 182)	Graphic and terrifying illusions and hallucinations associated with a traumatic event which arise spontaneously. (p. 194)	An innate, almost biologically based alarm response to a dangerous or life-threatening situation. (p. 174)
On edge and on guard against danger.	A procedure in which clients expose themselves to increasingly greater anxiety-provoking situations. (p. 182)	An anxiety disorder characterized by anxiety that is not associated with a particular object, situation, or event but seems to be a constant feature of a person's day-to-day existence. (p. 185)

Imaginal Flooding	Lactate	Lactate Theory
Obsession	Obsessive-compulsive Disorder	Outcry Phase
Panic Attack	Panic Control Therapy (PCT)	Panic Disorder
Post-traumatic Stress Disorder (PTSD)	Relaxation Training	Situationally Bound Panic Attack
Situationally Predisposed Panic Attack	Social Phobia	Specific Phobia

A theory of panic disorder proposing that the intense anxiety experienced during a panic attack results from an increase of lactate in the blood. (p. 177)

A chemical in the blood whose production is stimulated by physical exertion, and is found at higher levels in people with panic disorder. (p. 177)

A behavioral technique in which the client is immersed through imagination in the feared situation. (p. 182)

The first reaction to a traumatic event in which the individual reacts with alarm accompanied by a strong emotion. (p. 194)

An anxiety disorder characterized by the experience of recurrent obsessions or compulsions that are inordinately time-consuming or cause significant distress or impairment. (p. 187)

An unwanted thought, word, phrase, or image that persistently and repeatedly comes into a person's mind and causes distress. (p. 187)

An anxiety disorder characterized by recurrent panic attacks or constant apprehension and worry about the possibility of panic attacks. (p. 174)

Treatment that consists of cognitive restructuring, exposure to the bodily cues associated with panic attacks, and breathing retraining. (p. 178)

A period of intense fear and physical discomfort accompanied by the feeling that one is being overwhelmed and is about to lose control. (p. 174)

A panic attack that is triggered by anticipation of or exposure to a specific situation or cue. (p. 174)

A behavioral technique used in the treatment of anxiety disorders that involves progressive and systematic patterns of muscle tensing and relaxing. (p. 178)

An anxiety disorder in which the individual experiences several distressing symptoms for more than a month following a traumatic event, such as reexperiencing the traumatic event, emotional numbing, and increased arousal. (p. 192)

An irrational and unabating fear of a particular object, activity, or situation. (p. 179)

An anxiety disorder characterized by irrational and unabating fear that one's behavior will be scrutinized by others, causing the individual to feel embarrassed and humiliated. (p. 183)

A panic attack that is usually but not invariable triggered by exposure to a situational cue. (p. 175)

Thought Stopping	Traumatic Experience	Unexpected or Uncued Panic Attack

A panic attack that occurs in the absence of a specific situation or cue. (p. 174)	Disastrous or extremely painful event that has severe psychological and physiological effects. (p. 192)	A cognitive-behavioral method in which the client learns to stop having anxiety provoking thoughts. (p. 182)

CHAPTER 7
SOMATOFORM DISORDERS, PSYCHOLOGICAL FACTORS AFFECTING MEDICAL CONDITIONS, AND DISSOCIATIVE DISORDERS

CHAPTER AT A GLANCE

DISSOCIATIVE DISORDERS
Dissociative Identity Disorder
Dissociative Amnesia
Dissociative Fugue
Depersonalization Disorder
Theories and Treatment

SOMATOFORM DISORDERS
Conversion Disorder
Somatization Disorder
Body Dysmorphic Disorder
Hypochondriasis
Conditions Related to Somatoform
Disorders
Theories and Treatment

**PSYCHOLOGICAL FACTORS
AFFECTING MEDICAL
CONDITIONS**
Axis I Disorders
Psychological Symptoms
Personality Traits
Maladaptive Health Behaviors
Stress-Related Responses
Specific Psychological Factors

Alters	Behavioral Medicine	Body Dysmorphic Disorder
Continuous Amnesia	Concersion Disorder	Coping
Depersonalization Disorder	Dissociative Amnesia	Dissociative Fugue
Dissociative Identity Disorder	Emotion-Focused Coping	Factitious Disorder
Factitious Disorder by Proxy (Munchausen's Syndrome by Proxy)	Generalized Amnesia	Host

A psychological disorder in which an individual is dissatisfied and preoccupied with the idea that a part of his/her body is ugly or defective. (p. 211)	An interdisciplinary treatment approach in which behavioral techniques are used to help individuals gain control over their unhealthy bodily reactions. (p. 226)	Personalities developed in dissociative identity disorder that are not part of the core or host personality. (p. 228)
The means with which people attempt to reduce the sensation of stress. (p. 222)	A disorder in which individuals translate unacceptable drives or troubling conflicts into bodily motor or sensory symptoms that suggest a serious medical condition. (p. 208)	An amnesia in which individuals fail to recall events from a particular date, up to and including the present time. (p. 233)
A condition in which a person who is confused about personal identity suddenly and unexpectedly travels to another place. (p. 234)	A disorder in which a person is unable to remember important personal details and experiences, usually associated with trauma or extremely stressful events. (p. 233)	A disorder in which persons experience repeated distortions of mind-body perceptions without provocation by drugs. (p. 235)
A psychological disorder in which people fake symptoms or disorders because of an inner need to maintain a sick role. (p. 216)	A coping strategy in which a person does not change anything about the stressful situation itself, but, instead tries to improve his or her feelings about the situation. (p. 222)	A disorder in which an individual develops more than one self or personality. (p. 228)
The core personality of an individual. (p. 228)	A syndrome in which an individual cannot remember anything at all from his or her life. (p. 233)	A psychological disorder in which a person induces physical symptoms in another person who is under that individual's care. (p. 218)

Hypnotherapy	**Hypochondriasis**	**Hysterical Neurosis**
La Belle Indifference	**Localized Amnesia**	**Malingering**
Masked Depression	**Munchausen's Syndrome**	**Pain Disorder**
Primary Gain	**Problem-focused Coping**	**Psychological Factors Affecting Medical Conditions**
Psychoneuro-immunology	**Secondary Gain**	**Selective Amnesia**

The term Freud used for conversion disorder implying that the disorder was a physical reaction to anxiety. (p. 209)	A somatoform disorder in which an individual believes or fears that he or she has a serious illness, when in fact, he/she is merely experiencing normal bodily reactions. (p. 214)	A therapy technique in which the client is hypnotized and encouraged to recall past experiences while in a trance state. (p. 232)
Deliberately feigning the symptoms of physical illness or psychological disorder for an ulterior motive. (p. 215)	The most common form of dissociative amnesia in which an individual forgets all the events that occurred during a specified time interval. (p. 233)	A phenomenon where individuals display a lack of concern over the seriousness of their physical symptoms. (p. 209)
A somatoform disorder in which individuals believe they are experiencing unrelenting and unrelievable pain. (p. 2112)	A type of factitious disorder which is chronic in which the individual's whole life becomes consumed with the pursuit if medical care. (p. 217)	A term used to indicate an underlying depression that is covered or not obvious because another disorder exhibits its symptoms more prominently. (p. 211)
A diagnostic category which includes situations in which psychological or behavioral factors have an adverse effect on a medical condition. (p. 220)	A coping strategy in which the individual reduces stress by acting to change the stressful situation. (p. 222)	The avoidance of burdensome responsibilities because one is "disabled." (p. 219)
A dissociative disorder in which the individual fails to recall some, but not all, details of events that have occurred during a given period of time. (p. 233)	The sympathy and attention a sick person receives from other people. (p. 219)	A science that studies the relationship between stress, nervous system functioning, and the immune system. (p. 224)

Somatization Disorder	Somatoform Disorders	Stress Innoculation Training
Stress	Stressful Life Event	Stressor

A therapy in which individuals are taught to prepare for stressful events and are given help in practicing ways to control stress. (p. 227)

A group of disorders that includes a variety of conditions in which psychological conflicts become translated into physical problems or complaints that cause distress or impairment in one's life. (p. 208)

A disorder that involves the expression of psychological issues through bodily problems that have no basis in a physiological dysfunction. (p. 209)

The actual event that individuals perceive as threatening. (p. 221)

Another term for a stressor. (p. 221)

The unpleasant emotional reaction a person has when he or she perceives an event to be threatening. (p. 221)

CHAPTER **8**
SEXUAL DISORDERS

CHAPTER AT A GLANCE

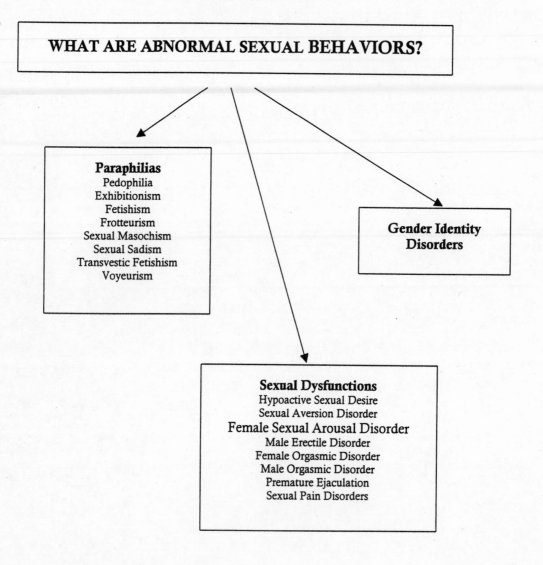

WHAT ARE ABNORMAL SEXUAL BEHAVIORS?

Paraphilias
Pedophilia
Exhibitionism
Fetishism
Frotteurism
Sexual Masochism
Sexual Sadism
Transvestic Fetishism
Voyeurism

Gender Identity Disorders

Sexual Dysfunctions
Hypoactive Sexual Desire
Sexual Aversion Disorder
Female Sexual Arousal Disorder
Male Erectile Disorder
Female Orgasmic Disorder
Male Orgasmic Disorder
Premature Ejaculation
Sexual Pain Disorders

Assigned (or biological) Sex	Covert Conditioning	Dysparenuria
Exhibitionism	Female Orgasmic Disorder	Female Sexual Arousal Disorder
Fetish	Fetishism	Frotteur
Frotteurism	Gender Identity	Gender Identity Disorder
Gender Role	Hypoactive Sexual Desire Disorder	Lovemap

A sexual dysfunction affecting both males and females that involves recurrent or persistent genital pain before, during, or after sexual intercourse. (p. 267)	A behavioral intervention in which the therapist instructs the client to imagine a highly negative experience when engaging in an undesirable behavior. (p. 250)	The sex of the individual that is recorded on the birth certificate. (p. 257)
A sexual dysfunction characterized by a persistent or recurrent inability to attain or maintain the normal physiological and psychological arousal responses during sexual activity. (p. 264)	A sexual dysfunction in which a woman experiences problems in having an orgasm during sexual activity. (p. 264)	A paraphilia in which a person has intense sexual urges and arousing fantasies involving the exposure of genitals to a stranger. (p. 249)
A person with the paraphilia of froteurism. (p. 252)	A paraphilia in which the individual is preoccupied with an object and depends on this object rather than sexual intimacy with a partner for achieving sexual gratification. (p. 250)	A strong, recurrent sexual attraction to a nonliving object. (p. 250)
A condition in which there is a discrepancy between an individual's assigned sex and gender identity, involving a strong and persistent identification with the other gender. (p. 257)	The individual's self-perception as a male or female. (p. 257)	A paraphilia in which the individual has intense sexual urges and sexually arousing fantasies of rubbing against or fondling an unsuspecting stranger. (p. 252)
The representation of an individual's sexual fantasies and preferred practices. (p. 256)	A sexual dysfunction in which the individual has an abnormally low level of interest in sexual activity. (p. 263)	The behaviors and attitudes a person has that are indicative of maleness or femaleness in one's society. (p. 257)

Male Erectile Disorder	Male Orgasmic Disorder	Masochism
Orgasmic Reconditioning	Paraphilias	Partialism
Pedophilia	Premature Ejaculation	Sadomasochist
Sensate Focus	Sexual Aversion Disorder	Sexual Dysfunction
Sexual Masochism	Sexual Orientation	Sexual Sadism

The seeking of pleasure from being subjected to pain. (p. 253)	Also known as inhibited male orgasm; a sexual dysfunction in which a man experiences problems having an orgasm during sexual activity. (p. 266)	A sexual dysfunction marked by a recurrent partial or complete failure to attain or maintain an erection during sexual activity. (p. 264)
A paraphilia in which the person is interested solely in sexual gratification from a specific body part, such as feet. (p. 251)	A disorder in which an individual has recurrent, intense sexually arousing fantasies, urges, or behaviors involving (1) nonhuman objects, (2) children or other nonconsenting persons, or (3) the suffering or humiliation of self or partner. (p. 245)	A behavioral intervention geared toward a relearning process in which the individual associates sexual gratification with appropriate stimuli. (p. 252)
A person who derives sexual pleasure from both inflicting and receiving pain. (p. 253)	A sexual dysfunction in which a man reaches orgasm well before he wishes to, perhaps even prior to penetration. (p. 266)	A paraphilia in which an adult's sexual urges are directed toward sexually immature children. (p. 246)
An abnormality in an individual's sexual responsiveness and reactions. (p. 260)	A sexual dysfunction characterized by an active dislike of intercourse or related sexual activities. (p. 263)	A method of treatment for sexual dysfunctions that involves the partners taking turns stimulating each other beginning with nonsexual stimulation and gradually progressing over time to genital stimulation. (p. 270)
A paraphilia in which sexual gratification is derived from activities that harm, or from urges to harm, another person. (p. 253)	The degree to which a person is erotically attracted to members of the same or opposite sex. (p. 257)	A paraphilia marked by an attraction to achieving sexual gratification by having painful stimulation applied to one's body. (p. 253)

Spectatoring	**Squezze Technique**	**Stop-start Procedure**
Transsexualism	**Transvestic Fetishism**	**Vaginismus**
Voyeur	**Voyeurism**	

A method for developing greater orgasmic control in the male in which the man or his partner stimulates him to sexual excitement and as he approaches the point of orgasm, stimulation is stopped. (p. 270)

A method of treatment for premature ejaculation in which the partner stimulates the man's penis during foreplay and squeezes it when he indicates that he is approaching orgasm. (p. 270)

The experience in which the individual feels unduly self-conscious during sexual activity, as if evaluating and monitoring his or her performance during the sexual encounter. (p. 263)

A sexual dysfunction that involves recurrent or persistent involuntary spasm of the musculature of the outer part of the vagina. (p. 267)

A paraphilia in which a man has an uncontrollable craving to dress in women's clothing in order to derive sexual gratification. (p. 254)

A term sometimes used to refer to gender identity disorder, specifically to individuals choosing to undergo sex reassignment surgery. (p. 257)

A paraphilia in which the individual has a compulsion to derive sexual gratification from observing the nudity or sexual activity of others.(p. 255)

A person with the paraphilia of voyeurism. (p. 255)

CHAPTER 9
MOOD DISORDERS

CHAPTER AT A GLANCE

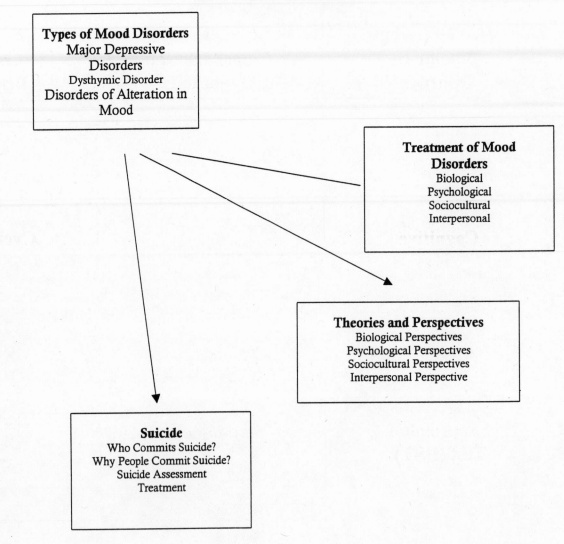

Types of Mood Disorders
Major Depressive
Disorders
Dysthymic Disorder
Disorders of Alteration in
Mood

**Treatment of Mood
Disorders**
Biological
Psychological
Sociocultural
Interpersonal

Theories and Perspectives
Biological Perspectives
Psychological Perspectives
Sociocultural Perspectives
Interpersonal Perspective

Suicide
Who Commits Suicide?
Why People Commit Suicide?
Suicide Assessment
Treatment

Attributions	**Bipolar Disorder**	**Bipolar I Disorder**
Bipolar II Disorder	**Catecholamine Hypothesis**	**Cognitive Distortions**
Cognitive Triad	**Cortisol**	**Cyclothymic Disorder**
Dexamethasone Suppression Test (DST)	**Dysphoria**	**Dysthymic Disorder**
Episode	**Euphoria**	**Hypomanic Episode**

The diagnosis used to describe a clinical course in which the individual experiences one or more manic episodes with the possibility of having experienced one or more major depressive episodes. (p. 285)	A mood disorder involving manic episodes—intense and very disruptive experiences of heightened mood, possibly alternating with major depressive episodes. (p. 283)	Explanations that people make of the things that happen to them. (p. 292)
Errors that depressed people make in the way they draw conclusions from their experiences. (p. 293)	A hypothesis that asserts that a relative shortage of norepinephrine causes depression, and an overabundance of norepinephrine causes mania. (p. 289)	The diagnosis used to describe a clinical course in which the individual experiences one or more major depressive episodes and at least one hypomanic episode. (p. 285)
A mood disorder that, compared with bipolar disorder, involves a less intense vacillation between states of euphoria and dysphoria. (p. 280)	A hormone involved in the mobilization of the body's resources in times of stress. (p. 290)	A negative view of self, world, and the future. (p. 293)
A mood disorder involving chronic depression of less intensity than major depressive episodes. (p. 280)	The emotion of sadness. (p. 280)	A method of testing neuroendocrine functioning by injecting the individual with dexamethasone, which in normal individuals, results in the suppression of cortisol. (p. 290)
A period of elated mood not as extreme as a manic episode. (p. 284)	The emotion of elation. (p. 289)	A time-limited period during which specific intense symptoms of a disorder are present. (p. 280)

Attributions	Bipolar Disorder	Bipolar I Disorder
Bipolar II Disorder	Catecholamine Hypothesis	Cognitive Distortions
Cognitive Triad	Cortisol	Cyclothymic Disorder
Dexamethasone Suppression Test (DST)	Dysphoria	Dysthymic Disorder
Episode	Euphoria	Hypomanic Episode

The diagnosis used to describe a clinical course in which the individual experiences one or more manic episodes with the possibility of having experienced one or more major depressive episodes. (p. 285)

A mood disorder involving manic episodes—intense and very disruptive experiences of heightened mood, possibly alternating with major depressive episodes. (p. 283)

Explanations that people make of the things that happen to them. (p. 292)

Errors that depressed people make in the way they draw conclusions from their experiences. (p. 293)

A hypothesis that asserts that a relative shortage of norepinephrine causes depression, and an overabundance of norepinephrine causes mania. (p. 289)

The diagnosis used to describe a clinical course in which the individual experiences one or more major depressive episodes and at least one hypomanic episode. (p. 285)

A mood disorder that, compared with bipolar disorder, involves a less intense vacillation between states of euphoria and dysphoria. (p. 280)

A hormone involved in the mobilization of the body's resources in times of stress. (p. 290)

A negative view of self, world, and the future. (p. 293)

A mood disorder involving chronic depression of less intensity than major depressive episodes. (p. 280)

The emotion of sadness. (p. 280)

A method of testing neuroendocrine functioning by injecting the individual with dexamethasone, which in normal individuals, results in the suppression of cortisol. (p. 290)

A period of elated mood not as extreme as a manic episode. (p. 284)

The emotion of elation. (p. 289)

A time-limited period during which specific intense symptoms of a disorder are present. (p. 280)

Indolamine Hypothesis	Learned Helplessness Model	Major Depressive Disorder
Major Depressive Episode	Manic Episode	Melancholic Features
Mixed Episode	Probands	Rapid Cyclers
Seasonal Pattern	Suicidal Intent	Suicidal Lethality

A mood disorder in which the individual experiences are acute, but time-limited, episodes of depressive symptoms. (p. 280)	A behavioral approach to depression that proposes that depressed people have come to view themselves as incapable of having an effect on their environment. (p. 292)	A hypothesis that proposes that a deficiency of serotonin causes depression. (p. 289)
A specifier for a depressive episode in which the individual loses interest in most activities, awakens much earlier than usual in the morning, has significant loss of appetite, and possibly psychomotor agitation or retardation and excessive feelings of guilt. (p. 281)	A period of euphoric mood with symptoms involving abnormally heightened levels of thinking, behavior, and emotionality. (p. 283)	A period in which the individual experiences intense psychological and physical symptoms related to a dysphoric mood. (p. 280)
Individuals with bipolar disorder who have four to eight mood episodes within the course of a year. (p. 286)	In genetic research, people who have the symptoms of a particular disorder. (p. 288)	A period of at least one week, during which the symptoms of both a manic episode and a major depressive episode occur in rapidly alternating fashion. (p. 283)
The dangerousness of a suicidal person's intended method of dying. (p. 302)	The level of commitment to taking one's own life (p. 302)	A specifier for a depressive episode in which the individual has varying symptoms according to time of year, with symptoms usually developing during the same months every year. (p. 281)

CHAPTER 10
SCHIZOPHRENIA
AND RELATED DISORDERS

CHAPTER AT A GLANCE

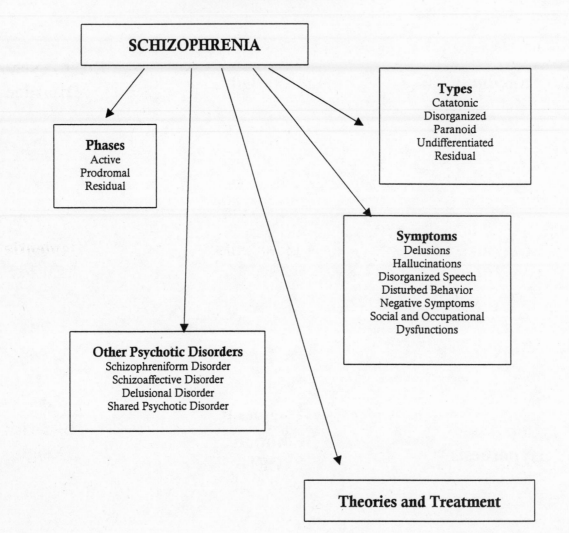

Active Phase	Affective Flattening	Alogia
Anhedonia	Avolition	Brief Psychotic Disorder
Cortical Atrophy	Delusional Disorder	Dementia Praecox
Dopamine Hypothesis	Expressed Emotion (EE)	High-risk Design
Labeling	Negative Symptoms	Neuroleptics

Speechlessness or a notable lack of spontaneity or responsiveness in conversation. (p. 314)	A symptom of schizophrenia in which an individual seems unresponsive and which is reflected in relatively motionless body language, facial reactions, and minimal eye contact. (p. 314)	A period in the course of schizophrenia in which psychotic symptoms are present. (p. 313)
A disorder characterized by the sudden onset of psychotic symptoms that are limited to a period of less than a month. (p. 321)	A lack of initiative, either not wanting to take any action or lacking the energy and will to take action. (p. 314)	A loss of interest in or ability to experience pleasure from activities that most people find appealing. (p. 314)
The term used by Kraeplin to describe what is currently known as schizophrenia—a degeneration of the brain that begins at a young age and ultimately leads to disintegration of the entire personality. (p. 312)	A disorder marked by a single striking psychotic symptom, an organized system of non-bizarre beliefs. (p. 324)	A wasting away of tissue in the cerebral cortex of the brain. (p. 327)
A research method in which investigators follow the lives of children who are considered to be at risk for developing schizophrenia because they have a biological parent with the disorder. (p. 329)	An index of the degree to which family members speak in ways that reflect criticism, hostile feelings, and emotional over-involvement or over-concern with regard to the schizophrenic individual. (p. 333)	A biological explanation for schizophrenia which proposes that delusions, hallucinations, and attentional deficits result from overactivity of neurons that communicate with each other via the transmission of dopamine. (p. 328)
A category of medications used to reduce the frequency and intensity of psychotic symptoms; also called major tranquilizers. (p. 335)	The symptoms of schizophrenia, including affective flattening, alogia, avolition, and anhedonia, that involve functioning below the level of normal behavior. (p. 314)	A social process in which an individual is designated as having a certain disease or disorder; once given this label the individual acts in ways that conform to the label. (p. 333)

Positive Symptoms	Premorbid Functioning	Process Schizophrenia
Prodromal Phase	Reactive Schizophrenia	Residual Phase
Schizoaffective Disorder	Schizophrenia	Schizophrenia Catatonic Type
Schizophrenia Disorganized Type	Schizophrenia Paranoid Type	Schizophrenia Residual Type
Schizophrenia Undifferentiated Type	Schizophreniform Disorder	Shared Psychotic Disorder

The gradual appearance of schizophrenia over time; contrasts with reactive schizophrenia. (p. 318)	The period prior to the onset of the individual's symptoms. (p. 319)	The symptoms of schizophrenia, including delusions, hallucinations, disturbed speech, and disturbed behavior, that are exaggerations or distortions of normal thoughts, emotions, and behavior. (p. 314)
A period in the course of schizophrenia, following the active phase, in which there are continuing indications of disturbance, evidenced by the same kinds of behaviors that characterize the prodromal phase. (p. 313)	The development of schizophrenia in response to a precipitant that provokes the onset of symptoms; contrasts with process schizophrenia. (p. 319)	A period in the course of schizophrenia, prior to the active phase of symptoms, during which the individual shows progressive deterioration in social and interpersonal functioning. (p. 313)
A type of schizophrenia characterized by a variety of bodily movement abnormalities. (p. 315)	A disorder with a range of symptoms involving disturbances in content of thought, perception, affect, sense of self, motivation, behavior, and interpersonal functioning. (p. 312)	A psychotic disorder involving the expression of a major depressive episode, a manic episode, or a mixed episode while also meeting the diagnostic criteria for schizophrenia. (p. 323)
A type of schizophrenia in which people who have been previously diagnosed with schizophrenia still show some lingering signs of the disorder, such as emotional dullness, social withdrawal, eccentric behavior, or illogical thinking. (p. 316)	A type of schizophrenia characterized by preoccupation with one or more bizarre delusions and auditory hallucinations that are related to a particular theme of being persecuted or harassed. (p. 315)	A type of schizophrenia characterized by a combination of symptoms including disorganized speech and behavior, delusions and hallucinations that lack a coherent theme, and flat or inappropriate affect. (p. 315)
A psychotic disorder in which one or more people develop a delusional system as a result of a close relationship with a psychotic person who is delusional. (p. 325)	A type of schizophrenia characterized by psychotic symptoms that are essentially the same as those found in schizophrenia, except for the duration and the chronic nature of the symptoms; specifically, symptoms usually last from 1-6 months. (p. 322)	A type of schizophrenia characterized by a complex of schizophrenic symptoms such as delusions, hallucinations, incoherence, or disorganized behavior that does not meet the criteria for the other types of schizophrenia. (p. 315)

**Smooth Pursuit
Eye Movements**

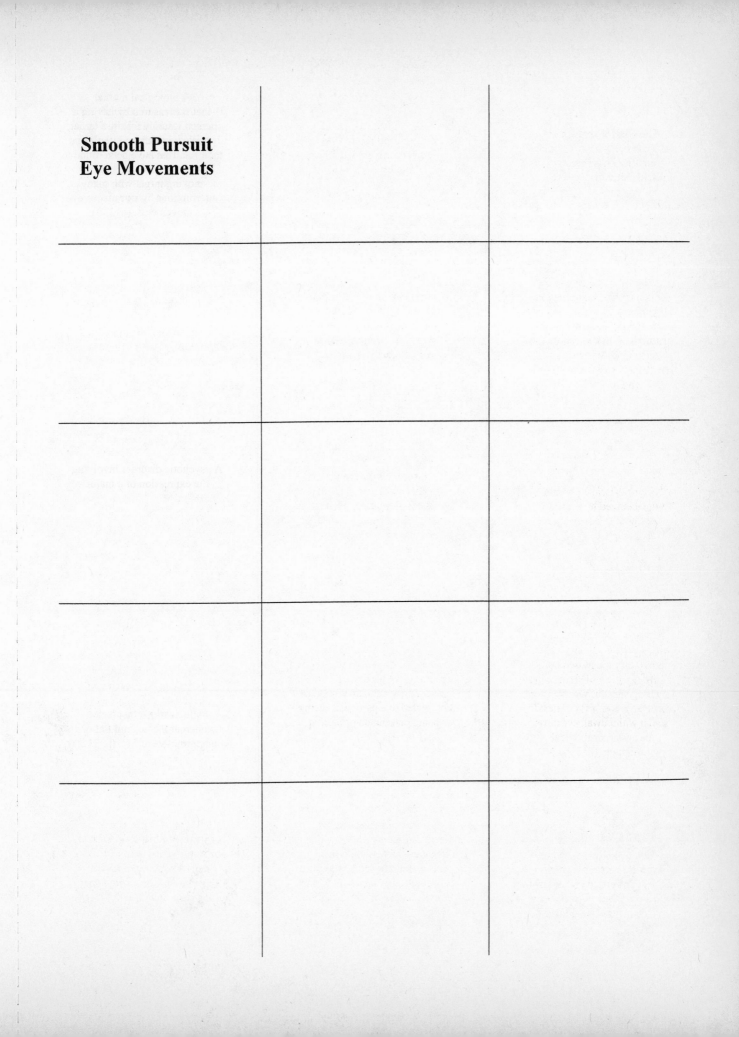

A biological marker that is measured by having a person visually follow a target; people with schizophrenia and their relatives have been found to show irregular pursuit of a moving target with many interruptions by extraneous eye movements. (p. 330)

CHAPTER 11
DEVELOPMENT-RELATED DISORDERS

CHAPTER AT A GLANCE

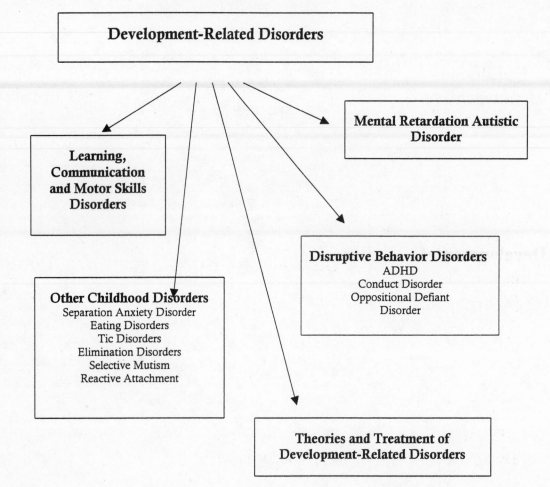

Development-Related Disorders

Learning, Communication and Motor Skills Disorders

Mental Retardation Autistic Disorder

Other Childhood Disorders
Separation Anxiety Disorder
Eating Disorders
Tic Disorders
Elimination Disorders
Selective Mutism
Reactive Attachment

Disruptive Behavior Disorders
ADHD
Conduct Disorder
Oppositional Defiant Disorder

Theories and Treatment of Development-Related Disorders

Asperger's Disorder	Attention-deficit Hyperactivity Disorder (ADHD)	Autistic Disorder
Childhood Disintegrative Disorder	Conduct Disorder	Coprolalia
Developmental Coordination Disorder	Disorder of Written Expression	Down Syndrome
Dyslexia	Echolalia	Encopresis
Enuresis	Expressive Language Disorder	Failure to Thrive

A pervasive developmental disorder involving massive impairment in an individual's ability to communicate and relate emotionally to others. (p. 349)	A behavior disorder of childhood involving problems with inattentiveness, hyperactivity, and impulsivity. (p. 356)	A pervasive developmental disorder in which the child maintains adequate cognitive and language development but becomes severely impaired in social interaction, and displays restricted, repetitive, and stereotyped patterns of behavior, interests, and activities. (p. 349)
The involuntary uttering of obscenities. (p. 364)	A development-related disorder that involves repeated violations of the rights of others and society's norms and laws; the childhood precursor of antisocial personality disorder in adulthood. (p. 357)	A pervasive developmental disorder in which the child develops normally for the first two years and then starts to lose language, social, and motor skills as well as other adaptive functions, including bowel and bladder control. (p. 349)
A form of mental retardation caused by abnormal chromosomal formation during conception. (p. 348)	A learning disorder in which the individual's writing is characterized by poor spelling, grammatical or punctuation errors, and disorganized paragraphs. (p. 354)	A condition characterized by marked impairment in the development of motor coordination. (p. 356)
An elimination disorder in which the child is incontinent of feces and has bowel movements either in clothes or in some other inappropriate place. (p. 364)	Parrot-like repetition of overheard words or phrases. (p. 350)	A learning disorder in which the individual omits, distorts, or substitutes words when reading and reads in a slow, halting fashion. (p. 354)
A condition in which the child does not grow physically and cognitively at a normal rate due to poor prenatal care or grossly inadequate and inattentive parenting. (p. 349)	A communication disorder characterized by a limited and faulty vocabulary, speaking in short sentences with simplified grammatical structures, omitting critical words or phrases, or putting words together in peculiar order. (p. 354)	An elimination disorder in which the child is incontinent of urine and urinates in clothes or in bed after the age when the child is expected to be continent. (p. 364)

Feeding Disorder of Infancy or Early Childhood	**Fetal Alcohol Syndrome (FAS)**	**Learning Disorder**
Mainstreaming	**Mathematics Disorder**	**Mental Retardation**
Mixed Receptive/Expressive Language Disorder	**Oppositional Defiant Disorder**	**Pervasive Developmental Disorder**
Phonological Disorder	**Pica**	**Reactive Attachment Disorder of Infancy or Childhood**
Reading Disorder (Dyslexia)	**Rett's Disorder**	**Rumination Disorder**

A delay or deficit in an academic skill that is evident when an individual's achievement on standardized tests is substantially below what would be expected for others of comparable age, education, and level of intelligence. (p. 354)	A condition associated with mental retardation in a child whose mother consumed large amounts of alcohol on a regular basis while pregnant. (p. 348)	A disorder involving the persistent failure to eat, leading to a loss of weight or failure to gain weight. (p. 364)
A condition, present from childhood, characterized by significantly below-average intellectual functioning (an IQ of 70 or below). (p. 347)	A learning disorder in which the individual has difficulty with mathematical concepts and tasks. (p. 354)	A governmental policy to integrate fully into society people with cognitive and physical disabilities. (p. 349)
A condition that begins in childhood and has a major impact on social and cognitive functioning; it involves serious defects in social interaction skills and communication skills, as well as odd behavior, interests, and activities. (p. 349)	A disruptive behavior disorder of childhood that is characterized by undue hostility, stubbornness, strong temper, belligerence, spitefulness, and self-righteousness. (p. 358)	A communication disorder in which the individual has difficulty understanding and expressing certain kinds of words or phrases, such as directions, or in more severe forms, basic vocabulary or entire sentences. (p. 356)
A disorder involving a severe disturbance in the ability to relate to others in which the individual is unresponsive to people, is apathetic, and prefers to be alone rather than interact with friends or family. (p. 364)	A condition in which individuals eat inedible substances, such as paint, string, hair, animal droppings, and paper. (p. 364)	A communication disorder in which the individual misarticulates, substitutes, or omits speech sounds. (p. 356)
An eating disorder in which the infant or child regurgitates food after it has been swallowed and then either spits it out or reswallows it. (p. 364)	A pervasive developmental disorder, occurring only in females, in which the child develops normally until between five months and four years of age, and then begins to show neurological impairments including a deceleration of head growth, stereotyped hand movements, lack of body coordination, language impairments, and social withdrawal. (p. 349)	A learning disorder in which the individual omits, distorts, or substitutes words when reading, and reads in a slow and halting fashion. (p. 354)

Selective Mutism	**Separation Anxiety Disorder**	**Stereotypic Movement Disorder**
Stuttering	**Tic**	**Tourette's Disorder**

A disorder in which the individual voluntarily repeats nonfunctional behaviors, such as rocking or head banging, that can be potentially damaging to his or her physical well-being. (p. 364)

A disorder of childhood characterized by intense and inappropriate anxiety, lasting at least four weeks, concerning separation from home or caregivers. (p. 362)

A disorder originating in childhood in which the individual consciously refuses to talk, sometimes accompanying this refusal by oppositional or avoidant behavior. (p. 364)

A tic disorder involving a combination of chronic movements and vocal tics. (p. 364)

A rapid, recurring, involuntary movement or vocalization. (p. 364)

A communication disorder that involves a disturbance in the normal fluency of speech that is characterized by sound repetitions or prolongations, broken words, blocking out sounds, word substitutions, or words expressed with an excess of tension. (p. 356)

CHAPTER 12
COGNITIVE DISORDERS

CHAPTER AT A GLANCE

Cognitive Disorders

Delirium

Dementia
Memory Loss
Aphasia, Apraxia, and Agnosia
Disturbance in Executive Functioning

Amnestic Disorders
Substance-Induced
Pick's Disease
Parkinson's Disease
Lewy Body Dementia
Frontal Lobe Dementia
Huntington's Disease
Creutzfeldt-Jakob Disease

Alzheimer's Disease
Diagnosis
Theories and Treatment
Biological Perspective
Environmental Perspectives
Medical Treatment
Behavioral Management of Symptoms

Agnosia	Akinesia	Amnestic Disorders
Amyloid Plaques	Aphasia	Apraxia
Bradykinesia	Broca's Aphasia	Caregiver Burden
Caregivers	Choline Acetyltransferase (CAT)	Creutzfeldt-Jakob Disease
Delirium	Dementia	Epilepsy

Cognitive disorders involving the inability to recall previously learned information or to register new memories.. (p. 373)	A motor disturbance in which a person's muscles become rigid and movement is difficult to initiate. (p. 379)	The inability to recognize familiar objects or experiences, despite the ability to perceive their basic elements. (p. 375)
A loss of the ability to carry out coordinated bodily movements that the individual could previously perform without difficulty. (p. 375)	A loss of the ability to use language. (p. 374)	A characteristic of Alzheimer's disease in which clusters of dead or dying neurons become mixed together with fragments of protein molecules. (p. 382)
The adverse effects on caregivers from the constant demands placed on them by their role. (p. 385)	A form of aphasia that involves disturbance in language production, but intact comprehension abilities. (p. 374)	A motor disturbance involving a general slowing of motor activity. (p. 379)
A neurological disease transmitted from animals to humans that leads to dementia and death resulting from abnormal protein accumulations in the brain. (p. 379)	An enzyme that is essential for the synthesis of acetylcholine. (p. 382)	The people (usually family members) primarily responsible for caring for a person with a chronic disease, such as Alzheimer's disease. (p. 385)
A neurological condition that involves recurring bodily seizures with associated changes in EEG patterns. (p. 372)	A form of cognitive impairment involving generalized progressive deficits in a person's memory and learning of new information, ability to communicate, judgement, and motor coordination. (p. 374)	A temporary state in which individuals experience a clouding of consciousness in which they are unaware of what is happening around them and are unable to focus or pay attention. (p. 372)

Executive Functioning	Frontal Lobe Dementia	Huntington's Disease
Lewy Body Dementia	Neurofibrillary Tangles	Parkinson's Disease
Pick's Disease	Pseudodementia	Substance-Induced Persisting Amnestic Disorder
Substance-Induced Persisting Dementia	Tau	Vascular Dementia
Wernicke's Aphasia		

A hereditary condition causing dementia that involves a widespread deterioration of the subcortical brain structures and parts of the frontal cortex that control motor movements. (p. 379)	A form of dementia that specifically involves the frontal lobes of the brain. (p. 379)	Cognitive abilities such as thinking, planning, organizing, and carrying out of behaviors. (p. 375)
A disease that can cause dementia and involves the degeneration of neurons in the subcortical structures that control motor movements. (p. 378)	A characteristic of Alzheimer's disease in which the material within the cell bodies of neurons becomes filled with densely packed, twisted protein microfibrils, or tiny strands. (p. 381)	A form of dementia similar to Alzheimer's disease with progressive loss of memory, language, calculation, and reasoning, as well as other higher mental functions. (p. 379)
An amnestic disorder caused by drugs or environmental toxins. (p. 373)	Literally, false dementia, or a set of symptoms caused by depression that mimic those apparent in the early stages of Alzheimer's disease. (p. 380)	A relatively rare degenerative disease that affects the frontal and temporal lobes of the cerebral cortex and that can cause dementia. (p. 378)
A form of dementia resulting from a vascular disease that causes deprivation of the blood supply to the brain. (p. 380)	A protein that normally helps maintain the internal support structure of the axons. (p. 381)	A form of dementia caused by the ingestion of substances, such as drugs, or exposure to toxins. (p. 377)
		A form of aphasia in which the individual is able to produce language but has lost the ability to comprehend so that verbal productions have no meaning. (p. 374)

CHAPTER 13
SUBSTANCE-RELATED DISORDERS

CHAPTER AT A GLANCE

Substance Use Disorders

Alcohol
Patterns of Use and Abuse
Immediate Effects of Alcohol Use
Long-Term Effects of Alcohol Use

Treatment for Substance
Abuse and Dependence
Biological
Behavioral
Cognitive

Substances Other than Alcohol
Stimulants
Amphetamines
Cocaine
Cannabis
Hallucinogens
Heroin and Opioids
Sedatives and Hypnotics
Anxiolytics

Abstinence Violation Effect	**Alcohol Dehydrogenase**	**Aldehyde Dehydrogenase**
Crack Cocain	**Cue Exposure Method**	**Delirium Tremens**
Depressant	**Disulfiram**	**Expectancy Model**
Hallucinogens	**Hypnotic**	**Korsakoff's Syndrome**
Methadone	**Potentiation**	**Relapse Prevention Therapy**

An enzyme that is involved in metabolizing alcohol. (p. 402)	A zinc-containing enzyme that breaks alcohol down into fatty acids, carbon dioxide, and water before it enters the bloodstream. (p. 398)	A sense of loss of control over one's behavior that has an overwhelming and demoralizing effect. (p. 399)
A physical condition consisting of autonomic nervous system dysfunction, confusion, and possible seizures associated with alcohol withdrawal. (p. 431)	A behavioral approach to alcohol treatment in which the individual is given a priming dose of alcohol, which initiates the craving for more alcohol; the person is then urged to refuse further alcohol. (p. 403)	A crystallized form of cocaine that is usually smoked. (p. 409)
An approach to alcohol dependence that focuses on cognitive-behavioral and social learning perspectives. According to this view, people acquire the belief that alcohol will reduce stress; will make them feel more competent; and will give them feelings of pleasure. (p. 399)	Known popularly as Antabuse, a medication used in the treatment of alcoholism that inhibits aldehyde dehydrogenase (ALDH) and causes severe physical reactions when combined with alcohol. (p. 402)	A psychoactive substance that causes depression of central nervous system activity. (p. 396)
A permanent form of dementia associated with long-term alcohol use in which the individual develops retrograde and anterograde amnesia, leading to an inability to remember recent events or learn new information. (p. 398)	Psychoactive substance that is used as a sleep medication. (p. 417)	Psychoactive substances that cause abnormal perceptual experiences in the form of illusions or hallucinations, usually visual in nature. (p. 414)
A treatment method based on the expectancy model, in which individuals are encouraged not to view lapses from abstinence as signs of failure. (p. 403)	The combination of effects of two or more psychoactive substances such that the total effect is greater than the effect of either substance alone. (p. 396)	A synthetic opioid that produces a safer and more controlled reaction than heroin and is used in treating heroin addiction. (p. 416)

Sedative	Stimulants	Substance
Substance Abuse	Substance Dependence	Substance Intoxication
Substance Withdrawal	Tolerance	Wernicke's Disease

A chemical that alters a person's mood or behavior when it is smoked, injected, inhaled, or swallowed in pill form. (p. 394)

Psychoactive substances that have an activating effect on the nervous system. (p. 407)

A psychoactive substance that has a calming effect on the central nervous system. (p. 417)

The temporary maladaptive experience of behavioral or psychological changes that are due to the accumulation of a substance in the body. (p. 394)

A maladaptive pattern of substance use manifested by a cluster of cognitive, behavioral, and physiological symptoms during a 12-month period and caused by the continued use of a substance. (p. 395)

The pattern of maladaptive substance use that leads to significant impairment or distress. (p. 395)

An acute condition associated with long-term, heavy alcohol use involving delirium, eye movement disturbances, difficulties in movement and balance, and deterioration of the peripheral nerves to the hands and feet. (p. 398)

The extent to which the individual requires larger and larger amounts of the substance in order to achieve its desired effects, or feels less of its effects after using the same amount of the substance. (p. 395)

Psychological and physical changes that occur when some substances are discontinued. (p. 394)

CHAPTER 14
EATING DISORDERS AND IMPULSE-CONTROL DISORDERS

CHAPTER AT A GLANCE

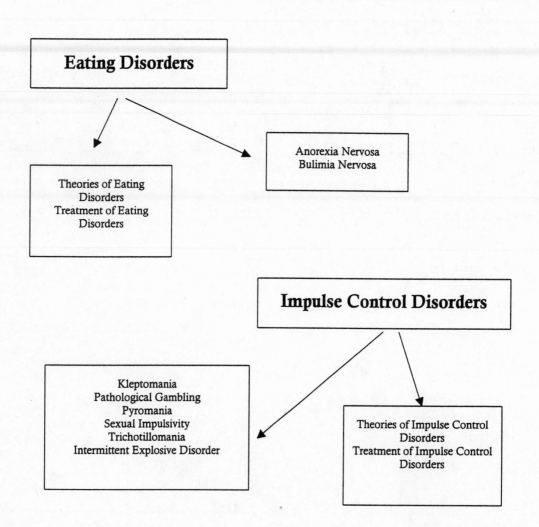

Eating Disorders

Theories of Eating Disorders
Treatment of Eating Disorders

Anorexia Nervosa
Bulimia Nervosa

Impulse Control Disorders

Kleptomania
Pathological Gambling
Pyromania
Sexual Impulsivity
Trichotillomania
Intermittent Explosive Disorder

Theories of Impulse Control Disorders
Treatment of Impulse Control Disorders

Anorexia Nervosa	**Big Win**	**Binge**
Bulimia Nervosa	**Impulse**	**Impulse-Control Disorders**
Intermittent Explosive Disorder	**Kleptomania**	**Nonpurging Type**
Pathological Gambling	**Purge**	**Purging Type**
Pyromania	**Sexual Impulsivity**	**Trichotillomania**

The ingestion of large amounts of food during a short period of time, even after reaching a point of feeling full, and feeling a lack of control over what or how much is eaten. (p. 470)	A gain of large amounts of money in one bet, which propels the pathological gambler into a pattern of uncontrollable gambling. (p. 460)	An eating disorder characterized by an inability to maintain normal weight, an intense fear of gaining weight, and distorted body perception. (p. 479)
Psychological disorders in which people repeatedly engage in behaviors that are potentially harmful, feeling unable to stop themselves, and experiencing a sense of desperation if their attempts to carry out the behavior are thwarted. (p. 456)	An urge to act. (p. 456)	An eating disorder involving the alteration between the extremes of eating large amounts of food in a short time, and then compensating for the added calories either by vomiting or other extreme action to avoid gaining weight. (p. 470)
A form of bulimia nervosa in which individuals compensate for what they eat by fasting or excessive exercise. (p. 470)	An impulse-control disorder that involves the persistent urge to steal. (p. 457)	An impulse-control disorder involving an inability to hold back urges to express strong angry feelings and associated violent behaviors. (p. 466)
A form of bulimia nervosa in which individuals force out of their bodies what they have just eaten. (p. 470)	To eliminate food through unnatural methods such as vomiting or excessive use of laxatives. (p. 468)	To eliminate food through unnatural methods such as vomiting or excessive use of laxatives. (p. 468)
An impulse-control disorder involving the compulsive, persistent urge to pull one's own hair. (p. 465)	An impulse-control disorder in which people feel uncontrollably driven to seek out sexual encounters and engage in frequent and indiscriminate sexual activity. (p. 463)	An impulse-control disorder involving the persistent and compelling urge to start fires. (p. 462)

CHAPTER 15
ETHICAL AND LEGAL ISSUES

CHAPTER AT A GLANCE

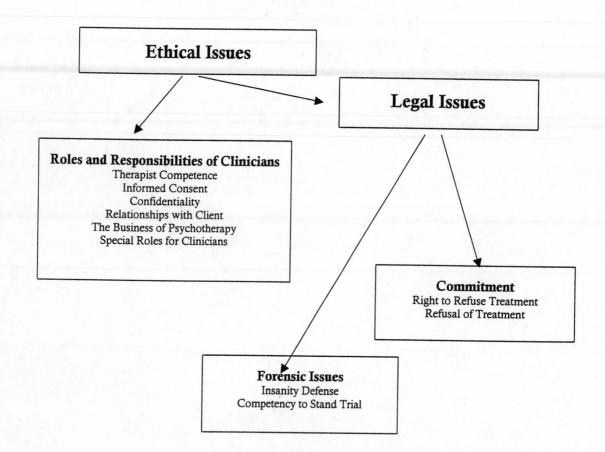

Ethical Issues

Legal Issues

Roles and Responsibilities of Clinicians
Therapist Competence
Informed Consent
Confidentiality
Relationships with Client
The Business of Psychotherapy
Special Roles for Clinicians

Commitment
Right to Refuse Treatment
Refusal of Treatment

Forensic Issues
Insanity Defense
Competency to Stand Trial

Commitment	Competency to Stand Trial	Confidentiality
Duty to Warn	Guardian ad Litem	Informed Consent
Insanity Defense	Least Restrictive Alternative	Mandated Reporting
Parens Patriae	Privileged Communication	

The principle that disclosures in therapy must be safeguarded by the therapist as private. (p. 453)

A prediction by a mental health expert of the defendant's cognitive and emotional stability during the period of the trial. (p. 464)

Legal procedures designed to protect individuals from doing harm to themselves or others through institutionalization or other forms of mental health treatment. (p. 456)

The process, often in the form of a written statement, in which a client participates in setting treatment goals, understands and agrees to the treatment plan, and knows the credentials of the clinician. (p. 452)

A person appointed by the court to represent or make decisions for a person (e.g., minor or incapacitated adult) who is legally incapable of doing so in a civil legal proceeding. (p. 455)

The clinician's responsibility to notify a potential victim of a client's harmful intent toward that individual. (p. 454)

The legal requirement that professionals notify appropriate authorities about cases in which children and certain other groups of vulnerable individuals are being abused. (p. 453)

A treatment setting that provides the fewest constraints on the client's freedom. (p. 460)

The argument, presented by a lawyer acting on behalf of the client, that because of the existence of a mental disorder, the client should not be held legally responsible for criminal actions. (p. 460)

Information provided by a client to a clinician that cannot be disclosed in a court of law without the client's permission. (p. 453)

The authority of the state to protect those who are unable to protect themselves. (p. 456)